GAY ICONS

ALSO BY GEORGES-CLAUDE GUILBERT

Madonna as Postmodern Myth:
How One Star's Self-Construction Rewrites Sex,
Gender, Hollywood and the American Dream
(McFarland, 2002)

GAY ICONS

The (Mostly) Female Entertainers Gay Men Love

GEORGES-CLAUDE GUILBERT

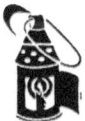

McFarland & Company, Inc., Publishers

Jefferson, North Carolina

ISBN (print) 978-1-4766-7433-9
ISBN (ebook) 978-1-4766-3301-5
LIBRARY OF CONGRESS CATALOGUING DATA ARE AVAILABLE

BRITISH LIBRARY CATALOGUING DATA ARE AVAILABLE

Front cover image of Judy Garland, 1930s; *insets* Madonna *(upper)* "Ray of Light" photograph 1998; Bette Davis, early 1940s (all images Photofest)

Manufactured in the United States of America

McFarland & Company, Inc., Publishers
Box 611, Jefferson, North Carolina 28640
www.mcfarlandpub.com

Acknowledgments

I wish to thank the following people for the support and/or inspiration they provided: Chloé Boreham, Eddy Chevalier, Anne Crémieux, Kevin Drif, Credence Fogo Sol, Justin R. Garcia, Lisa Goodrum, Anthony Guilbert, Régis Hélie, Blair Markowitz, Sébastien Mignot, Élise Pereira Nunes, Aaron Smith, Hélène Tison, Brenda R. Weber, and especially the late and much missed Alexander Doty.

Table of Contents

THE PERFORMERS

Table of Contents

We revere the ruby slippers because we believe they can make us invulnerable to witches (and there are so many sorcerers pursuing us nowadays); because of their powers of reverse metamorphosis, their affirmation of a lost state of normalcy in which we have almost ceased to believe and to which the slippers promise us we can return; and because they shine like the footwear of the gods [Rushdie 1994].

Introduction

In the movie *In & Out* (Frank Oz, 1997), the whole town of Greenleaf wonders about the sexual orientation of Howard Brackett (Kevin Cline), who teaches at the local high school. One of the clues that make him suspect is his profound admiration for Barbra Streisand, whose essential records he owns and whose songs he knows very well. Can we infer from this suspicion that some performers are so systematically and universally identified as gay icons that even the heterosexuals of small-town Indiana are aware of that iconicity?[1] Possibly. Does this mean that the people of Greenleaf all understand exactly what it is about Barbra Streisand that particularly delights gays? Of course not. In the early 1990s, Madonna's gay iconicity had reached such heights in the U.S. that the heterosexual high school boys who liked her music hid that reprehensible taste, lest they be mistaken for gays (and obviously still-closeted high school gays hid it too, for fear of being found out). This does not mean everyone understood the mechanisms of it all.

In the same order of ideas, David Halperin shows us the degree of notoriety of the "gay cult status" of Joan Crawford, using the example of the movie *Heathers* (Michael Lehman, 1989): the high school students played by Winona Ryder and Christian Slater murder "two football jocks at their high school and disguise the murder as a gay double suicide, they establish the sexual identity of their victims [...] by planting on them [...] a number of telltale 'homosexual artifacts,' as they call them—including mascara, a bottle of mineral water, and, most notably, a 'Joan Crawford postcard'" (Halperin 2012: 149).

Gay icons are usually very well known by the general public, sometimes lionized by that public, but not necessarily for the same reasons that made them gay icons.

1

Introduction

What is a gay icon? How is a gay icon formed? What are the aesthetic and political functions of the gay icon? What role does she play in the gay community? How does she contribute to the diffusion of gay culture? How does she contribute to the complexification or decomplexification of sexual identities and gender identities?

Originally, as everyone knows, an icon was a religious image, painted on wood, and used for worship. Twentieth- and 21st-century icons are the sacred images of a secular society; they help construct a collective identity and delineate the zeitgeist.

The *a minima* definition of a gay icon could be a celebrity who is particularly liked by gays. Being particularly liked by gays is often lucrative.[2] But such a definition is clearly insufficient.

This book means to address the question in more detail, looking at interesting women and seeing what interesting things they might indicate about gay culture in particular and society in general. The relatively small space given to female gay icons in dictionaries and encyclopedias of gay culture is quite surprising.

"Gay men and divas, fags and femmes fatales: we are bound together by a logic we dimly understand," Edward R. O'Neill writes (*Camera Obscura* 65: 14). I mean to take at least tentative steps toward the understanding of that logic. "Icons such as Judy Garland, Barbara Stanwyck, and Barbra Streisand [...] deserve close scrutiny for their enduring appeal and influence on queer audiences," Luca Prono says (Prono 2008: XI). I wish to undertake that close scrutiny here.

Generally speaking, this book means to be restrictive and picky, because sadly the term "gay icon" has been dreadfully overused lately. It is not as shallow or commercial a term as some journalists would have us believe. As Graham Norton and Pat Reid have it, "now that the gay community has become mainstream, the title of Gay Icon has become—to put it mildly—slightly cheapened." That is undeniable. Norton and Reid add that the term "is bandied about by the straight media in an effort to make otherwise dull losers seem the tiniest bit interesting—oh, and because Brian the gay bloke in the office said he liked them" (Norton & Reid 1999: 12).

That "the gay community has become mainstream"[3] remains to be established, but it is tempting to admit that sizable portions of gay *culture* have indeed become mainstream, and it is true that most media seem at the very least aware of the existence of gay icons. One could indeed argue that gay culture has always been mainstream: look at the most revered painters, sculptors, writers, filmmakers and fashion designers—but this book is no place for that debate.

Strictly gay icons will be discussed, not lesbian icons. Lesbian icons are fewer and more difficult for a non-specialist to analyze. Obviously, though, some of the gay icons featured here are also lesbian icons, including Marlene Dietrich, Greta Garbo and Katharine Hepburn. But surely performers such as Ellen DeGeneres, Melissa Etheridge, Jodie Foster, Gina Gershon and Me'shell Ndegeocello correspond much more closely to the expected definition of a lesbian icon than to that of a gay icon.

Some might wonder why this book speaks only of gay icons, as opposed to LGBT, LGBTQ, LGBTQ+, LGBTQI, LGBTQIA, LGBTQIA+, LGBTQIAPK, or even LGBTQQIP2SAA if not LGBTQUILTBAG icons. The simple reason is that it is hard to establish that it would be relevant. Surely those ever-growing acronyms are more useful in daily life and in legal matters than in the examination of diva veneration. I admit my vocabulary might seem contradictory at times, as there are moments when "queer icons" might work much better than "gay icon" to voice my ideas about this or that celebrity and her public. In October 2016 I was puzzled by the expression "icône queer" applied to Jaden Smith and to the band La Femme in the French press. It is easier to see, though, why people such as Antony (and the Johnsons), now known as Anohni, Bruce LaBruce, Skunk Anansie or Peaches might be seen as queer icons.

As for the general difference between "gay" and "queer," without worrying about applying the terms to icons for a moment, it seems possible in this day and age to simplify the debate with the following generalization: gays tend to be modern, consumerist, assimilationist, essentialist (in matters of sexual orientation, sometimes even in matters of gender), and to espouse social/sexual categories. In contrast, queers tend to be postmodern, less consumerist, constructionist[4] (in matters of sexual orientation and gender), and to reject social/sexual categories. This book would certainly be seen as abominably mainstream and vanilla by homocore artists or queercore activists and queer punks if they took the time to flick through its pages, but that will not stop me from using the verb "to queer," as no other will do in certain passages. Conchita Wurtz queered the Eurovision song contest in 2014 when she sang "Rise Like a Phoenix" in an evening dress and heels and sporting a black beard—she did not "gay it up." Nevertheless, this book is not about queer icons and does not mean to be unduly concerned with academic and publishing trends: in 2017 there are many more gay boys out there in the real world than politically savvy queers well-versed in queer theory—these gay boys worship good old gay icons, not fashionable political figures. There is certainly room, however, for another book, equally stimulating but with less cross appeal, dedicated to queer icons and transgender icons.

Only female performers will be considered here. Male gay icons correspond to another logic altogether and could provide the topic for another book. Indeed, the vast majority of male gay icons are desired by the gay men who iconize them, and the following pages will soon show that this book is more concerned with identification than with desire. Naturally, a gay male may simultaneously identify with and desire a male singer or actor, but desire will usually overcome identification in the iconizing process. Besides, one finds totally brainless actors playing utterly uninspiring roles and leading lethally boring lives hailed as gay icons in inane press articles simply because they are deemed extremely sexy. That is not the kind of dynamic I wish to explore at this point. The greatest gay icons have always been women, anyway, as this book notably hopes to make plain.

I say "female performers," but I am not concerned here with some hypothetical feminine essence; drag luminaries Divine, RuPaul or Sharon Needles are featured because it matters little for the demonstration that they happen to have been born genetically male, or to have appeared in public out of drag. Genetically speaking, this book is about 67 females and three males, some might say.

As it happens, in the sense in which I use the phrase, "gay icon" is sometimes almost conflated with "diva." In *Queer: The Ultimate User's Guide* (2002), Simon Gage *et al.* look at the restricted dictionary definitions and then state that the term "diva" now means, besides the obvious,

> a huge voice, an even bigger ego and the balls to use it—throw in a penchant for sparkly dresses, a hint of real life tragedy and "my man done me wrong" torch songs and you've got a very loose definition. And only gay men can truly [...] appreciate the nuances and humor of this image of overblown femininity, they've lip-synced to their voices in front of the mirror more times than they care to remember, and the lyrics.... Show us a gay man who doesn't know what it feels like to have tragedy in their life? In a nutshell, these women are who gay men would want to be if they were born a different gender [24].

Introduction

The gay icon is usually beautiful, by most people's standards, and quite widely seen as attractive and desirable. In movies, she is the object of Laura Mulvey's would-be controlling male gaze, obviously, but she is also hailed as gorgeous and dynamite-hot by gay men, who gaze at her with fondness without wanting to own her and/or demean her. The gay icon wears beautiful dresses that contribute to her iconicity: Greta Garbo in Adrian, Marlene Dietrich in Irene, Mae West in Elsa Schiaparelli, Rita Hayworth in Jean Louis, Cher in Bob Mackie, Rihanna in Giorgio Armani...

I have also decided to restrict myself to durably famous people—if not actual international stars (Guilbert 2002: 12–13)—for it baffles me to see ephemeral celebrities such as American talent-show winners or even mere runner-ups described as gay icons when the public all but forgets their names by the time the next season starts, and no one knows them outside the U.S.

Worse, some British newspapers will without scruple describe a participant in a reality television program as a gay icon although her looks are moderately acceptable, her look consists of a pair of jogging pants and a sports bra and all she does is sit around all day in a loft discussing trivia without the least concern for grammar. Plus, no one has even ever heard of her outside the British Isles.[5]

Some of our icons owe their status more to their career (cinematic or musical), others more to their biography. Most owe it to a delicate combination of the two. Indeed, and as we will see, it is when the biographical intrudes into the artistic, or even the diegetic (and vice versa), that gay iconicity reaches its maximum potential and functions at its optimum level. Some conditions are evidently more propitious for the emergence of a gay icon than others, as I hope to illustrate. It is not necessary to raise awareness of LGBTQ+ issues, actively support LGBTQ+ rights, speak out against discrimination and homophobia, and be involved in AIDS charities to be a gay icon, but it helps.[6]

In his blog *Slaves of Academe*, Oso Raro confides that he has been reflecting upon the Star and her "relationship to gay self-conception." He explains: "Like most gay men, my life has been influenced by an intense identification with the Star, whether in film, television, or music. For many of us, I think this is a complex nexus of desire, longing, mentoring, and modeling, shaped by things like race, gender, and sexuality in subtle but

5

powerful ways." Raro discusses some of the qualities of the gay icon: "strength, resiliency, resistance to conventional gender norms. Controversial and complicated women marching to the beat of their own drum." All they need to add to that is Hollywood glamour.[7]

The gay icon tends to be heterosexual. Sometimes she is a fighter, sometimes a long-suffering victim; in any case, she's a strong personality, who often ends tragically. She is a star, and no one becomes a star without encountering some pitfalls on the way. The fighter gay icon has learned to defend herself, to fight for her rights and her freedom. She is often a "brassy, bombastic, over-the-top diva," as Bobby Hankinson says. They are the best kind.[8]

I used to think, mistakenly, that gay icons necessarily belonged to one or the other category, the triumphant dominatrix or the sobbing doormat, but I gradually realized I was wrong. Many of them belong to both categories simultaneously, and others keep moving from one to the other, going through phases, as it were. So a gay icon can be a depressed drama queen, a tragic martyr who belts out torch songs about it all, or Queen of the Universe, all about strength and emancipation. After all, isn't contradiction a necessary condition of stardom (Morin 1957: *passim*; Guilbert 2002: 91–110)?

David Halperin writes:

> For lots of gay men, Joan Crawford, the Golden Girls, Lady Gaga, and many other camp icons continue to exercise a certain power and appeal, though mainstream gay commentators like [Andrew] Sullivan, who would prefer that they didn't, assert that they don't. That seemingly confident assertion, however, expresses not a fact but a wish—and one that is not likely to be fulfilled anytime soon [Halperin 2012: 258].

I myself do not agree with Andrew Sullivan on this score, as on many others. Indeed, if I did I would not have decided to write this book.

People like Sullivan would like to have us think that gay icons are on the way out, that with "homosexual lifestyles" becoming somewhat banal, gay marriage being legalized all over the place, they have become irrelevant or obsolescent. It is wrong to narrowly associate gay icons with the closet or with the lack of civil rights for gays. And it is wrong to suppose that everyone is out or about to be. Just because many men are coming out of the closet does not mean everybody is, everywhere. It still very much depends on social background and geography. The same debate rages when it comes to camp.[9] I do not believe camp is on its way out, far from it. However, this not mean that the logic of camp remains exactly the same as it always was. Too many people assume that if a woman is a gay icon she is necessarily camp. That is not true at all. Jacqueline Bouvier Kennedy Onassis is certainly a gay icon, but it is harder to claim that she was or did camp. Andy Warhol promoted the gay iconization of Jackie Kennedy, just as he promoted the gay iconization of Marilyn Monroe and Elizabeth Taylor. I once bought a t-shirt with her face on it and a quote underneath: "What does my hairdo have to do with my husband's ability to be president?" That t-shirt was camp, undoubtedly, but when Kennedy said words to that effect I am not certain that she was. We now know better. Jack Kennedy was the first president of postmodern politics. Jackie's glorious bouffant hairdo had *everything* to do with her husband's chances of being elected—if not his ability to govern the U.S. adequately. Her clothing mattered a great deal; her Oleg Cassini outfits went down in history. Anybody wearing a pink pillbox hat today would be camp, but Jackie wasn't— although camp and queer readings of her are possible, as Roberta Mock reminds us (Mock 2003: 20–37). Wayne Koestenbaum published a whole (splendid) book about it (Koestenbaum 1993/2001). Jackie Kennedy does not get an entry in this book simply because she was not technically in show business. I could, however, have included her, if only on the strength of all those magazine covers that featured her alongside movie stars, extraordinarily pitting her against Elizabeth Taylor as if they were playing on the same turf. After all, the Kennedys were all about *la politique spectacle*.[10]

Admittedly, many heterosexual, genetically female gay icons do tend to be camp. And that does not mean they are not queer in some way— *pace* those of my colleagues who see camp as a thing of the past and queer as the future.

Let us examine one cliché that is not infrequent among extremely gay-friendly ladies: the "gay man trapped in a straight woman's body" trope.[11] Madonna has often claimed she is one, for example, to British TV host Michael Parkinson in November 2005.[12] Rose McGowan has often said it, notably in July 2011.[13] Lady Gaga has said it, repeatedly.[14] Victoria Beckham declared it in December 2007.[15] Mila Kunis said it, too.[16] She apparently likes calling herself a "fairy princess." Courtney Love said it about herself and her daughter Frances Bean Cobain, in 2008.[17] Pamela Anderson declared it in 2012.[18] And I must admit quite a few of my female friends have said they are…

Roberta Mock puts it much more crudely as in the epigraph of her article "Heteroqueer Ladies: Some Performative Transactions between Gay Men and Heterosexual Women.": "My ex-husband once told me that I was 'a gay man with a cunt.'"

This phenomenon is clearly linked to notions of "fag-haggery." Self-professed fag hags are often the ones who claim to be gay men trapped in heterosexual women's bodies.[19] Indeed some of them go too far in their fantasy of becoming gay men. In a very funny passage of her book *The Diva Rules*, Michelle Visage describes the excess: "And that is where my greatest transformation happened: I became a gay man. I wanted Max and Cesar, everyone in my family, and all these kids along the river to know that, though I was white, a biological female, and hetero, I was one of them," until one of her voguing friends said to her: "Guuurl, I'm worried about you. […] We love you very much. You're one of us. You're already in our family, so please do yourself a huge favor and stop acting like a faggot" (Visage 2015: 61–63).

Mock's phrase "heteroqueer ladies" provides a working category of analysis that could, I imagine, allow one to refrain from speaking of "camp women" or "fag hags," and it is without qualms that one could pronounce all female gay icons "heteroqueer ladies." The fact that the heteroqueer lady, the blazing gay icon both on and off screen (or on and off stage), often gets the leading man, the actor, the singer, or the boy toy who is so desirable in the eyes of gay men and often proportionally gorgeous, favors the gay iconization process. One of the most common foibles of gay men is their tendency to fall for straight men. It is easy to interpret this as a manifestation of internalized homophobia (this book is no place for this debate), but the fact is that this foible reinforces gay men's identification. A song like Britney Spears' "Womanizer" (2008), for instance, works wonders, and not just because of its video.

When discussing gay icons, there is an issue that cannot be skirted: the numerous people who believe in the necessity of a Pygmalion whenever they see a star (often phallocratic men who cannot tolerate the idea of self-made women, let alone self-made female stars), cannot conceive of a gay icon uncreated by some man pulling the strings (more or less) in the shadows. Although it is true that icons are made and not born, it is not true that icons never make themselves. Some creators, such as Alfred Hitchcock (Grace Kelly, Kim Novak), are particularly iconogenic. Marlene Dietrich, for her part, owes much of her gay iconicity to director Josef von Sternberg. But that is not to say he was her Pygmalion and she was nothing more than a docile Galatea, on the contrary—even if she curiously claimed so herself on occasions.

Similarly, a second topic (linked to the previous one) cannot be avoided here: the possibility of gay misogyny at work in the process of gay iconization and the practice of diva worship.[20] No matter how ardently one wishes it did not exist, one cannot but observe occasional manifestations of this evil—but it will not dwelt on it unduly, because it is undeniably a marginal and uninteresting phenomenon.[21] Some misguided feminists see elements of misogyny in the very practice and dynamics of gay iconization. It is true that diva worshippers laugh good-naturedly when their idols stumble. Some might even parody them. But as the verifiable cliché goes, the best parodies come from a place of love. Playful mockery and affectionate derision should not be mistaken for dislike. It might be argued that on the contrary, drag queens' parodying antics, for example, stem out of fondness and regard. Gay men in drag all over the world pay comic tributes to gay icons.

The problem is complicated by different schools of feminism, which do not necessarily see misogyny in the same places. Some second-wavers tend to consider all male to female drag as intrinsically misogynistic, which seems inane to me. Perhaps some comic drag queens ferociously lampoon women, thus possibly giving the appearance that they dislike them, but even those tend to do so with immense tenderness. As for glamorous drag queens, anyone with even a moderately rational mind who watches their show and talks to them later will tell you that we are dealing more with adoration and admiration—to put it mildly—than anything else.

Reasonable feminists realize that misogyny is much more rampant among straight men than among gay men. In the tradition of pantomime dames, perhaps, some straight actors in drag playing evil stepmothers are misogynistic, but even that is not so obvious—Dame Edna Everage, who basically comes from that tradition, is certainly not misogynistic.

After all, what credit can one give to such accusations of misogyny when the second-wave "star" Germaine Greer has become dreadfully transphobic and sees all transwomen as insults to a generic, terribly essentialist category of individuals called "women"? Indeed, a group of like-minded women goes as far as to see in transwomen a form of symbolic rape of all ciswomen. Should we even dignify such horrors with a response?

There will always be feminists who are convinced that men cannot do feminism simply because they are men. There will always be feminists who think that male privilege is not any different when it comes to gay men and that gay men cannot understand the oppression suffered by women. It is not a competition, but maybe they should wonder if they can understand the oppression suffered by gay men. Gay men get beaten up simply because they are gay. Fifteen-year-old boys kill themselves because they feel that they might be gay.

If gay boys indulge in a little bit of escapism and find tools to help construct themselves as non-self-hating individuals in the adulation of a gay icon or two, then I am all for it. If they enjoy and/or practice camp and it helps them survive the homophobia of their surroundings, I say go for it.[22]

In 1988, Andrew Ross "faulted camp for reconciling people with their own oppression. [...] Feminist critics also pointed out the misogynistic character of camp, which, in spite of its many female icons, is rooted in a troubling interest with waste and decay, relating them, in particular, to women's aging bodies" (Prono 2008: 54). I myself have never viewed camp as inherently misogynistic. I do see how camp may have an interest in waste and decay and aging bodies, but I do not find this troubling: indeed, it can be quite the opposite.

To be entirely truthful, I must quote a few gay men who are themselves in the business of worshipping gay icons and faintly suspect that their worship might contain misogynistic elements. It is true that gay men love their divas to be occasional train wrecks. This makes the identification process even more efficacious. So many gay men have train-wreck phases themselves, Japhy Grant writes in *Queerty*:

> This week we look at the women we adore despite—or because of—the adversity they face, both real, imagined and self-inflicted. Now, to be totally honest, there's a whiff of misogyny in our collective love of tragic women, though at the end of the day, who doesn't love a good melodrama? Whether they lived hard and fast and short or lingered on into a faded oblivion, these are the women who've inspired the gay community to keep your chin up no matter what the world throws at you—and that no problem can't be solved with a sensible pump.[23]

Pick yourself up, "put on your red shoes and dance the blues,"[24] train-wreck divas are telling us. Are there more train-wreck stories among lesser divas? Hollywood underdogs? Ill-used actresses?[25] Possibly. Andrew Ross claims:

> Garland, Davis, and the other queens of Hollywood are one thing. María Montez, Tallulah Bankhead, Carmen Miranda, and Eartha Kitt are another. If they are also figures celebrated by gay camp, then it is not for their thespian talents or for their stylized parodies of femininity. On the contrary, the widespread cultivation of these exploited actresses (*Myron*'s cult of Montez, in Gore Vidal's novel, is representative) is inevitably tinged with ridicule, derision, even misogyny [Ross in Cleto 1999: 328].

I beg to differ. To me, Montez, Bankhead, Miranda and Kitt are gay icons in exactly the same way as Garland or Davis. They can be equally "celebrated by gay camp," they do have worthwhile thespian talents, and their stylized parodies (or it is pastiches?) of femininity are as precious as Davis'. I believe that in every process of gay iconization, there are elements of straightforward admiration for some qualities (beauty, singing, acting, dancing, humor), along with healthy elements of ridicule and derision. In the same way that gay men have learned through the ages to not take themselves and each other too seriously (this is one of the aspects and uses of camp, obviously), to poke fun at themselves and each other, of course they are not going to take their cultural enthusiasm entirely seriously, and of course they are not going to worship without a pinch of (camp) salt.

It is true that Gore Vidal's character Myron is a bit misogynistic (which is not to say that Vidal was), but I do not think he is really representative of anything. Admittedly, there are gay misogynists, just as there are homophobic women, but the ones I have encountered tend to worship Greek and Latin classics, politically dubious novelists and sportsmen, not show-business divas.

Perhaps we can be content with the notion that some gays' enthusiasm for some gay icons is ambivalent. Mark Simpson explains:

> [B]eing a gay icon is not simply about love. It's more usually about a fierce, frightening ambivalence towards women or a desperate, driven identification. Any woman who hears that she's a gay icon should immediately check her back for knives and make sure her feet haven't been welded to a plinth.
> The word "icon" itself means "image" or "statue"—a representation of a sacred personage which is itself regarded as sacred. Gay icons are representations of Woman that are revered far more than women. Which is why being dead helps,

but if you happen to be inconveniently alive gays will bury you under sycophantic, hysterical praise (see Liza Minnelli).[26]

Surely those jocular words constitute food for thought, even if the generalization is excessive. The third question that cannot be bypassed here is the accusation of cultural terrorism that might be hurled at me. Who am I to claim to know what gay men like? And what is a gay man anyway? Am I guilty in spite of myself of essentialist typology? And how can I infer that they share anything else than the fact that they are sexually attracted to males? Besides, a couple of gay men I know like car-racing, heavy metal, soccer and dislike Madonna as much as they dislike Barbra Streisand. They disapprove of this book because they see themselves as evidence that not every gay man is into musicals and melodramatic belting. My answer to all of those legitimate misgivings is, I suppose, the informal and unscientific statistics I have gathered, coupled with decades of reading and observation (in music stores, bookstores, pubs, bars, cafés, restaurants, nightclubs, and the poster-covered walls of people's apartments). Not every gay man loves all those larger-than-life women, admittedly, but a great many do, as the bibliography at the end of this book helps establish. In addition to these books, I have used websites of every description; in discussions such as this, it is healthy to look beyond academe.

It is hard to discuss gay icons without resorting to the expression "gay sensibility." Susan Sontag speaks of "camp sensibility" in her 1964 "Notes on Camp." Many writers use either or both expressions. They are indubitably problematic.

Etymologically, such expressions harken back to the senses and sensory perception, they have to do with emotions; whereas it is easy to see camp as a relatively intellectual phenomenon (and I don't mean "intellectual" in the sense that only people with a higher education might enjoy camp, I mean "intellectual" in the sense of having to do with the mind, not with the heart.). Admittedly, Sontag herself specifies, "It is not a natural mode of sensibility" and goes on to speak of camp's love for "the unnatural" (Sontag 1969: 277). I myself might be prepared to speak of "sensibility" as long as it is clearly established that we are dealing with a sensibility that has been forged in time, for example, through practices of resistance, as opposed to anything innate—as in, gays like extraordinarily camp singers because they have a gay sensibility.

Introduction

As David Halperin writes, "I do not claim there is one and only one gay culture, shared by all gay men—or that the cultural practice of male homosexuality is unitary, whole, autonomous, and complete in itself" (Halperin 2012: 17). But that does not stop us from identifying unifying characteristics in gay cultures (at least in the U.S., the UK, Australia, and to a lesser extent France, Italy, and Spain[27]), and thus a form of "gay sensibility."

My problematics are also circumscribed according to geography and sphere of existence. I have deliberately concentrated on English-speaking gay icons (if not native speakers, at least women who became famous in an English-speaking country). The vast majority of my icons are American. I have regretfully refrained from discussing French gay icon Sylvie Vartan (1944–) in an entry of her own, however interesting she might be, because not enough people have heard of her in the Anglophone world. Susan Sontag claimed in 1964 that "what the French call yé-yé" is camp (Sontag 1969: 280). Vartan was certainly yé-yé in the 1960s, and she has always been a practitioner of camp. As a matter of fact, there is little camp in French popular culture (compared to Anglophone popular culture). Vartan played Las Vegas. She has an American husband and a famous American nephew, actor Michael Vartan. Early on, she developed a rather unique singing style that is to sound what a pout is to visuals. She has loudly moaned her way through more than five decades of a very successful career; in France she is a huge star as well as a gay icon, and she has been exquisitely enshrined by camp artists Pierre et Gilles. Indeed the gay artists Pierre et Gilles have made it their artistic mission to portray as many important gay icons as they can, knowing that their postmodern art is itself a literal iconization process (consider their kitsch religious influences). Beautified by them, the gay iconicity of transgender singer Marie France and of Lio, Madonna, Kylie Minogue, or Arielle Dombasle increases tenfold. They have also worked (including on videos) with male gay favorites such as Marc Almond.

Along the same logic, I have decided not to include French gay icon Barbara (1930–1997), perhaps more of a lesbian icon, although she certainly has a huge gay following in France. Her songs are poems, a little on the intellectual side, extremely beautiful and extremely sad. Tall and slightly butch, she was always dressed in black, with a bit of red. She belongs to the category of singers French producer and journalists promote as *grandes dames.* Indeed she is so much of a revered *grande dame* that the last time I listened to a presentation about her at a French cultural studies conference, the academic spoke nothing but admiring compliments for 20 minutes, as opposed to elements of research. I myself have been known to gush, but I always strive to remain at least moderately academic.

As for Italy, it has certainly had its share of flamboyant gay icons, such as the divine Milva and the immeasurably camp Mina. Both singers have delighted generations of gay men both in Italy and abroad. In all probability, Mina's song "E Poi" (1973) is the most diva-ish of her repertoire. I strongly recommend it to anyone who has just broken up with a significant other and is indulging in extreme self-pity. Her own French, Spanish and English versions, although not quite so melodramatic, offer their share of over-the-top fun. The fact that in the video, Mina is basically in bridegroom drag, complete with white carnation in her lapel, does nothing to diminish her gay iconicity.

I did not include Princess Diana (1961–1997) either, because she was not exactly a show-business personality (although this is disputable, the British royal family being all about public performance). She was certainly a regal diva, and was supposed to become the queen of the United Kingdom; she was the idol of many queens of the United Kingdom and elsewhere, who cried many tears when she died in that gruesome Parisian tunnel.

Nor did I include Barbie, having limited myself to actual human beings, although many concur she is indeed a tremendous gay icon, what with her impossible figure, her pink camper and her sequins and glitter. There are now queer readings of Barbie all over the place and marvelous parodies of her adventures on the Internet.[28]

This is a historical and contemporary catalogue of gay icons that intends to entertain as well as to edify. This book means to leave no epistemological stone unturned, no aesthetic dimension unobserved and no political aspect neglected. Each individual entry is conceived to provide additional comments, to complement this general introduction and help form the beginning of an understanding of gay iconicity. I hope after my readers have read the 70th entry, they will have fewer doubts about what makes a gay icon and what role a gay icon holds in society. Judging from a cursory look at web fora, where people tear each other apart trying to decide who is really a gay icon and who is not, the question is topical.

Finally, where do I speak from? First, I undertook this book as a work of love, because I am basically a fan, most profoundly. Starstruck is my middle name. To a question about my religion I started answering "diva worshipper" back in the 1970s.[29] Second, I write as someone who devoted several years of study to Madonna and wrote a book about her. Indeed, a great deal of my research and output have been about exceptional women: Carson McCullers, Madonna, my glamorous Vietnamese grandmother[30]... I am an American studies/cultural studies/gender studies professor, I am a second-wave constructionist feminist, I teach queer theory and post-modern theory, and I believe all of these female gay icons have something interesting to tell us about gender construction. Mostly, I believe that most of these icons are empowering both for gay men and for women.[31] I do not claim to be objective, even if I always strive to be scholarly.

I also decided to write this book in the hope that not *all* the young gay men who stumble upon it are convinced that now that gay marriage is legal in a great many Western countries, we no longer need gay cultural history. On the contrary, I believe that making a *tabula rasa* of it all would be a dreadful mistake. Just as it would be naïve to suppose that all gay men will come out now that they can get married, it is naïve and overly optimistic to think we do not need sites of resistance and queering practices any longer. That we no longer need identification and disidentification practices (Muñoz 1999). Besides, camp and the worship of divas are more than that. Professing we do not need them any longer is a bit like claiming that now that African Americans can (supposedly) vote everywhere and Barack Obama has been president, there is no more need for them to practice specific cultural techniques of resistance for them. Unfortunately, it is silly and irresponsible to think that racism and homophobia are gone, as recent political events have shown. Maybe in 2096.[32]

As for those ageist youngsters who think Britney Spears, say, is already a bit too old at 35, I would like to convince them that she is still relevant and that there are much older—or even deader—gay icons who are really worth their attention. I offer 70 here, and if some reproach me for my enthusiasm, which they think reeks of nostalgic gay clichés and might be used to reinforce homophobic clichés, I can only say, in the immortal words of Gloria Gaynor, I will survive.[33]

THE PERFORMERS

Julie Andrews (1935–)

"There is no such thing as a gay sensibility," the cultural critic and journalist Jeff Weinstein once said, "and yes, it has an enormous impact on the arts." This is true. I, for example, am a gay man, but I would rather have bamboo shoots pressed slowly through my eyeballs than listen to Barbra Streisand sing (or act or direct or...). I like loud, jangly guitar pop, found *Brokeback Mountain* kind of dull, and, at least since the age of four, have never done drag. On the other hand, I know every single word of *The Sound of Music*. Homosexuals are not homogeneous [Ness 2006].

This article could have been quoted at the beginning of the Barbra Streisand entry below. Julie Andrews happens to be the first entry, because they are in alphabetical order, and this quote serves well to prolong the Introduction. Indeed even the embedded Jeff Weinstein quote could have served as an epigraph. Undeniably, homosexuals are not all the same, but isn't it interesting that although Patrick Ness dislikes Streisand, he is an Andrews aficionado? When you start reading his declaration of difference, seeing he dislikes Streisand, is unmoved by Ang Lee's movie and likes "straight" pop, you expect him to continue listing his tastes, perhaps including violent sports, Ernest Hemingway, Norman Mailer, waxing his car on Sunday and chopping wood—but no, he talks about *The Sound of Music* (Robert Wise, 1965).

Leslie Bennetts interviewed Julie Andrews for *The New York Times* in March 1982 and mentioned the contrast between her squeaky-clean family-friendly roles in *Mary Poppins* (Robert Stevenson, 1964) and *The Sound of Music* and her impersonation of a gay Polish count in *Victor/Victoria* (Blake Edwards, 1982). "Does Mary Poppins have an orgasm? Does she go to the bathroom? I assure you, she does," Andrews replied.[1] Her answer is linked to the porous frontier between dramatis persona and real-itatis femina in the mind of the public, which I have examined elsewhere (Guilbert 2002: *passim*),[2] and which will be significant in several entries below. Interestingly, Andrews chose to establish that Mary Poppins has orgasms, not merely that she has sexual relationships. For those who thought the character/actress was such a goody two shoes that she was a virgin or an abstinence advocate, she makes it clear that this is not the case, but she also insists upon the fact that she actually enjoys sex to the point of orgasm—lest she be suspected of having dutiful intercourse, forcing herself for the patriarchy but really finding it repulsive ("close your eyes and think of England"). In fact, not only does Poppins/Andrews have sex, but she is so *au fait* of it all that she even unblinkingly accepts the idea of gay sex. As Leigh W. Rutledge reminds us, *Victor/Victoria* opened everywhere to mostly enthusiastic reviews. Only Christian newspapers and overly intellectual critics objected. The comedy achieved "in some ways, what nearly thirteen years of gay liberation have not: an impression on the general public's consciousness of homosexuals as compassionate and likable people who should be left alone to live and love as they please" (Rutledge 1992: 187). Such an achievement could only reinforce Andrews' gay iconicity.

Yvonne Tasker, for her part, points out that Andrews' main costume in the movie partakes of a practice that has been a gay favorite for decades: "One of the most recognizable images of female-to-male cross-dressing in the world of entertainment is that of the female star body clothed in male evening dress: an image associated with cabaret stars such as Josephine Baker, and with stars of the 'classic' cinema such as Dietrich" (Tasker 1998: 23).

Julie Andrews, admittedly, had such a neat, pure, quasi-virginal image in the days of *The Sound of Music*, with that "fresh" makeup meant to look like an absence of makeup, that it might be hard for younger readers to imagine how big a gay icon she was and still is—although surely, such unadulterated wholesomeness had to be suspicious. Her popularity with the gays did not wait for *Victor/Victoria*.[3] It was her powerful four-octave voice, to a large extent, that triggered it—that voice she tragically lost in 1997 when she underwent calamitous surgery in New York, supposedly to remove a lone nodule from her vocal chords.

Andrews herself has never fully understood her gay icon status, although she feels flattered, as she told *The Guardian* in 2004: "I'm that odd mixture of, on the one hand, being a gay icon and, on the other hand, having grandmas and parents being grateful I'm around to be a babysitter for their kids. And I've never been able to figure out what makes a gay icon, because there are many different kinds."[4] Andrews never seemed to fully comprehend the camp irony that was associated with older icons such as Joan Crawford or Bette Davis, but she suspected that longevity had something to do with their status.

In *Mary Poppins*, she takes us back to those sweet days of childhood, when we knew we loved Dick (Dick Van Dyke/Bert) and loved the way he dressed and moved, without quite realizing all the dimensions of the attraction. He was not merely funny. We wanted to snap our fingers and see our room clean itself up, we wanted to dance with Bert in his striped jacket in some English park and sing "Supercalifragilisticexpialidocious" too—gaily.

Brett Farmer wonders about Andrews being the object of cult devotion in a queer culture context. He does see that she presents "few of the attributes regarded as intrinsic to the standard gay icon (excessive emotionalism, camp flamboyance, personal suffering, and/or a schizoid persona, to cite the usual suspects)," but he also notes that she displays others, "nostalgic wholesomeness, civility, and bourgeois propriety [...], that would seem about as far from the traditional semiotics of queer divadom as imaginable." He goes on to venture that perhaps that is why she has come to occupy a literally unique place among gay icons, and quotes those who declared, more or less in jest, that Julie Andrews more or less made them gay, such as Wayne Koestenbaum, Michael Musto, Cherry Jones, Kate Neilsen, and Brett Farmer himself (Farmer in Doty 2007: 144–145).

Gays like sing-along movies, and Julie Andrews is the undisputed queen of sing-along movies, finding serious competition only in *The Rocky Horror Picture Show*'s Tim Curry. In fact, Julie Andrew broke all sorts of box-office and album sale records throughout her career. Gay men love women who break records—they like women who break things, period.

Lauren Bacall (1924–2014)

In 2010, an ill-reputed biography by Darwin Porter entitled *Humphrey Bogart: The Making of a Legend* claimed that the actor was terrified of being gay, and slept with a thousand women before he met Lauren Bacall simply to reassure himself. If this is true, more than anything it shows that Bogart entertained the strangest conceptions in sexual matters—although, isn't it interesting that he chose Bacall, precisely (Porter 2010: 97)?

How many actresses ever wore a skirt or a pair of pants quite the way Bacall did? She famously wore clothing that was cut like men's, and that made her smolderingly sexy. She was style incarnate, her speaking voice almost rivaled Marlene Dietrich's (no one's speaking voice actually rivals Marlene Dietrich's, except perhaps Amanda Lear's). Sultry looks, smoky voice, iconic style, all she needed to complete the picture was to write interesting books, which, along with her politics, delighted many gay readers.

Many of Bacall's films are unforgettable, notably *The Big Sleep* (Howard Hawks, 1946), *Key Largo* (John Huston, 1948), and *Designing Woman* (Vincente Minnelli, 1957). In the tremendous *Written on the Wind* (Douglas Sirk, 1956), Bacall is upstaged by Dorothy Malone but remains highly prized.

In *To Have and Have Not* (Howard Hawks, 1944) when she asks, "Anybody got a match?" standing against the wall in the hotel corridor, her voice, her eyes and her gestures were enough to make her an instant gay icon. The way Humphrey Bogart and Lauren Bacall throw and catch that box of matches is terribly iconic—that hardly needs telling, as it is so universally accepted as such. The extraordinary potential for insolence, rebellion, even explosion that she conveys in those remarkable scenes, along with the feeling that she has seen the world and been through a lot, is astonishing when you reflect that she was 19 when she shot the movie. Indeed, she even claims she was still a virgin (Bacall 1994: 108).

In *By Myself* she remembers being educated to be "a nice Jewish girl":

[N]ice Jewish girls didn't smoke—weren't fast—nice Jewish girls had character. "Don't chase a boy, ever—if he wants to see you, he'll call; if not, forget him." But what were you to do if your head was filled with dreams of beauty, glamour, romance, accomplishment, and if you were stuck with being tall, ungainly (I didn't know I was "colt-like" until a critic said I was), with big feet, flat chested—too young to have finished high school at fifteen, too inexperienced, shy, frightened to know what to do with a boy when I did have a date? [Bacall 1978: 2].

Precisely. Surely all these elements helped turn her into a gay icon. In *Now* she writes: "Yet I'm called a legend by some, a title and category I am less than fond of. Aren't legends dead? Isn't that what makes a legend, not being around anymore? Or sometimes I'm called a special lady of films and theater, which makes me feel like a dowager empress" (Bacall 1994: 104). She does have a point, as some of our gay icons reach even more gay iconicity when they pass away, and are even more readily declared "leg-endary" (pronounced as RuPaul would). But when Bacall wrote this in 1994, she *was* a legend. People remember the lucky Bacall of the 1940s, who at the end of the day went home to the extraordinarily butch Bogie, finding rest and comfort in his manly arms. After she took off her sharp suit, they no doubt had torrid sex and then smoked a dozen post-coital cigarettes in their inimitable ways. How cool can you get? Many gays envied her, many gays adored her.

Lucille Ball (1911–1989)

In 1980, People asked Lucille Ball, the star of *I Love Lucy* (CBS, 1951–1957), her opinion of gay rights: "It's perfectly all right with me. Some of the most gifted people I've ever met or read about are homosexuals. How can you knock it?" (Rutledge 1992: 148)

Lee Tannen wrote a book entitled *I Loved Lucy: My Friendship with Lucille Ball*. "In it he recalled a mutual friend telling Ball how gay men adored her and how her curiosity was piqued when she learned about a gay bar in West Hollywood that played marathons of *I Love Lucy* episodes," Jeremy Kinser reminds us. "Tannen later told *Out* magazine, 'Lucy Ricardo was the true gay icon, [and] the underdog who was always trying to prove herself, and I think many gay men can identify with that.'"[5]

There is every cause to suspect that women cannot become full-fledged Hollywood stars if they have brown (i.e., colorless) hair,[6] at least since Hollywood went color. You need black, red, or blond hair. Since the 1960s it can be ash blond, but in the 1950s it was really either black, red, or platinum blond. If you express that theory in class, some students will try to find a counter example. Julia Roberts often comes to the rescue. However, it is easy to point out that she only became a star with *Pretty Woman* (Garry Marshall, 1990), in which her brown hair had acquired distinctly auburn highlights, if not actually red. That theory may be slightly far-fetched (Bette Davis was sometimes brown-haired in black-and-white movies), but it is based on observation: it takes drastic statements to give birth to a star, be they aesthetic or otherwise. At the very least, this is true of gay icons. Who needs a half-baked look? Every white woman's hair is naturally brown, for Pete's sake. A blazing icon is artificial, she is radical, her hair should be raven black, black as night, black as the heart of the "baddest bitches."[7] Or she should be a peroxide blonde, like Monroe and all her wannabes, because platinum blondes have more fun and gentlemen prefer blondes—because blondes rock. Otherwise, she can be a flaming redhead, the type of red or orange that could only ever come out of a bottle, like Rita Hayworth or Lucille Ball or David Bowie in the early 1970s.

Lured (Douglas Sirk, 1947) has often been called a film noir, which it is not, but it is a piece of curio, well worth seeing, if only because it is directed by Sirk and stars Ball. Naturally one prefers Sirk's melodramas, and there are elements of his habitual fare here, but *Lured* (aka *Personal Columns*)—a remake of *Pièges* (Robert Siodmak, 1939)—offers a vibrant Ball as a taxi-dancing smart mouth who collaborates with the authorities to catch a murderer and is oddly exciting for the viewer. The movie boasts the hyper-elegant George Sanders, soon to co-star in the all-time gay favorite *All About Eve* (Joseph L. Mankiewicz, 1950). Sanders was married to gay icon Zsa Zsa Gabor in 1949 and to her sister Magda Gabor in 1970. As we will see later, he spent a considerable part of his life surrounded by gay icons.

Like Lee Tannen, some might be tempted to say that Lucy Ricardo, the *I Love Lucy* show character, not Lucille Ball, was the gay icon. That is really beside the point. Fictional gay icons may well be found, such as Jessica Rabbit, but they are not the subject of this book. What matters most is that the conflation between dramatis persona and realitatis femina was fruitful and wide-ranging in *I Love Lucy*, just as it would be decades later with Alexis Morell Carrington Colby Dexter Rowan and Joan Collins, to give but one example at this stage.

Lawrence Applebaum writes about being fascinated by the makeup worn by Lucille/Lucy: "I didn't know what 'drag' was, but Lucy was always dressing up as someone else. The Queen of the Gypsies, Superman, even the first Drag King on television (singing in that barbershop quartet). Somehow Lucy managed to be glamorous frozen in a freezer with icicle eyelashes! I was in love." Applebaum also notes the striking friendship between Lucy and Ethel, which is easy to read as very positive from a feminist viewpoint and gives us an insight into another explanation for the show's continuing popularity with gay men: "[I]t seems Ethel was the first fag hag of the '50s: Lucy's slightly overweight sidekick, always ready with a campy one-liner" (Applebaum in Montlack 2009: 57).

One should not forget that Ball changed the rules of television sitcoms forever when she opted for the systematic use of the three-camera filming technique, which allows modern sitcoms to be shot in front of a live audience without interrupting the show while getting different complementary camera angles.[8] Gays love their sitcoms. This was incredibly modern of her, but even more modern was the way she fell in love with a Cuban musician and pressured the conservative network executives into hiring him, creating, in a rather feminist and pioneering way, Desilu Productions (the first independent television production company in the U.S.). Equally modern was her private investment towards the *I Love Lucy* pilot. Ball was her own boss in more ways than one, and she was definitely ballsy, the way gays like their icons to be.

Tallulah Bankhead (1902–1968)

Tallulah Bankhead grew up in Alabama, where one of her childhood friends was Zelda Sayre—later Zelda Fitzgerald—with whom she shared a rebellious streak. A larger-than-life actress, Bankhead vied with Mae West for the title of Queen of Camp. She came up with *bons mots* and Wildean aphorisms with a remarkable sense of timing and a splendid talent for apropos lines. One does not really need to go any further than resorting to four legendary Bankhead quotes to drive the point home.

When a producer suggested she replace Marlene Dietrich in a movie, Tallulah Bankhead replied: "I always did want to get into Marlene's pants" (Porter 2007: 271).[9]

"Daddy warned me about boys and booze, but he never said anything about girls and cocaine."[10]

To the robed thurifer, waving his censer in the air in an Anglican church: "I love the drag, darling, but do you know your purse is on fire?"[11]

The fourth quote we find in a Truman Capote book. Bankhead was at a party with writer Dorothy Parker and they were gazing at Montgomery Clift, who had passed out with drink.

> "He's so beautiful," murmured Miss Parker. "Sensitive. So finely made. The most beautiful man I've ever seen. What a pity he's a cocksucker. [...] I mean, he is a cocksucker, isn't he, Tallulah?"
>
> Miss Bankhead said: "Well, d-d-darling, I r-r-really wouldn't know. He's never sucked my cock" [Capote 1986: 110–111].

Who needs more? Of course, a woman who speaks such lines, a woman who is always corrosively humorous, venomous, and questions traditional visions of gender and sexual orientation decades before Judith Butler is going to be hailed as a gay icon. Dorothy Parker herself has often been said to be a (literary) gay icon—like Carson McCullers or Anne Rice. Indeed, if the old-fashioned expression "a friend of Dorothy" designates a male homosexual, this is seemingly due to two women, *The Wizard of Oz*'s Judy Garland and the writer Dorothy Parker, a gay icon, who famously declared: "Heterosexuality is not normal, it's just common."[12]

People still discuss whether or not the part of Margo Channing in all-time gay favorite *All About Eve* (Joseph L. Mankiewicz, 1950) was based on Tallulah Bankhead. Apparently not,[13] but *se non è vero, è ben trovato*, as they say in Italy.[14]

Husky-voiced Bankhead came from a well-to-do, conservative, Southern Democratic family. She often disagreed with them on various political issues, such as Civil Rights. Excessive in every domain, she spoke too much, spent too much, had too much sex, drank too much booze, took too many drugs, etc. After a few attempts at success in the U.S., she emigrated to London, England, to work in the West End.

Joe, the Closet Professor, writes:

> For seven years Bankhead was the toast of London. British audiences adored her, whether the content was classy or tawdry. A group of aficionados who emulated Tallulah (gallery girls) would cheer whenever she made an entrance and, delighted, she would wave back at them, saying, "Thank you dahlings." She was an extremely accessible star and would happily greet her fans at the stage door, signing autographs, inquiring as to their health, sometimes even making them guests in her home.[15]

After that, hard-partying Bankhead went back to the U.S. to star in Broadway plays. She was mostly a theatrical actress, but she did have one big movie hit, *Lifeboat* (Alfred Hitchcock, 1944). In this respect she is a unique gay icon because many gay men love her although they have only ever seen her in *Lifeboat*. They were too poor to travel to New York to see her on stage, or they were nine and living on the other side of the pond when she died, and yet they love her, notably because of what they heard or read about her. "Over the years stories of her merry debauchery have been passed from generation to generation."[16]

In *Lifeboat* Bankhead plays the glamorous journalist Connie Porter. It is because of her that this Hitchcock movie should be watched, even though it is not generally counted among his best. In *Die! Die! My Darling!* (Silvio Narizzano, 1965), aka *Fanatic*, a Hammer film, Bankhead reaches wonderful levels of camp, being chillingly terrifying and terribly amusing at the same time. This gothic movie was deliberately trying to compete with *What Ever Happened to Baby Jane?* (Robert Aldrich, 1962), which will be covered below, in the way it took an aging gay icon and gave her an outré part.

Tallulah Bankhead was The Black Widow in two 1967 episodes of the television series *Batman* (Fox 1966–1968). Considering that series is one of the campest ever, and definitely a gay classic, this was an inspired piece of casting that could only reinforce the camp quotient of both product and actress in a marvelous synergy.[17]

It seems Bankhead had affairs with a number of men and women (Billie Holiday, Mercedes de Acosta, Marlene Dietrich, Greta Garbo and Joan Crawford are rumored to have dabbled with her).[18] She is even said to have had a threesome with Dietrich and Howard Hughes.[19] Such gossip, linked to a scathing wit and the fact that she inspired the creation of Disney's Cruella de Vil in *One Hundred and One Dalmatians* (1961), can only endear her to gays.

Shirley Bassey (1937–)

In "This Is My Life," Shirley Bassey proclaims that this is who she is, this is her actual life, this is the person she is under the makeup. That is why drag queens all over the world like miming the lyrics to this song in their act. One begins the song looking as glamorous as possible: hyperfeminine, a sheath dress, a glitzy wig, and a pair of evening gloves. Then at the end, one wipes off one's eye shadow with a majestic motion, one ruins one's lipstick with an emphatic gesture of the back of one's hand, and finally one tears off one's wig, belting out that this is who one truly is. With the melodramatic accents of Bassey, it works wonders. It should be noted that this song is not to be confused with gay icon Eartha Kitt's song of the same title.

Jean-Pierre, aka Lee Allen, drag queen extraordinaire in the enchanted Cannes of the 1970s and 1980s, had turned this classic into a much more subversive number.[20] Cleverly, he used Vic Damone's version, beginning the song in leather pants and a Perfecto leather jacket, looking very butch indeed. He wore a black leather cap and mirror Ray-Bans, standing still with his legs apart and his hands in his pockets, moving his shoulders in a subtle way that screamed masculinity. At the point in the song when his colleagues who did the Bassey version in those days took off their dresses and/or their wigs then started wreaking havoc on their makeup, Jean-Pierre took off his cap, without missing a beat or the least inflection of Vic Damone's manly version. Out cascaded a long blond wig, reminiscent of French gay icon and singer Sylvie Vartan's hair. He then took off his glasses to reveal gorgeous almond eyes, heavily made-up and sporting three pairs of fake eyelashes glued together. Then he removed his jacket and tore off his pants, in the manner of strippers (how did the world go round before the invention of Velcro?). At this point the audience realized that the pants were extremely long so as to hide his stiletto heels until the reveal. The creature thus unveiled wore a figure-hugging red dress, evocative of Rita Hayworth in *Gilda* (Charles Vidor, 1946). The song ended with Jean-Pierre striking nightclub singer poses. Strangely enough, that song is originally Italian: "La vita" was written by Bruno Canfora and Antonio Amurri. In fact, Shirley Bassey originally sang it in English and Italian, in 1968, with a rather strange Italian accent. Since then there have been interesting remixes of the song. Bassey's 1979 disco version, the one Jean-Pierre's colleagues used, was an instant gay hit in clubs—or was it an instant hit in gay clubs?

Shirley Bassey recorded the theme song for the James Bond movie *Goldfinger* (Guy Hamilton, 1964). My parents bought the single. On the sleeve of the vinyl record was a picture of British actress Shirley Eaton (the 1964 Bond girl), lying in bed on her stomach, her naked body entirely spray-painted gold. Not knowing any better, I thought *this* was the Shirley Bassey whose name was featured above the photograph ("Goldfinger La chanson du générique par Shirley Bassey"). I can be forgiven, I was only five—it never occurred me that the voice I instantly fell for did not sound so white, and no, I do not believe that is a racist thing to say. Bassey being non-white is part of the attraction for gays, but this notion is even more relevant when it comes to singers such as Gloria Gaynor, as we will see. *Goldfinger* is a gay favorite because of this song, but also, undoubtedly, because of the lesbian character with the marvelously evocative name Pussy Galore.

When Bassey sings *Sweet Charity*'s "Big Spender" in 1967, she appropriates the trashy glamour and the chutzpah of many a Bob Fosse creature and anticipates Chaka Khan (sometimes dubbed a gay icon). Unsurprisingly, that song is a gay favorite—many products associated with Bob Fosse notoriously are. It is basically an ode to prostitution, or at least to sugar-babying in nightclubs.[21] In gay clubs, beautiful young men and unprepossessing old men know a lot about that exchange system. *Sweet Charity* brings to mind Gwen Verdon, who was so stupendous in the stage musical in 1966, by all accounts. Verdon is an icon to many gays, although my (young) students on either side of the Atlantic have no idea who she is. I disagree with David Van Leer, who thinks that when *Sweet Charity* was adapted for Hollywood in 1969, "the role went without success to Shirley MacLaine, who was overtaxed by the part's singing and dancing" (Van Leer 1995: 170). On the contrary, one might be tempted to think that this is one of MacLaine's most interesting roles, one that helped make her something of a gay icon.

When Bassey covers "Can't Take My Eyes Off You," she is contributing to a noteworthy phenomenon: a 1967 Franki Valli song that has been covered hundreds of times all over the globe, but most notably by gay favorites and gay icons, among them Sheena Easton, Gloria Gaynor, Pet Shop Boys, Amanda Lear, Heath Ledger, Frida Lyngstad, Mina, Michelle Pfeiffer, Diana Ross, Jimmy Sommerville, and especially the transparently named Boys Town Gang. This song echoes a debate that has divided psychoanalysts, feminists and feminist psychoanalysts for decades, one that is frequently raised in gender studies classes: how do you experience desire? Do you experience desire strictly through your eyes or through your other senses (as well)? Most people would agree to say that men desire through sight (cf. Laura Mulvey's "male gaze"), whereas women also desire through smell and hearing.

Your girlfriends will often rave about a man's voice or smell, but their brothers will barely register such "details" in women, and merely concentrate on visuals. What people fight over is whether this difference (which is verifiable on a daily basis, just ask around) is innate or learned. Complete constructionists believe it is totally acquired. In the song she claims that she simply cannot believe just how beautiful the addressee is, and as a result she cannot help constantly gazing at the addressee. She very much wants to hold the addressee, feeling the stirrings of love, which is so wonderful that she feels grateful she is on this planet. The song goes on to state that if the speaker feels feeble and desperately needs the addressee, it is entirely due to the physical appearance of the addressee. There is nothing to indicate that any conversation has taken place; we are really dealing with lust at first sight, i.e., purely visual, superficial desire, unembarrassed by other considerations. In a heterosexual context this might be problematic—in a gay context, not so much.

Alas, some might argue that Bassey has lost the right to be a gay icon (possibly like Donna Summer, although as we will see, Summer's crimes may be worse). Many see gay iconicity as something that is earned, deserved, something one ought to strive to remain worthy of at all times. Gays like their icons to be at least minimally feminist. In an interview with the *Daily Mail* in 2015, Bassey expressed horrendous anti-feminist sentiments: she believes women should not be pilots, firefighters, policewomen or soldiers, among other appalling ideas. In fact, it is tempting to attribute such sexist garbage to senility.[22] And it does not take much digging to find out that she uttered homophobic tripe long before 2015. When she saw the kiss between her friend Peter Finch and Murray Head in *Sunday, Bloody Sunday* (John Schlesinger, 1971) she was "sick" to the point of having to exit the movie theater (Russo 1987: 211). Still, how can you not shiver when she intones that she is utterly alone in the world, not owning a single thing, and helplessly in love and in lust with the addressee of her song?

Marisa Berenson (1947–)

The granddaughter of fashion designer Elsa Schiaparelli, Marisa Berenson started her career as a model and then graduated to acting. In 1973 she declared: "I, for one, have become a big fan of homosexuals. I've become a fag moll really. There's nothing more fun than fags" (Rutledge 1992: 58). Obviously, such statements are immensely problematic. As I said in my introduction, women do not need to be fag hags to become gay icons. Besides, many gay men might take exception with the sweeping generalization at play here. Probably more so today than back in 1973, when they took any sympathy they could get. Such a generalization implies that all fags are the same and that they are all "fun," a notion that can easily be disproved. However, there was a measure of camp and humor in this and in everything else she said and did in public, so she is forgiven.

Can gay men be happier with declarations such as the following by Sigourney Weaver? Jase Peeples quoted her reaction to being celebrated by Geeks OUT in April 2013:

> I am extremely touched and thrilled to be honored by Geeks OUT as a queer geek icon and muse. It means so much to me that my work has been relevant and encouraging to the LGBT community. I support each and every one of you to be exactly and gloriously who you are and all you can be. The planet needs your individuality and talent and power to make it a more humane and respectful and fantastic place, where everyone is valued and celebrated equally. So rock on and geek out, my friends. Have a wonderful time tonight. Thank you again for this awesome honor [...]

Peeples concludes: "It's warm and fuzzy moments like this that remind us Weaver is far more than an LGBT icon or ally, she's a genuine friend of the community as well."[23] We do not have to agree with him. Weaver is clearly more of a lesbian icon, as indicated by the lesbian reaction to the Alien quadrilogy (cf. Smyth in Burston & Richardson 1995: 124).

One thing that gay men have in common, of course, is their desire for men. That is something they also share with heterosexual women, especially those who have not been successfully brainwashed by the patriarchy to believe they can only desire their husband or at least the man they love. This is something that Berenson understood early in the day both on and off screen. Gay men identify with her in *Barry Lyndon* (Stanley

Kubrick, 1975), but even more so (and more easily) in gay favorite *Cabaret* (Bob Fosse, 1972), with gay icon Liza Minnelli. As the pure Natalia Landauer who becomes crazy with lust ("the fire") for Fritz she is tremendous; and the contrast with the slutty Sally Bowles (Liza Minnelli) is immensely enjoyable (more on Sally Bowles below). Berenson also appeared in the gay cult film *Death in Venice* (Luchino Visconti, 1971) and other films.

She spent quite a lot of time, particularly in the 1970s, in legendary clubs such as New York's Studio 54 in the company of glamorous gay boys and cocaine-sniffing stars. She had a series of impressive lovers and husbands, including both a Rothschild and gay favorite and Visconti creature Helmut Berger. All this can be read about in her book *Moments intimes* (Berenson 2009: *passim*).

Louise Brooks (1906–1985)

Not only is it heavily advised to be a very blonde blonde, a very raven brunette or a very flamboyant redhead to become an icon, it is also useful to have a look, besides having looks. Dancer and actress Louise Brooks, originally from Kansas, had a look. Indeed, she shocked her admirers when she appeared long-haired in *Overland Stage Raiders* (George Sherman, 1938). Before that annoying move, her signature black bob hairdo had contributed immensely to her celebrity.

Louise Brooks starred in the silent movie *Die Büchse der Pandora* (*Pandora's Box*, G.W. Pabst, 1929), which "featured what is probably the first explicitly drawn lesbian character on film" (Russo 1987: 24). Many people worldwide thought she was a real-life lesbian. Brooks starred in two dozen movies, but all you really need to remember is *Die Büchse der Pandora* and *Tagebuch einer Verlorenen* (*Diary of a Lost Girl*, G.W. Pabst, 1929).

What makes Brooks a remarkable exception in this book is that not only is she a gay intellectuals' icon, as it were, but she also became a gay icon more than two decades after the fact. Indeed these two elements are linked. When she made those movies in Europe, Americans almost ignored her, and Europeans did not immediately hail her as a unique and unforgettable performer. Her cult status came much later, starting in the 1950s, as the result of the rediscovery of her work by Parisian film buffs, followed by American academics and feminist scholars (people such as Henri Langlois and Mary Ann Doane). In 1982 she reinforced this phenomenon when she published her fascinating autobiography, *Lulu in Hollywood*.

Brooks inspired Adolfo Bioy Casares' science fiction novel *The Invention of Morel* (1940). She also inspired Liza Minnelli's look as Sally Bowles in *Cabaret* (Bob Fosse, 1972). The Italian graphic artist Guido Crepax modeled his beautiful comic book heroine Valentina (1965–1996) on her.[24] In gay favorite *Death Becomes Her* (Robert Zemeckis, 1992), Isabella Rosselini's look as Lisle von Rhoman is partly based on Louise Brooks. There are many more such examples.

What we are dealing with is an uncanny conflation of actress Louise and character Lulu, linked with an embodiment of the (1920s) zeitgeist (however belated): the liberated flapper. A self-destructive streak, a deep I-Don't-Care-About-Anything-Really attitude, a superior intelligence and a complicated love life and sex life (more or less bisexual), including a one-night-stand with Greta Garbo, it would seem, helped forge her retrospective but nonetheless vivid gay iconicity. Some are still debating if Brooks was a superbly talented actress or if indeed she acted at all: the iconic result is the same.

Maria Callas (1923–1977)

For various reasons, Maria Callas is the only opera diva (the only proper diva, the only actual diva, some would say) in this book. I know literature, popular music, cinema and television (especially from the U.S.) relatively well, but I am about as knowledgeable in classical music and opera as I am in quantum physics. However, even the least operatic of queens know this operatic queen, and can even identify her voice when it is used in some tampon commercial on television. I do know a lot about gay favorite Jacqueline Bouvier Kennedy Onassis, and funnily enough it is through my studying her that I got interested in Maria Callas via their common lover Aristotle Onassis.

In Terrence McNally's play *The Lisbon Traviata* (1989), as well as in his play *Master Class* (1995), the Callas gay cult is stoked. That cult is also perceivable in how Callas' singing is used in the gay-themed movie *Philadelphia* (Jonathan Demme, 1993) and in the biopic of gay activist Harvey Milk, *Milk* (Gus Van Sant, 2008).

Wayne Koestenbaum's fascinating book *The Queen's Throat: Opera, Homosexuality and the Mystery of Desire* (1993) has a great deal to say about gay men's love of opera and about Callas. Glenn McNatt has read him too.[25] He explains:

> Gay men are attracted to opera precisely because its extravagant displays of emotion and willfulness express a secret realm of feeling denied them in the "straight" world. Callas—in her life and art the supreme exemplar of that extravagance, and of the terrible price it exacts from those who indulge it—is a gay icon because she willed her art into being out of terrible private suffering and made that suffering public. [...] "Gays are considered a dispensable population. Listening to Callas, we become less dispensable: we find a use, a reflection, an elevation. For political, ethical, combative, and ineluctable reasons, I consider my interest in Callas to be a piece of my sexual and cultural identity." [...] Callas is a gay icon, too, because she celebrated female wrath and willfulness and because such behavior so wholeheartedly exceeded the bounds of acceptable gender behavior of her era. "Displays of masculine power," Koestenbaum writes, "are alienating and depressing (they reflect patriarchy's sway), but displays of feminine power show the universe executing an about-face. [Callas'] vengeful volleys give us courage, and inspire us as we struggle to be open and not closed, serene and not erased, human and not degenerate."[26]

The Italian director Pier Paolo Pasolini is a well-known addiction among gay film buffs. He got Callas to play Medea in *Medea* (Pier Paolo Pasolini, 1969), in which gorgeous Laurent Terzieff plays the Centaur. Arianna Huffington writes about the soprano's "fascinating" and "unlikely" friendship with Pasolini: "Maria, who, at her most petty, had exploded against both Marxists and homosexuals, had found in Pasolini, a passionate Marxist and a notorious homosexual, not just a friend but, as she was to say after his death, a brother" (Huffington 2002: 177).

The Italian director Luchino Visconti is also a vivacious cult among gay film buffs—and not just because of his pet actor Helmut Berger doing Marlene Dietrich in *The Damned* (*La caduta degli dei*, 1969). Huffington writes, "It was she who sought him out, and she who cleared the way into La Scala for him. He had the entire Milanese establishment against him—those who did not mind his homosexuality objected to his Communism and vice versa. But Maria was the reigning queen and Maria wanted Visconti" (Huffington 2002: 68).

Callas is typically, like Eva Perón,[27] a woman who remains mysterious enough to make you keep buying biographies of her and watching European biopics of her, even bad TV movies sometimes—and still she eludes you. Callas knew everything there was to know about the alienation of vulnerable people. Gay men often know a lot about that too. Gays love a diva shrouded in mystery: mystery equates with glamour. Interestingly, Callas is disliked by many "classical" opera lovers, who take exception to her unusual voice (which eventually abandoned her). In many ways a trainwreck story, Callas' biography delights the gay fan who likes reading about painful struggles with weight, doomed affairs with politicians and millionaires, supercharged diva behavior and occasional self-destructive excesses. The new biopic, *Callas* (Niki Caro, 2017), with Noomi Rapace in the title role, has a lot to live up to.

Naomi Campbell (1970–)

Naomi Campbell is practically the reason the word "supermodel" had to be invented. "Top model" would not have sufficed to describe the degree of glamour and fame she reached. She was one of the modeling stars of the 1990s who quickly grew very rich: Cindy Crawford, Linda Evangelista, Christy Turlington, Claudia Schiffer.... Her first appearance in the public arena was in Bob Marley's video for "Is This Love" (1978). She was seven. At 15, she was spotted by the manager of a modeling agency while shopping in Covent Garden. She soon signed with Elite Model Management. Even before she came of age she graced the cover of the British version of *Elle* and the British edition of *Vogue* (where few black women had appeared). After that she stopped counting. By now, she has notoriously appeared on more than 500 magazine covers across the globe.

Today Naomi Campbell is as famous for her violent tantrums as for her modeling. In 2009 she assaulted a photographer with her handbag. At that time *The Mirror* published a reminder of her most publicized past antics, amusing and relevant enough to warrant a long quotation:

> February 2000: Pleads guilty to a 1998 assault on Georgina Galanis, her then assistant. Campbell had assaulted Galanis with a telephone in a hotel room and threatened to throw her out of a moving car. November 2004: Accused of allegedly head-butting personal assistant Amie Castaldo in the face, biting her on the lip and yanking her to the ground by her hair [...]. August 2005: Accused of leaving actress friend Yvonne Scio "covered in blood" after a row over a skimpy outfit. [...] March 2006: Hit housekeeper Ana Scolavino with jewel-encrusted mobile phone. Given five days' community service in 2007. July 2006: Allegedly slapped assistant Amanda Brack and beat her around the head with a BlackBerry. Settled out of court. October 2006: Naomi was arrested after an alleged assault on her drugs councilor. June 2008: Naomi paid out "thousands of pounds" to Slovakian housekeeper Ivana Lovas who took her to court claiming she was a victim of racial and sexual discrimination. June 2008: Naomi carried out 200 hours' community service for kicking and spitting at police after going "berserk" on an aircraft at Heathrow. January 2009: Naomi reaches a settlement with former maid, Gaby Gibson, who claimed that she verbally and physically abused her.[28]

Campbell is also known for her clashes with rival celebrities such as Tyra Banks and former Spice Girl Victoria Beckham. Like some of her competitors, she seems to have decided early in her career that she wanted to be present on every front. She "wrote" a novel entitled *Swan* (1994). The blurb claims: "Naomi Campbell's first novel is both runway romance and front-cover thriller, a page-turning, appetite-whetting invitation to the extraordinary world of fashion. It is a novel told with the undeniable force of experience, but it is above all a story for everyone who's gone from schoolgirl to supermodel in their dreams." If not exactly the worst thing one could read, it is excessive to call it a page-turner. Clearly it was calculated to please teenage girls and gay men. Campbell also released a (much more entertaining) book of photographs of her, simply entitled *Naomi* (1996). Besides, she recorded an album entitled *Baby Woman* (1994). It was understandably trashed by the critics, for the most part. But one hears much worse on the radio. The album was a commercial success in Japan but a relative failure in the rest of the world.

Campbell has appeared in numerous music videos for artists such as George Michael and Michael Jackson, as well as in movies and television series. She has worked with the most glamorous fashion designers and the best photographers, including Richard Avedon, Steven Meisel, Herb Ritts, and Mario Testino. Since 2013, she has regularly been featured as a judge in several versions of the show *The Face*, in the U.S., the UK and Australia. It's called diversification.

Alongside her modeling career, Naomi Campbell has developed new activities and participated in numerous humanitarian projects in collaboration with people such as Nelson Mandela and the Dalai Lama, and with organizations such as UNESCO.

In 2010, she testified at the trial of Charles Taylor, Liberia's former president, who was charged with war crimes and crimes against humanity. At the hearing she recounted her meeting with Taylor and talked about receiving a few "little diamonds." She said she talked about that gift to her agent Carole White and to actress Mia Farrow, the very next day. She also claims to have given the diamonds to charities, a story that was corroborated by an official of the Nelson Mandela Foundation. Her testimony was damning for Charles Taylor and confirmed how the war in Sierra Leone was fueled in the 1990s.

Like Madonna, Campbell got involved with the Kabbalah community at some stage. She has been linked romantically in the media to various interesting men, including Flavio Briatore, Eric Clapton, Adam Clayton, Robert De Niro, Vladislav Doronin, Terrence Howard, Lenny Kravitz, Guy Laliberté, Sergio Marone, Mike Tyson, and Usher. If one is to believe the tabloids (notably the Italian ones, which adore her), she only ever dates very rich men, and that makes gay men dream.

Like many of the gay icons featured in this book, she has her own range of cosmetics and perfumes. Unfortunately the gamut of celebrity perfumes often tend to be distributed in cheap supermarkets instead of glamorous perfume stores, and they often smell like it too.

In an insightful article entitled "Gay Men's Revenge," Susan Bordo starts with a well-known quote by John Berger from his book 1972 book *Ways of Seeing* about the fact that in the arts and in commercials, "men act and women appear" (Bordo 1999: 21).

> Where do we stand today? [...] Not surprisingly, the situation is postmodern pastiche. The old world [...] has become a cartoon. The macho man of the glowering underwear ads and the action hero movies are comic-book creations, virtual self-parodies. Our culture's icons of feminine "appearance," the movie stars

and models, are now cyborgs, perfected by plastic; the way they "appear" to us is always retouched, often computer altered. The daring "reversals" suggested by contemporary images of power-babes and languid young men, while they may seem revolutionary, finally have something familiar, even cartoon-like about them, depending as they do on such literal and highly dualistic notions about activity and passivity, power and vulnerability, who asserts and who "receives." "Acting" and "appearing" themselves, of course, have always been something of a false duality. All that attention to appearance women have engaged in is hardly passive preening; it is hard work. At the same time, the man who tries to be as tough as the Marlboro man is, of course, attempting to "appear" a certain way. Nowadays, the duality is even less meaningful, as the cultivation of the suitably fit "appearance" has become not just a matter of sexual allure but also a demonstration that one has the "right stuff": will, discipline, the ability to stop whining and "just do it." Image making is the main industry of our culture, and when it comes to one's own body, it is a full-time job.

These lines fit hardworking Campbell, her career and entourage, in many different ways (they also fit a few other gay icons in this book, and many male gay icons). She is totally plastic in the best sense of the word (for lookist gays, that is). It is said that when Spike Lee decided to employ her in *Girl 6* (1996), he insisted she take off the green contact lenses she wore in her photo shoots, which he thought indicated a form of internalized racism. Those lenses did little to decrease her plasticity or her "plasticness," as it were. Campbell's participation in Madonna's very gay book *Sex* (1992) is pure postmodern plastic, like the participation of the plastic cowboys and comic-book sadomasochists who, like her, "appear."[29] Hurrah for Photoshop, who needs reality, many superficial gays might say. In 2015, she had a sexy bitch "cyborg" part, Camilla Marks, in the series *Empire*, created by gay director/producer Lee Daniels, in which she was all about artifice and gay iconicity—although she was not quite so iconic as the great Taraji P. Henson playing the feisty Cookie. Out gay actor Jussie Smollett, who plays the gay son in *Empire*, is friends with Naomi Campbell and loves Madonna.[30] He and Campbell appear together in UK gay magazine *Attitude*, where she claims:

"I have been surrounded by gay men my entire life [...] and because I have grown up working in the creative and fashion industries, many of them have become like family to me." [Gay stylist Edward] Enninful regularly refers to Naomi as his sister. "I've always said without gay men, I wouldn't be where I am today." Where she talks the talk, she walks the walk. As a child, possibly hinting at her future work with the gay community particularly the lucrative charity initiatives for the amfAR (the Foundation for Aids Research), she adored Boy

George and Culture Club. "He was my childhood idol and I'm glad to be able to call him a personal friend," she says. [...] "As a fan, I feel lucky to have appeared in two Culture Club videos." [...] And true to her lethal instinct for the power of camp, she simply adores *Drag Race*. "Naomi Smalls is amazing. Ru's show has brought so many talented performers to the public. I'm pleased to see that drag culture is being accepted more in the mainstream."

Naomi was there for the start of it all. "I have fond memories, from the Nineties in New York, of the colourful characters from the House of Xtravaganza, so it is humbling to be looked upon as a fashion icon by this community. All I can say is, the love, adoration and support is mutual."

Seriously, though, how can you not love this woman?[31]

In the television series *Star*, also created by Lee Daniels, Campbell plays Rose Crane, rock star wife, addict and mother. One only has to watch her express disdain, saying, "She's positively repulsive is what she is," with a designer dog on her lap, to understand how her iconicity works (season 1, episode 2).

Mariah Carey (1969–)

Mariah Carey is undeniably a diva and has often been mocked in the press for her prima donna behavior—which some of us find endearing—as well as for her poor fashion choices. If she had only recorded *one* particular song, her version of "Without You" (1994), she would probably be a gay icon, seeing as she reaches record levels of torch-singing in her rendition. Gays buy her albums in great numbers, even if they often snub her poor cinematic efforts. She has sold more than 200 million albums. When she sang a duet with fellow gay icon Whitney Houston, "When You Believe" (1998), trying to out-torch her older friend and/or rival, thousands of gay Houston aficionados became her fans.

The website TheGayUK speaks of the "11 Mariah Carey Songs Every Gay Boy Needs In His Life" and claims that "there's nobody that quite manages to fulfil their Diva quota like Mariah. In among the glitter, butterflies and working out in five inch heels, she's written some belters to help you get through the darkest moments of your life."[32] The song "Hero" (1993) is generally seen as a gay anthem.

Mariah Carey

I am sometimes chagrined when a performer is said to be camp and I myself do not see it immediately. Is there something wrong with me? Gage *et al.* call Mariah Carey "so camp it's almost frightening" (Gage *et al.* 2002: 20). I must confess I had not thought her so. Using Christopher Isherwood's distinctions loosely (Isherwood in Cleto 1999: 51),[33] maybe I could extricate myself from this by declaring her low camp, as opposed to, say, Whitney Houston, who's camp; in the same way I could call Maria Callas and Montserrat Caballé high camp, Bernadette Peters and Sylvie Vartan camp, and Paris Hilton and Sheila low camp. Looking at glam rock, several incarnations of David Bowie were camp, or maybe even high camp, especially Ziggy Stardust, whereas Gary Glitter was never anything but low camp, just like Suzi Quatro, Alvin Stardust, Sweet, and Slade. Whether or not Carey is low camp, at any rate, she is certainly excellent at adding layer after layer of pathos to torch songs, delighting many a gay man in the process. Camp, notoriously, is to a large degree in the eye of the beholder.

Clearly Carey has a weight problem, which anyone watching her perform through the years can recognize, even without reading tabloids. In the summer of 2017 she showed off a rather inflated body in her Caesar's Palace show in Las Vegas, which prompted many jokes about her dancers' weight-lifting. Apparently it did not cross her mind to alter her style and wear less revealing and/or less figure-hugging costumes. Good for her, some would say. Presumably she constantly goes on and off diets (like so many of the women discussed in this book, notably Britney Spears). Many gays relate to this.

Gays know they are the most lookist and fattist bitches on the planet, and they need to stay in shape if they want to remain on the market, just like Mariah (or not?). She often feels like she is about to go entirely train wreck on us and then seems to stay just this side of it. On December 31, 2016, she made a complete fool of herself in Times Square, as her short New Year's Eve show turned into a cataclysm. Obviously her ardent fans forgave her, and her official reaction consisted of a tweet saying: "Shit happens. Have a happy and healthy new year everybody! Here's to making more headlines in 2017." What can one do to recover from such a disaster, broadcast all over the planet? Drugs? Alcohol? Chocolates? Are the comfort that gay iconicity brings her and her reliance on her gay fan base enough to reassure her?

Cher (1946–)

Cher is the living goddess of many gays, vying for the title of reigning Regal Diva with Madonna now that Joan Crawford, Bette Davis and Judy Garland are gone. Cher is a mistress of reinvention, and gays love reinvention (and not just because they often had to reinvent themselves to reinforce the doors of their closets). Even if many of today's gays are very essentialist when it comes to sexual orientation (it serves their assimilationist politics, the "Hey I was born this way, you have to give me gay marriage and gay parenting" stance), they are happily often constructionist when it comes to gender (otherwise gay icons would not exist). They know that femininity is a construction and they love a good story. They love hyperfemininity because they know no little girl comes out of her mother's womb wiggling her bottom, pouting and craving sequins. I have no doubt that every morning Cher (and other gay icons before or after her, such as Amanda Lear and Madonna) wakes up, stands in front of her mirror and wonders, hmm, what version of femininity am I going to perform this time? Or if not every day, maybe every two years or so.

Cher's biography, discography, televisionography and filmography are fascinating and impressive. Cher is an immense actress who won a well-deserved Oscar for *Moonstruck* (Norman Jewison, 1987); the way her character, Loretta Castorini, asserts herself is forever branded in every film buff's psyche. She was flabbergasting in *Mermaids* (Richard Benjamin, 1990).[34] That movie offers splendid quotes for those of us who love female characters such as Mrs. Flax, free and independent and uninhibited. Mrs. Flax claims that there are two important things that a woman should know, one of which is driving. She also tells her teenage daughter, when gazing upon a 26-year-old man, that "a real woman is never too old." In *The Witches of Eastwick* (George Miller, 1987) Cher is Alexandra Medford, an over-the-top bewitching witch who triumphs at the end and delights gay viewers worldwide with fellow witches/feminists Jane Spofford (Susan Sarandon) and Sukie Ridgemont (Michelle Pfeiffer).

The tremendous television show *RuPaul's Drag Race* is constantly preoccupied with divadom and gay iconicity. RuPaul's drag queens are inspired by gay icons, they pay weekly tributes to gay icons, they lip-sync to the songs of gay icons, and occasionally they even satirize gay icons when they play the "Snatch Game."

Around the globe, hundreds of drag queens have done Cher at one point or another. I myself have seen quite a few "Chers" perform on three continents. Now the world has Chad Michaels, who does Cher magnificently and has even had plastic surgery to look more like her, to the point that he sometimes looks more like Cher than Cher does. Such are the paradoxes of the constructed femininity of gay icons.

Like many a gay icon, Cher is a fag hag. I always use the term in its most positive sense, as I have said, and in no way do I ever imply that fag-haggery is a prerequisite for gay icons. Some think fag-haggery is ill-advised, perhaps because they entertain negative notions of what constitutes a fag hag.[35] I see fag hags as independent women with feminist leanings who like gay culture and enjoy the company of gays, gays who provide a welcome break from the harassment they sometimes suffer in other quarters. Cher has often voiced her support for gays. She declined an invitation to perform at the Winter Olympics in Russia in 2013 because of the rampant and unchecked homophobia that affects and sometimes kills LGBT people in that country.

"Believe" (1998) and "Strong Enough" (1999) are gay songs in exactly the same way Gloria Gaynor's "I Will Survive" (1978) is a gay song (cf. below). They helped Cher conquer a whole new generation of gay boys, as my disco-dancing students told me back then.

In the *Routledge Encyclopedia of Queer Culture*, edited by David A. Gerstner, John Forde writes that the daughter of Sonny Bono and Cher, Chastity Bono, "achieved gay iconic status in her own right when she came out as a lesbian in 1995" (Forde in Gerstner 2006: 94). This was before she became a he by the name of Chaz Bono. I am not certain Chastity Bono ever was a gay icon, she was presumably something of a lesbian icon, but I am quite certain Chaz Bono is a trans icon now. Of course, there is something in the fact that this particular brave person is the daughter of über-gay icon Cher that can only make gays marvel.

In a Vegas club whose name I forget, in 2003, I greatly enjoyed a female female impersonator (a genetic woman in female drag), whose name eludes me, in her performance as Cher. The singing was interesting and to the point, the looks and the look acceptable, but the Cher talk between two songs was very convincing indeed. At some point she stood on the edge of the stage and dragged up a nine- or ten-year-old boy. He answered all of her questions with gusto, and laughed good-naturedly when she went on at great length about being a "major older babe." But then she asked him for a kiss, and he screamed, "No way!" At that point, my traveling companion and I idly surmised that this boy was going to grow up straight. More seriously, Cher's "major-older-babeness" is very much part of her attraction. She has aged so slowly and so well, with all the plastic surgery and other artifices that show-business money can buy. Surely she is reaching some sort of limit these days. Unless she sells her soul to the devil there will come a time when she will look ancient regardless of what she does. But how many other people can claim that they looked better in the 1980s and 1990s than in the 1960s and 1970s—and I am not merely referring to her nose?

Before turning to dance music and after her hippyish period, Cher had acquired some degree of "street cred" as a rock 'n' roll chick, riding motorbikes and hanging out with tough guys. Gays love rock 'n' roll chicks (at least those who wear lipstick), and gays love fantasizing about tough bikers.

The following long quotation, an onstage, between-songs lesson in gay-iconicity-reinforcement, is self-explanatory:

> Thank you. Ok. Wait. I have to get my serious, put my serious outfit on. I have outfits for every move. Serious jacket. Serious hat for my naturally blond hair. And what's an outfit without a whip? [cheers] Thank you. So. What did you think of my entrance? [cheers] Yes, it was very fabulous, wasn't it? Actually, it's worked every, every place but in Cleveland. And, in Cleveland a, uh, chandelier came down and I was hanging up there like some sort of transvestite piñata. And, it was very sad and a little scary. But, you know, I don't care, because I wanted to make the show really fabulous. [cheers] I wanted it to be really fabulous because it's the last time I'm doing it. [Boos] You know what? Give me a freakin' break, okay? I've been an evil freakin' diva for forty freakin' years! [cheers] And there's all these young girls, and they're coming to take, well they're not gonna take my place, but they're gonna take somebody's place. J-Lo and Britney, and all those girls, you know. [Boo] Anyway, if you wanna know the truth, why I wanted to make it so fabulous? I have a motive, okay? And that is, I thought, I'm gonna make this show so fabulous, and then I'm gonna say, follow this, you bitches [cheers]. But I mean that with humility and love. You know, how I am. Alright, so now we're turning to this part that I've always wanted to do, this kind of ring master whatever it is, ring master cum I don't know what, because we're getting near to the fabulousness. Okay so, ladies and gentlemen! And flamboyant gentlemen! Boys and girls and children of all ages! Welcome to the Cherest show on earth! And this is the official beginning of the Cher show right now, and follow this, you bitches.[36]

Venomous commentators might call this mercenary crap, they might sneer that Cher simply knows on which side her bread is buttered, but that would be simplistic. The truth is that there is a real synergy between Cher and gays. Obviously she exaggerates everything all the time; that is the whole point. She practices camp, and camp is exaggeration. It would not work as well if she did not repeat the words "fabulous" or "bitches." She is self-conscious to the extreme: camp is self-conscious. She forges gay vocabulary and gay vocabulary forges her. She has often claimed her show was the last one ever, but we never believe her, and we are right not to, because then she returns, ever more flamboyant, like the flamboyant gentlemen she winks at in the audience.

Cher sang in an orange wig with David Bowie. Cher sang a great many flamboyant duets with a great many gay icons and gay favorites, including Tina Turner. Cher sang in Elvis drag. Cher likes saying that she spent her time singing and dancing naked around the house as a child, and that she still does it—the only difference being that now she gets paid for it. Cher is a gay icon feminist and role model. On January 21, 2017, she graced the anti–Donald Trump women's march in Washington, D.C., in black and cream, alongside fellow gay icon feminist and role model Madonna, who wore black and red.

Joan Collins (1933–)

Joan Collins began her career in the English theater, but she found herself in Los Angeles in the 1950s. Her father was a theatrical agent, her sister dreamt of celebrity in any domain at any cost. In 1950s Hollywood, there were the platinum blondes and the raven-dark brunettes (plus a couple of flamboyant redheads). The blondes were in no way threatened by Collins, who was encroaching upon Elizabeth Taylor's territory. In *Land of the Pharaohs* (Howard Hawks, 1955), she radiated with already exaggerated femininity, verging on camp, but she had not yet reached the pinnacle of the 1980s. It is only with her role in the television series *Dynasty* (ABC, 1981–1989) that Collins' gay iconicity really took off. That series is the exact equivalent of *Dallas*, the characters tear each other apart in as determined a way, in the same power tournaments and money games linked to oil—in Colorado rather than Texas. That being said, the differences are far from negligible: in *Dallas* people are either unattractive or indifferent-looking, in *Dynasty* everyone's beautiful. In *Dallas* people are either badly dressed or dressed indifferently, in *Dynasty* people wear divinely cut luxury clothing, especially Alexis Morell Carrington Colby Dexter Rowan, played by Joan Collins. The same rules apply to the hairdos. The *mise en scène* in *Dallas* consists broadly of a couple of extremely simple positions: the men stand with their hands on their hips, thrusting their genitals forward, or with one hand on one hip and the other holding a glass of bourbon. The women sit with their legs crossed, a glass of bourbon in hand. The *mise en scène* in *Dynasty* offers a lot more variety, notably in how it allows Collins the opportunity to always move gracefully, to be superb, glamorous, and 100 percent artificial.

There is a marvelous confusion between the character and the actress, a conflation gleefully maintained by gays. The magazines spoke in the 1980s (and occasionally still speak) more of Alexis than of Joan, even when discussing the *realitatis femina*. Discussing star identification, Richard Dyer explains: "The 'truth' about a character's personality and the feelings which it evokes may be determined by what the reader takes to be the truth about the person of the star playing the part" (Dyer 1979: 125). Every week many gay bars and gay clubs in the U.S. (and elsewhere) showed the episode of the week "live" while recording it on a VCR to play it again and again for their patrons. The gays organized Dynasty nights in bars or houses filled with people who wore Dynasty costumes—or should I say Dynasty drag?

Alexis is a woman, but she is devoured by ambition in a way that is usually the province of men in televised fiction (men such as J. R. Ewing). Gays tend to see her as a feminist heroine, a feminist role model. When it comes to *Dynasty*, feminists tend to be divided into two clans: the constructionist or constructivist clan (although this group did not really call itself that until the 1990s publication of books and articles by Judith Butler, Eve Kosofsky Sedgwick and Teresa de Lauretis), tends to approve—i.e., the third wave is pro–Alexis. On the other hand, the essentialist feminists of the second wave, those differentialists who still believe that women are genetically programed to be less violent, less ambitious and more nurturing, see her as a man in drag and find that she harms the feminist cause. What they dislike most is how she uses traditionally male weapons to conquer power, including extreme corruption, but *also* abundantly uses the traditional weapon of females to move ahead: seduction. She sways her hips and flutters her fake eyelashes with nonpareil dexterity, she sleeps with men who can help her social ascent and is a serial wife. The two cult catfights involving Alexis and her rival Krystle (Linda Evans) polished Collins' gay iconicity. One of them took place in a house, the other in a water-lily pool.

In 2002 Collins married a man 32 years her junior, Percy Gibson, her fifth husband. She is a cougar, and gays love cougars. She has her own cosmetics company and a wig business called Dynasty. She is very involved in various charities, to the point that she was ennobled by the British royal family in 2015.

Her younger sister Jackie Collins (1937–2015), a best-selling novelist, is also very popular with gay men. One only need look at photographs of the pair in their elaborate makeup, black leather and leopard prints, in full drag, as it were, to understand why (I recommend Google Images). Jackie Collins wrote scorching-hot popular novels in which bitches sometimes ruled the world. Some were adapted for the movies with her sister in a lead role. Joan Collins herself has penned a few rather camp books, including works of fiction.

The *Routledge Encyclopedia of Queer Culture* tells us that *Dynasty* "attracted a devoted gay following for its ground-breaking gay characters and the camp bitchiness of its star, Joan Collins. [It] established Collins as a Bette Davis–like gay icon." That entry also rightly reminds us that the "yo-yo-ing sexuality" of Alexis' son Steven "reflected the producers' ambivalent attitudes towards positive presentations of homosexuality" (Forde in Gerstner 2006: 196). Obviously, the sexy Steven was an added bonus for *Dynasty*'s gay audience, but Alexis would have been quite enough to attract gays in droves.

Tony Thorne, who authored the *Bloomsbury Dictionary of Modern Slang*, thought it fit to mention Joan Collins in his definition of camp. He gives two examples, including this: "'You, Joan [Collins,] have earned your place with Judy, Marlene and Marilyn in the great camp pantheon of the sky.' Howard Jacobson, *Sunday Correspondent*, 17 September 1989." In matters of style, *Dynasty* and Joan Collins had a great influence in the

1980s, but gays are still buying Alexis collectors dolls in the 2010s. Dynasty hairdos were all the rage for a while, as well as those celebrated power suits, those shoulder pads that Alexis constantly sported, reminiscent of Joan Crawford.

Joan Crawford (1904–1977)

Marjorie Rosen writes: "[T]he actress whose vibrant chorines and dancing flappers most vividly catch the tone of the Jazz Age is Joan Crawford. [For] Scott Fitzgerald, Crawford—perhaps because in her roles she reminded him so much of Zelda—represented the flapper at her most headstrong and desirable" (Rosen 1973: 103). Perhaps that is one of the first clues to Crawford's inordinate gay divadom. Flappers and Zelda Fitzgerald and Zelda's friend Tallulah Bankhead and occasional friend Dorothy Parker are gay hits. Crawford has certainly been the object of a very great deal of gay devotion for the past nine decades.

"One of the odd things about camp is that it is often associated with extraordinary devotion by gay men for female stars," writes Patrick Higgins in *A Queer Reader* (Higgins 1993: 244).[37] Other critics see nothing odd about it. Joan Crawford was a queen of camp and a gay icon for four decades. Is it relevant to establish degrees of camp in leading ladies? Possibly linked to the degree of that devotion? These are important questions. One can enjoy establishing classifications for one's own pleasure, but does it bring much to the debate that this book is trying to present? Some declarations may be found puzzling, such as the indispensable Corey K. Creekmur declaring that Garbo and Dietrich are "less campy" than Davis, Crawford and Garland. What exactly does he mean by that? And would he also say that Garbo and Dietrich are "less camp" than Davis, Crawford and Garland? If not, what is the nuance he establishes? A grammatical one (Creekmur in Stein 2004: 4)?

David Trinidad, for his part, evokes the spectacular and now legendary feud between Bette Davis and Joan Crawford, part of their attraction by gays.[38] He asks stimulating questions. "Why have I always been drawn to them? Why are most (if not all?) gay men, sooner or later, attracted to them? Something in our blood, our DNA? Rare is the homosexual who can resist their theatricality. Perhaps that fascination is acquired, passed one to the other? How else does one learn at which altar to worship?" (Trinidad in Montlack 2009: 51–52). That feud has generated many pages of writing. People enjoy quoting their favorite lines related to that feud. "According to some, Joan Crawford was never a class act to begin with. 'She's slept with every male star at MGM except Lassie,' snorted arch-rival Bette Davis" (Stephens 1998: 22).

When a gay man thinks of Crawford, he thinks of her forced but tremendous smile, her hair, her shoes, and her shoulder pads. He also thinks of that feud with Davis. Gay readers were vastly entertained by *Bette & Joan: The Divine Feud*, by Shaun Considine. The author tells many stories that are treasures, including this one: "[W]hen Crawford was cited as being a major influence on the fashion of the 1930s and the 1940s, Davis growled, 'What in the hell did she ever contribute to fashion—except those goddamned shoulder-pads and those tacky fuck-me shoes?'" (Considine 1989: 29–30). Well, precisely: without meaning any disrespect to Davis, "those goddamned shoulder-pads" and "those tacky fuck-me shoes" are what the game is all about. Crawford would not be such a gay icon without those clothes and those shoes. Nor would Lana Turner and many others. Someone ought to write a book about gay men and their high-heel fetish. Fuck-me pumps are all the rage. If you're having a rational feminist day, you might see six-inch Louboutins as impractical, you might think that if a man threatens a woman wearing Louboutins, she will not go far running in them. If you're having a more fanciful feminist day, you might imagine her flare up with righteous anger and pluck out her would-be rapist's eyes with her spike heels.

Many have commented upon Crawford's padded shoulders. Pam Cook writes: "Joan Crawford, who plays Mildred, is an ambiguous sexual figure as a star with a history of playing 'independent women' roles, emphasized in this scene by the broad shoulders of her coat" (Cook in Kaplan 1980: 78). Most LGBTQ+ history specialists agree that they see adoptive families of sorts in 20th-century urban gay circles. Your family rejects you, their straight culture is not your culture, so you acquire your gay culture not only by making "spontaneous" forays into cinematic and televisual gems but also by mixing with older gays, friends, lovers or sugar daddies or johns. The phenomenon is very Greek and quite fascinating. In addition to novelists, poets, and playwrights, that culture includes Broadway musicals, gay cult movies, and gay icons. In the 21st century, the Internet has notoriously replaced older gays in that educational role—to a large extent, anyway.

Interestingly, Joan Crawford was already a gay icon when *Mommie Dearest* (Frank Perry, 1981) was released. But the biopic added a new layer to her gay iconicity, drawing younger gays to her. As David Halperin recalls: "Joan Crawford, with her impossibly arched eyebrows and gargantuan shoulder pads, was a camp icon long before *Mommie Dearest* even went before the cameras. Thanks to Faye Dunaway's performance in the film, Joan Crawford rose to the position of camp's High Priestess, and fans wouldn't have it any other way" (Halperin 2012: 177). Today, even 20-year-olds are illegally downloading Joan Crawford movies. When the miniseries *Mildred Pierce* (HBO, 2011) came out, many young gays went back to the Crawford movie, judging that Kate Winslet, however talented, could not possibly compete with the immortal diva in the original *Mildred Pierce* (Michael Curtiz, 1945).

Ever since the release of Christina Crawford's *Mommie Dearest* (1978), which details the ill-treatment she and her brother suffered at the hands of the gay icon, and even more since the release of its movie adaptation three years later, journalists and biographers have wondered about the degree of the narrative's truth. Again I am strongly tempted to declare, according to the proverb, *se non e vero, e ben trovato*. No one—at least no gay fans—really cares whether *Mommie Dearest* is all true or partially true or not true at all. What is the use of "truth" when you can enjoy that cult scene with the wire hangers and that cult line "No wire hangers ever!"? Pure camp has little use for historical accuracy. In the age of the Internet, the colorful "No wire hangers ever!" meme is everywhere.[39]

Crawford's work in *The Women* (George Cukor, 1939) is magnificent and has not been praised enough. Daniel Harris acknowledges her performance as follows:

> In that tour de force of bitchy camp, *The Women*, the all-female cast speaks in two distinct accents: the harsh American cockney of the kitchen help [...] and the high-society, charm-school intonations of the Park Avenue matrons [...]. Only Joan Crawford, the inimitable Crystal Allen, a social-climbing shopgirl who claws her way to the top, can speak in both accents as the occasion requires [Harris 1997: 9].

Golden-age Hollywood offered "several stories in which strong women characters defy convention, only to be brought to the brink of ruin by their bold behavior. Before the closing credits, however, they are rescued from their shaky precipice and repositioned in a more socially acceptable space." Marguerite J. Moritz appropriately exemplifies this practice with *Mildred Pierce* (Ringer 1994: 123).

People who are not familiar with Crawford's early work should know that it is worth making the effort to see her silent movies, for she was already iconic—at least in the splendidly titled *Our Dancing Daughters* (Harry Beaumont, 1928), *Dream of Love* (Fred Niblo, 1928), *The Duke Steps Out* (James Cruze, 1928), and *Our Modern Maidens* (Jack Conway, 1928). She handled the transition to talkies brilliantly with *Untamed* (Jack Conway, 1929), in which she plays wild girl Bingo. Untamed Crawford went through a bad patch in the late 1930s, box-office-wise, but she pulled through. Crawford won an Academy Award for her performance as *Mildred Pierce*. She had stayed home, claiming to be ill with pneumonia. To this day, most people seem to think she was faking it, fearing the Oscar would go to Ingrid Bergman for *The Bells of St. Mary's*. Crawford received the media at home, having apparently applied her makeup upon receiving the news of her victory. She was nominated two more times, for *Possessed* (Curtis Bernhardt, 1947) and *Sudden Fear* (David Miller, 1952).

As extraordinary as this may sound, Crawford starred in *Grand Hotel* (Edmund Golding, 1932) with Greta Garbo. Alas, you never see the two together on the screen. This is the movie when Garbo so memorably gets to say, "I just want to be alone" (and not "I want to be alone," as most people misremember). Some have trashed their acting in *Grand Hotel*, but others find that they are sufficiently iconic to not worry about acting or dancing. Ethan Mordden judges that Crawford dances "with the deftness of a Tyrannosaurus Rex," and that she "makes no attempt to be anything but Crawford" (Mordden 1988: 109–110). Of course, fans might fail to see a problem in Crawford being Crawford (whatever that might mean). Presumably we are talking about Crawford the public persona, as opposed to, say, Lucille Fay LeSueur, the *realitatis femina*? As Christina Crawford's book *Mommie Dearest* indicates, before the eponymous movie, perhaps the icon herself did not always know when to stop acting. I understand why some moviegoers might object to Neanderthaloid actor Gérard Depardieu always being Gérard Depardieu in every single one of his movies, the same exaggeratedly masculine, overweight, very Gallic French-man, but Crawford? Please. That is like deploring that all of Marlene Diet-rich's good movies use the same tricks of chiaroscuro and have her sing cabaret songs in a tuxedo, i.e., they involve her being Dietrich (more on that below).

In the classic *Johnny Guitar* (Nicholas Ray, 1954), Crawford is Vienna, a magnificent gender-bender in pants (not long enough), a cowgirl loved by lesbians and gays alike. At nearly 50, she radiates with beauty, strength and determination. Her lips are redder than ever and her rictus more pro-nounced than ever. She is particularly striking at the end in her blue jeans and red shirt (before she dons a dead cowboy's black jeans, yellow shirt and red tie). That movie is practically all about gender, and Crawford hov-ers between the sublime and the ridiculous throughout. "A man can lie, steal ... and even kill. But as long as he hangs on to his pride, he's still a man. All a woman has to do is slip—once. And she's a tramp!" Some of her contemporaries saw her as a "tramp." Crawford was allegedly bisexual and allegedly liked bisexual men. She is rumored to have had affairs with a string of men and women, including actresses such as Marilyn Monroe. She had four husbands, starting with Douglas Fairbanks, Jr., himself rumored to have been bisexual. In public, she appeared alone or with her children. Famously, Crawford did what it took to please the fans: always the star, she never went out without the whole works—in full drag, as it were. She constantly posed for the photographers, very patiently.

We can only agree with David Munk when he claims: "Only by revis-iting the ideas of brilliant gay minds like [Quentin Crisp's] can we find true insight into mythic figures like Joan Crawford." Why? Because she is "an actress whose popularity and longevity, like all cultural figures of such mythic proportion, says as much about the psychology and emotional needs of the people who worshipped her as it did about her."[40] Munk then quotes Crisp, who writes: "Without any natural gifts except for ballroom dancing, as Miss Crawford once said, she nagged herself into being a com-petent actress [to become famous]. Even her fans were aware of her tech-nical weaknesses [...]." Later he declares: "If she had any ability as an actress, it was never for pretending to be somebody else; it lay in trans-forming her face into a mask of fear or hatred or grief."[41] It is those masks gays love, always—notably the mask she wears in *What Ever Happened to Baby Jane?* (Robert Aldrich, 1962), which will be covered in the Bette

Davis entry. Gays, of course, love an evil queen, and it is well-known that Crawford inspired Walt Disney's evil queen in *Snow White and the Seven Dwarfs* (1937).

Miley Cyrus (1992–)

The singer, songwriter and actress Miley Cyrus was born and raised outside Nashville. She is the daughter of performer Billy Ray Cyrus. The youngest female gay icon mentioned in this book, Miley Cyrus has undergone a remarkable evolution since her Disney days. When you reach fame playing the average Miley Stewart who morphs into the sprightly Hannah Montana at night in the television series *Hannah Montana* (Disney 2006–2011), when the media and the producers conspire to maintain the utmost confusion between the realitatis femina and the two dramatis personae for years, is it any wonder you eventually want to rebel, kicking the Disney empire with your studded Doc Martens and doing kinky things with teddy bears? Other Disney kids managed to acquire some edge after they were released into the real world, such as Christina Aguilera, Justin Timberlake, Ryan Gosling and Britney Spears.

In many ways, girls like Miley Cyrus can never win: whatever they do there will always be a strong backlash both in the mainstream media and in cyberspace. When Cyrus twerks, she is accused of pillaging African American culture[42]; when she expresses a healthy interest in colorful forms of sexuality, she is faulted for being an opportunistic slut with herd instincts; when she expresses herself like a strong, independent young woman, she is called vulgar. Her performance at the 2013 VMAs was particularly controversial. In particular, many feminists had something to say about it. As Cyrus herself declared, "Madonna's done it, Britney has done it, anyone that's performed on the VMAs, you know? You're always going to make people talk. You might as well make them talk for like two weeks rather than two seconds. I've been laughing about all the news because everyone else is so serious."[43] This kind of statement delights gay men.

It seems Cyrus began advocating LGTBQ rights when she was barely out of childhood. She has performed with drag queens and trans activists (notably at the VMAs in 2015). She has even recorded LGBTQ-themed songs such as "Bang Me Box" (2015). She claims to be pansexual,[44] and presumably approves of the P in LGBTQIAP. The tabloids abundantly discussed the relationships they claimed Cyrus had with Patrick Schwarzenegger, Liam Hemsworth or Victoria's Secret model Stella Maxwell.[45] In October 2016, she gave *Variety* an insightful interview in which she reported questioning gender and sexuality early on.[46]

As the media often remind us, Miley Cyrus' godmother is Dolly Parton, providing the only famous example of godmother/goddaughter icons, as opposed to mother/daughter icons such as Judy Garland and Liza Minnelli. In November 2016, Cyrus and Parton sang the 1974 timeless song "Jolene" together on *The Voice*, backed by the quintet Pentatonix, giving us a very palpable sense of the transmission of gay iconicity.[47]

Dalida (1933–1987)

It is interesting to observe the evolution of the looks and look of French performer Dalida, along with the evolution of her voice, and compare them with those of her producer brother Orlando.[48] The singer Dalida was not extremely famous in the Anglophone world, but she sold more than 170 million records (in comparison, Madonna has sold more than 300 million records and the Beatles more than 600 million). She was Franco-Italian, born and raised in Egypt. She recorded songs in many different languages and acted in French, Italian and Egyptian movies. In Dalida and her brother's subtle, gradual changes, we see an astonishing fusion that borders on the transgender. They both cultivated their low-voiced Italian-accented French, systematically rolling their Rs, like few Italian immigrants, even after a decade in France (besides, growing up in Egypt, they already spoke French). That accent served Dalida's career in the same way as British actress/singer Jane Birkin's English accent in French helped hers (although she is not featured in this book, some have called Birkin a gay icon). As the progressive blondeness of both Dalida and Orlando (who were very dark in the 1950s) increased, their eyebrows became fairer and thinner and their voices met halfway in an amazing degenderization process, with the same tone. It would seem that Orlando progressively accepted himself and finally came out of the closet. Some biographers and some websites attribute Dalida's popularity among the gay community to her own sensitivity to gay issues, which is said to be linked to Orlando's homosexuality[49] and that of several of her show-business friends. Dalida is even said to have convinced politicians Robert Badinter and François Mitterrand to demedicalize and decriminalize homosexuality. This is a bit naïve, but she may have helped.[50] Dalida's gay iconicity in France and elsewhere owes little to her own position on homosexuality. Clearly, the fact that she publicized her support for the cause (for example, by appearing at Pride marches) in no way harmed her in that domain, but that support was made public years after her crowning.

So Dalida is a gay icon, as everyone agrees, but why? Some claim it is because she looks like a man in drag. I often heard that very sentence in the 1970s. More politely, people said she had masculine features. She did have a squarish jaw, a straight nose, and a relatively deep voice. In the old-style drag cabaret clubs of Paris such as Cabaret Michou, you will find Dalida impersonators whose resemblance to their model is uncanny; sometimes they sing rather than lip-sync and the vocal resemblance is equally uncanny.

The cougar phenomenon, if indeed it is a phenomenon,[51] is a splendid example of applied feminism—although the expression itself is clearly a poor, antifeminist choice of word, implying as it does that women who date younger men are predators. Since the dawn of time, the patriarchy has been brainwashing women to convince them that they are less worried about the firmness of male flesh than the opposite. Upper- and upper–middle-class men leave their wives the minute their belly is distended, replacing them with younger ones. Yet the forsaken wives believed in the durability of their love, sincerely believing that their sweaty husbands' fat beer bellies did not disgust them during each weekend's hurried coitus. Obviously, they were also motivated by economic considerations.[52] The cougar is liberated from her sisters' yoke, she is in tune with her sexual desires as an independent woman, she deems the hard body of her 20-something lover, with his splendidly defined Apollo's belt, much sexier than the flabby body of her ex-husband (who has trouble keeping up with the energy of his nubile wife—which serves him right).

Dalida magnificently exemplified the lust that a woman can feel for a much younger man with her song "Il venait d'avoir dix-huit ans" (1973). She also recorded it in English as "He Must Have Been Eighteen," in Italian as "Diciottanni," in Spanish as "Tenía dieciocho años," and three other languages. Many women who are past, say, 35, even among the most enlightened, even among those who are prepared to call themselves moderate feminists (at least in some domains), believe that they are structurally incapable of desiring a young man, as if some genetic encoding made it impossible from the moment they are not so young anymore themselves. This is utterly silly; we are simply dealing with the weight of the patriarchy. The cougar understands this and behaves like those millions of mature heterosexual men around the world, stopped by nothing and no one from showing that they desire the smooth flesh of an 18-year-old girl more than the wrinkly, flaccid flesh of women their own age. Naturally, this does not mean that the cougar—like an aging gay man—will not feel terrible when she examines her crow's feet and drooping eyelids in the mirror in the morning.

The gays are the worst in that domain, notoriously. Ageism, looism and especially fattism are rampant, as I have said. Unsurprisingly, a gay man wrote, "Il venait d'avoir dix-huit ans." Pascal Sevran knew the horror of seeing his body and face go to shreds: he was the proverbial pathetic old queen, whereas the young gays are always 20 or even younger. They may come and go in rapid succession, they may even occasionally look similar, but this in no way diminishes their power of seduction, their painful beauty and the cruelty of the degeneration of their admirer. The tragedy was beautifully illustrated in *Death in Venice* (Luchino Visconti, 1971), adapted from Thomas Mann. Singing such a song, how could Dalida not be a gay icon? We now know that in 1967, at age 34, she was pregnant by an 18-year-old Italian and had a clandestine abortion, which made her barren. That song was made for her in every possible sense.

Indeed, today's cougar is supposed to be happy with her lot and have no regrets. At the end of Dalida's 1973 song, though, the speaker finds herself alone and sad, dumped by the kid. Generally speaking, Dalida was unhappy in love; she is the French Judy Garland in more ways than one. Every time she fell in love, the man was psychologically fragile and ended up committing suicide. In 1967, her Italian lover, singer Luigi Tenco, shot himself in the head. She tried to kill herself. In 1970, her ex-husband Lucien Morisse also shot himself in the head. In 1983, her ex-boyfriend, Richard Chanfray, aka the Comte de Saint Germain, suffocated himself with exhaust fumes. In 1987, after many unhappy relationships, often with married men, Dalida finally killed herself, opting for a barbiturate overdose and making a beautiful corpse. Bob Henderson puts it thus in *Loverboy Magazine*:

> Dalida is our go-to when we want to bathe in self-pity. When you've gone through the most horrific break up, drawn the curtains, got a bottle of whiskey, smashed your phone and put "Je Suis Malade" on, desperately searching for some cigarettes which you gave up. And try not to think too much about the suicide note she left the world on 2 May 1987. "Life has become unbearable for me. Forgive me."[53]

Three decades after her death, gay men still spend a fortune on collector's CD boxes. Let it not be forgotten that in addition to singing delightfully sad torch songs, Dalida sang disco music that European and Canadian gays still dance to in nightclubs.

Bette Davis (1908–1989)

One could argue that if Garland is (according to most) the number-one gay icon in the 1939–1969 period, and if Madonna and her elder Cher have been fighting for the title in more recent years (it is entertaining to try to determine who history will regard as the number-one gay icon of the early 21st century), then Bette Davis and Joan Crawford are close behind.

Davis is particularly liked by gays not only for her cold, hard bitch aspects but also for her "masculine" sides. Autumn Stephens writes:

> One of the most hated divas in Hollywood, Bette Davis certainly didn't wind up as "the first lady of the American screen" by making nice. Tenacious, temperamental, and unafraid to pick a fight, Davis [...] clawed her way to the top [...]. Davis was no great beauty, and apparently no great shakes as an actress, either,

in her younger days [...]. Davis [...] finally engineered her own big break in 1934 [playing] loathsome Mildred Rogers in *Of Human Bondage*. [Other] actresses [did not care] to be cast as a spiteful bitch, but Davis won an Academy Award nomination for screaming things like "You cad! You dirty swine!" [Stephens 1998: 18].

Davis was sometimes very forceful indeed, and quite butch, so much so that she evoked a man in drag—which did little to dispel her gay appeal. In her movies she is never better than when she is a total bitch. "Like most gay men and drag queens [...], I adore the bitches of Hollywood," says "pagan lesbian" Camille Paglia (Paglia 1998: 44).

David Halperin confirms:

> Some female figures that are gay male icons are quite repellent to straight women (starting with Joan Crawford and Bette Davis in Robert Aldrich's 1962 movie, *What Ever Happened to Baby Jane?*). Many gay male cultural practices are therefore not masculine or feminine or "two-spirited," nor do they exactly demonstrate a combination of masculine and feminine characteristics or a condition halfway between male and female. Rather, they imply something else, something unique, or at least a particular formation of gender and sexuality that is specific to some gay men and that has yet to be fully defined [Halperin 2012: 317].

Halperin then evokes the infamous Rosa Moline, played by Bette Davis in *Beyond the Forest* (King Vidor, 1949), whose celebrated bitchy line "What a dump!" has been voted #62 movie quote by the American Film Institute. The scene is a staple of gay culture and was used by Edward Albee in his "crypto-gay play" *Who's Afraid of Virginia Woolf?* (1962) (Halperin 2012: 21–22). David Van Leer also shows how Edward Albee's play *Who's Afraid of Virginia Woolf?* (1962) is immersed in gay culture, notably with Martha's allusions to Bette Davis' career and to the line "What a dump!" (Van Leer 1995: 22–23). Mary Ann Doane reminds us of the fact that she is "the epitome of excessive female desire" in *Beyond the Forest* (Doane 1987: 65)—marvelously so, it must be said. Of course, in the general public's mind, excessive female desire and bitchiness are linked.[54]

Bette Davis herself has a few things to say about her bitchiness: "I do not regret one professional enemy I have made. Any actor who doesn't dare to make an enemy should get out of the business." And this: "I was thought to be 'stuck-up.' I wasn't. I was just sure of myself." And also: "I know I've been a perfect bitch. But I couldn't help myself" (Stephens 1998: 19).

Dark Victory (Edmund Goulding, 1939), which Antoine Sire calls "a cathedral of melodrama" (Sire 2016: 174), is a "woman's picture," as its press book claimed. Indeed, many of the gay icons featured in this book have at one point or another acted in women's pictures—one of the reasons for their iconicity, because such films represent a welcome change from testosterone-packed action movies (cf. Doane 1987: 29–30). *Dark Victory* and *Now, Voyager* (Irving Rapper, 1942),[55] in which Davis' boring spinster Charlotte Vale morphs into a sophisticate socialite, are among the top gay favorites in Davis' filmography. Sky Gilbert sums up, as if speaking for thousands of gay boys:

> I adore old (pre–1960) films for their camp [...]. *All About Eve* and *Now, Voyager* are my bible and my handbook. I've lived my life with the shadows of Bette Davis and Joan Crawford crossing through my dreams. These women were allowed to experience *life*—all the pain and passion that a little gay boy was supposed to hide. That's probably why I like dressing in drag and acting like a movie star [Gilbert 2000, 196].

At least Davis knew on which side her bread was buttered. She might have been bitchy, but she did not despise her fans. In 1962 she declared that actresses who claimed they didn't care for their fans were liars or totally lacked common sense. Fans make actresses, and that is particularly true for gay icons and their gay fans (Surowiec in Farinelli & Passek 2000: 151).

The surest way to judge the degree to which a movie and its actresses are a cult is to look at their gay-made parodies. Richard Dyer writes:

> This feeling is present in the early sixties in Los Angeles by the Gay Girls Riding Club, a group of friends who met on Sundays for horse riding, brunch and home movie making. Shown in the Los Angeles gay clubs, they were a series of campy films parodies, including [...] *Roman Springs of Mrs. Stone*, *What Really Happened to Baby Jane* and *All About Alice*. The same sensibility informs the films of the Kuchar brothers, an amazing outpouring of wild trash parodies with titles like *I Was a Teenage Rumpot* [...] [Dyer 1990: 143].

Any playful tribute by John Waters and Divine to any movie or diva corresponds to the same logic. *What Ever Happened to Baby Jane?*, a huge gay cult film, is Dav most "monstrous" movie. You could almost see it as her doing low camp, whereas she does high camp in *All About Eve*. Sky Gilbert calls *What Ever Happened to Baby Jane?* "a camp battle" (Gilbert 2000: 91). The number-one gay favorite among Bette Davis vehicles will probably remain *All About Eve* (in which gay icon Marilyn Monroe played a small part). In it Davis delivers the legendary line "Fasten your seatbelts, it's going to be a bumpy night," so often misquoted as "Fasten your seatbelts, it's going to be a bumpy ride," which makes more sense. "'Male actress' Charles Pierce and a couple of drag queens actually helped popularize the quote. His impression of Davis is flawless" (Frederick 2016: 93).

Paul Roen reminisces about *All About Eve*: "As for Margo Channing, she could pass for The Mother of Us All; the role is apparently modeled on Tallulah Bankhead, but the way Bette Davis plays it is pure, unadulterated drag queen."[56] There are so many reasons for this movie's gay cult appeal (Roen 1994: 26). *All About My Mother* (*Todo sobre mi madre*, Pedro Almodóvar, 1999) pays a splendid tribute to *All About Eve* and to Bette Davis that will be discussed below. No doubt there will be other such tributes in the 21st century.

Lana Del Rey (1985–)

In 2012, singer Lana Del Rey exploded in the public consciousness, notably with two songs, "Blue Jeans" and "Video Games." Soon she became the victim of a terrible kabala, the likes of which have rarely been seen in show business. The haters were mostly straight white men.

The explanation for this amazing hostility is that it is the result of a central misunderstanding, sociologically fascinating, based mostly on surprisingly dated and very unqueer values.

What most of Lana Del Rey's detractors seem to resent is the fact that she has totally reinvented herself to become a camp pop diva and gay icon. Born Elizabeth Woolridge Grant in 1986, she started singing at an early age. She recorded albums and performed under the names of May Jailer and Lizzy Grant. It remains unclear when precisely she started using the inspired pseudonym Lana Del Rey (with this spelling, though traces of Lana Del Ray remain on the Internet). She changed her name, looks, and look, and hoped that her early fans would not desert her as she turned camp and acquired a few million extra fans. Her first "proper" album, as it were, titled *Born to Die*, was released in January 2012. In November 2012 she re-released *Born to Die* (*The Paradise Edition*), with eight more songs, much like Lady Gaga (another gay icon and camp practitioner) re-released *The Fame* (2008) as *The Fame Monster* (2009), with eight more songs. Since then, three even camper albums have been released: *Ultraviolence* (2014), *Honeymoon* (2015) and *Lust for Life* (2017).

As far as her looks were concerned, Lizzy Grant was undeniably not unpleasant to look at, with averagely pretty features and an averagely nice body. Moreover, if her looks were not something to write home about, her look was an indifferent one, being pre-camp, and her songs, averagely harmonious, were not particularly conceptual.

Unimaginative critics, uninspired reviewers and bloggers with indistinct agendas reproach her for a lack of authenticity, or sincerity, as if she were a pre-punk 1970s rock band or some other such artist. Notably, she has been bitterly accused—as if it were a crime and as if it somehow affected her music—of having resorted to plastic surgery. Gays love plastic surgery, gays love artifice. Oscar Wilde would have approved of plastic surgery if it had existed in his time, Oscar Wilde did not think highly of sincerity in art.

It is easy to show that, on the contrary, today's best postmodern pop is precisely all about reinvention and camp artifice, and that criticizing Del Rey for such features makes little sense. A great many gay men buy her records, as evidenced by a quick Googling session and a look at social networks. Obviously, seeking the hypothetical *realitatis femina* behind the dramatis persona Lana Del Rey is a fruitless endeavor that manifests a singular failure to grasp the reality of today's pop, especially gay-iconic pop.

Curiously, people have made less of her voice change: she decided to drop her voice (lower), which is very interesting, artistically speaking. The inauthenticity reproach is amusing. Why isn't it voiced more often when, say, British white women sing like American black women? There are plenty of those around.

Shouldn't Lana Del Rey be commended for the ingenuous and coherent way she has constructed her career and persona? Her lyrics are rife with literary allusions, notably to gay favorites such as Walt Whitman or Tennessee Williams, three gay favorites. As a postmodern artist she does not worry about distinctions between high and low. Elizabeth Grant studied metaphysics at Fordham, but Lana Del Rey just hung out with cool gangsters and musicians and drug-addicted artists.

Funny how all those dated ideas, those post–Frankfurt School, post–Bourdieu notions of recuperation have come back with a vengeance, only for Lana Del Rey's benefit (no one seems to think gay icon Lady Gaga should use her own name and get rid of the makeup). In this postmodern post–Madonna age, that often sounds a bit silly. Lana Del Rey would easily fit into a debate about the difference between popular culture and mass culture and would be used in contradictory ways, depending on the speaker's vantage point.

Whether a rich daddy's girl or an indie Web 2.0 sensation (this was debated all over the place in 2012), Lana Del Rey embodies (as did other gay icons before her) the American Dream. She knows it, she had decided she would, and she sings about it and shoots videos about it. However, her take on the American Dream is highly playful and ironic. In her videos, she amusingly recycles all sorts of clichéd American Dream images, half rebel, half success story. If you listen closely to her lyrics, you realize that she has no illusions about life, love, society, or the American Dream. She just likes writing and singing about it. And many gay men will continue listening as she does. Writing moody songs and releasing videos with elaborate aesthetics, as she does, can only reinforce her gay iconicity.

Her lyrics and visuals show that she is unafraid of taking risks. She is attacked by feminists for her songs of submissive love, often involving daddy types, but gays (notably twinks) with daddy issues know what it means to be in love with the wrong guy, they know what it means to be aware of the fact that even though your relationship is politically incorrect, you choose to stay. He is older, he is tattooed all over, he is muscular and selfish, he treats you badly and you crawl back for more. The feminists who trash her tend to mistake the dramatis persona Lana Del Rey or the personae of the speakers of her songs with the realitatis femina Elizabeth Woolridge Grant, but gay boys know better. And they would even if she had not given them the song "Music to Watch Boys to" and its extraordinarily gay video (2015).

In July 2017 when *Lust for Life* came out, *Billboard* explained why she was a huge "muse to gay fans around the world." She is misunderstood, and has had to struggle, like gays. She is the queen of melancholy, she is camp, *Billboard* concluded.[57]

60

Catherine Deneuve (1943–)

I asked a dozen of my young gay students what immediately came to mind when hearing the words "Catherine Deneuve." I expected them to come up with *Les Demoiselles de Rochefort* (*The Young Girls of Rochefort*, 1967), but that only came second. They thought of *The Hunger* (Tony Scott, 1983) first, a very sleek movie in which Catherine Deneuve plays Myriam, an ancient vampire who moves superbly and disports herself with Susan Sarandon. The fact that many critics deem it a bad movie is entirely beside the point. Yes, it is filmed like an MTV music video or a commercial (which is where Tony Scott came from), but that only helped iconize Deneuve even more in the eyes of gay aesthetes. That role alone might have been enough to make her a gay icon, if she had not been one already. In *The Hunger*, Catherine Deneuve looks devastatingly gorgeous in a totally artificial way. She wears tremendously stylized clothing, she is in charge, she is immortal, she sucks (the blood of) men and women alike, and she goes clubbing with David Bowie (they even patronize a club where Bauhaus performs). Generally speaking, she rocks.

The filmmaker Jacques Demy (1931–1990) was a gay gay-icon maker married to feminist filmmaker Agnès Varda (1928–). He chose Deneuve for two cult films, *Les Parapluies de Cherbourg* (*The Umbrellas of Cherbourg*, 1964) and the aforementioned *Les Demoiselles de Rochefort*, which made a substantial contribution to her gay iconization. They are remarkably camp in the most colorful way. More recently, Catherine Deneuve starred with Fanny Ardant and other delightful actresses in *8 Femmes* (*8 Women*, François Ozon, 2002), a very gay movie in every possible sense. In between, she worked for dozens of pseudo-intellectual directors (sometimes gay) and specialized in annoying movies or irritating comedies, or at best boring pot-boilers—but she is always forgiven. In the same order of idea, she only marginally damaged her LGBTQ+ following when she sued the Canadian lesbian magazine *Deneuve* in 1995–1996, which had to change its name to *Curve*.

Deneuve has played a lesbian or bisexual four times, in film she has been a masochist, a prostitute, an incestuous woman, the wife of a pregnant man, etc.[58]

Deneuve has been photographed by every significant photographer in the Western world. She even married one: David Bailey. One should never underestimate the power of photographers in the making of icons. An icon is an image, photographers create images. See what gay photographer Herb Ritts, to name but one, contributed to the iconization of Madonna. Remember Cecil Beaton[59] and Richard Avedon? More recently, gay photographer David LaChapelle has contributed to the career of quite a few gay icons.

In addition to Bailey, Deneuve had affairs with talented and striking men, including filmmaker Roger Vadim (with whom she had a son, actor Christian Vadim) and Marcello Mastroianni (with whom she had a daughter, actress Chiara Mastroianni). Vadim is notorious for dating or marrying the most gorgeous actresses, such as Jane Fonda—and often giving them fabulous parts. For decades Deneuve was close to fashion emperor Yves Saint Laurent (and his companion, businessman Pierre Bergé, who survived him) and that is one of the factors that made her such an elegant fashionista, one of the most regal of our icons.

In the 1990s, when asked if she was thinking of resorting to plastic surgery at some point, Madonna used to reply that she would when Catherine Deneuve gave her the address of her surgeon. This presumably finally happened. Deneuve's facelifts have been extraordinarily neat. One need not base such observations on any press article or biography (although they help, but simply on one's own gazing at her face in film and on television every single year since 1967 and *Les Demoiselles de Rochefort*. She clearly started at an early stage, which surely is the best way to go about it, and she must have found an extremely talented practitioner, as Madonna observed. Only one facelift was a bit of a failure, her antepenultimate at the time of writing, it would seem. They distorted her mouth, but it was subsequently put back. In September 2017 her smile was starting to look slightly like the Joker's, but she was still gorgeous and she remains a powerful gay icon.[60] Similarly, singer and actress Sylvie Vartan had a bad automobile accident in 1970 and had to have a great deal of reconstructive surgery. The U.S. surgeons she picked invented a new face for her, working with what they had, and she still has that exact same face 50 years later, more or less. Gays love such stories.

Deneuve is a vigorous feminist,[61] an anti–death-penalty activist[62] and a supporter of LGBT rights. She is always unafraid to speak her mind. One of the things people lament about her is that she is icy. This has even been corroborated by some autobiographers, such as John Fraser. So? Why should a gay icon avoid icy behavior? Who does not love an ice queen? When you are so astonishingly beautiful, you can afford to be icy, some might hold.

As for those who claim that the other blonde of French cinema, Brigitte Bardot, is a gay icon, they must be deaf. Even if some gay men might have once been tempted to iconize her (notably when she sang Serge Gainsbourg songs), they have now heard her spew off about gays and Muslims and immigrants and presumably believe that even four lines in a book of this sort is more than the wretched woman deserves.

Marlene Dietrich (1901–1992)

In the 1920s, Dietrich played all sorts of run-of-the-mill parts in German movies and plays, day and night. Later at night she frequented the cabaret clubs of Berlin. Obviously this is where she learned her trade, more than anywhere else, observing the drag queens on stage; meaning she learned to construct glamour and hyperfemininity and to do camp, all of which suit her divinely, her gay fans think. Some biographers claim that Dietrich is the one who taught drag queens, so perhaps we could establish that there were fruitful exchanges during those decadent nights— pun intended. Some say she cleverly modeled her Dietrich star persona on Greta Garbo's (Doty in McLean 2011: 142).

In *The Blue Angel* (Josef von Sternberg, 1930), Dietrich is Lola Lola, the unscrupulous kept woman, the femme fatale who lures poor Professor Rath to ruin and despair, literally turning him into a clown. Paying to enjoy a young person's beauty is very widespread among gays. Our society is ageist on the whole, but gays are even more ageist than heterosexuals, and old gays are often prepared to don the mantle of the sugar daddy and spend a lot of money to enjoy the ardent youth and supple beauty of a mercenary catamite.

In *Morocco* (Josef von Sternberg, 1930), Dietrich plays the sugar-babying cabaret singer Amy Jolly. Amy is in love with burning hot legionnaire Tom Brown, played by Gary Cooper. In the Moroccan nightclub, she sings while in male drag: tuxedo and top hat, bow tie and flat shoes. She kisses a woman in the audience on the lips and moves and smokes exactly like a man in 1930. None of that was liable to displease the gays, obviously. Indeed, without getting into the Pygmalion debate here, all the films Dietrich shot with Josef von Sternberg are, quite simply, the stuff gay icons are made of. He was clearly a maker of gay icons.

In 1932, Dietrich is *Blonde Venus* (Josef von Sternberg, 1932). On stage in a nightclub, with a background of jungle tribal drums, a menacing gorilla (clearly coded as male) walks around in chains. Behind him, white women in blackface and afro wigs dance with spears. The gorilla takes off his fat hands, which turn out to be gloves. The gorilla turns out to be a white woman in a gorilla suit. He beheads himself, and he is a she: she is Helen Faraday, aka Helen Jones, she is Marlene Dietrich. She is a blonde. She takes hold of a blonde wig and dons it, the wig is pierced by an arrow. Dietrich is even blonder with the wig. Here she is in triple drag: interspecies drag, gender drag (one assumes the gorilla is male) and racial drag. The song she sings, "Black Voodoo," evokes (black) magic, witchcraft, the spells of the sorceress who gets men to crawl at her feet, begging. The message is a bit ambiguous, however, because it reveals the half-latent racism of the creators of the day (even the more progressive ones), all the more so because the moves of the gorilla are framed by the difficult words of a stammering black barman who is very much a caricature. In *Blonde Venus*, she sings in a man's tuxedo again, white this time. In *Shanghai Express* (Josef von Sternberg, 1932) she says, "It took more than one man to change my name to Shanghai Lily" and you can die happy, having heard that line. If you're a gay fan, you will want to see all the movies she made between 1930 and 1961.

Both on- and off- screen, androgynous Dietrich shows that masculinity and femininity are ever-fluctuating and extremely relative constructions. In her daily life, Dietrich often wore trousers; this was rare in the 1930s. She took what and who she wanted. Although married to Rudolf Sieber (and never to anyone else), she seemingly had strings of Hollywood lovers, along with French actor Jean Gabin and American President Jack Kennedy. Moreover, she wasn't insensitive to the charms of women and presumably had mistresses (I choose to believe a substantial percentage of the dozens of biographies I have read), including the (in)famous Mercedes de Acosta, who also frequented Greta Garbo's bed. One even reads rumors that Dietrich and Garbo had an affair in 1925—a very pleasant thought, surely, a bit like Athena and Aphrodite having an affair. What's not to like?

In her old age, however, Dietrich seemed to go out of her way to alienate her faithful gay public with her horrendous autobiography (1984), wherein she abundantly lies, denying just about everything that made her a gay icon, pretending she never had another ambition in life than to be a good housewife and make lovely dinners for a lovely husband before going to bed early. Happily, no one believed her.

I still treasure my vinyl records of her, singing in German in that amazing, very low voice in those 1960s and 1970s recordings, so much better than her early singing voice, which was sometimes high.

New York actor James Beaman is known both for his Lauren Bacall drag show and for his Marlene Dietrich cabaret piece *Black Market Marlene* at the beginning of this century. As he sees it:

> Of course there is a connection between impersonation and films. As young people, that's how we study the great stars. It is also a very gay phenomenon. Gay kids and gay people in general have a secret life and part of that life is looking for ourselves in our icons, and particularly the old-time movie stars who represented an idealized way of living. They were completely out of the norm yet revered for it—a dream of any outcast in society! [...] I have always loved classic films, and as a kid my parents let me stay up whenever a classic was on the late show. [...] I can quote entire films! So of course, the great movie divas—Davis, Dietrich, Garland—these are the icons that female impersonators do the most. They combined female allure with masculine power—these contradictions have particular resonance for gay men who find themselves caught between roles in our culture [Mayne in Gemünden & Desjardins 2007 : 373].

Sternberg and Dietrich were ideally suited to each other, producing camp together and working to develop the (gay) iconicity of the diva. Even Susan Sontag said: "Camp is the outrageous aestheticism of Sternberg's six American movies with Dietrich, all six, but especially the last, *The Devil Is a Woman*" (Sontag 1969: 285).

Jack Babuscio writes:

> To explain the relation of Sternberg to camp it is necessary to return, briefly, to the phenomenon of passing for straight. This strategy of survival in a hostile world has sensitized us to disguises, impersonations, the significance of surfaces, the need to project personality, the intensities of character, etc. Sternberg's

films—in particular the Dietrich films from *Morocco*, 1930, *The Devil Is a Woman*, 1935—are all camp insofar as they relate to those adjustment mechanisms of the gay sensibility. But they are also camp in that they reflect the director's ironic attitude towards his subject-matter—a judgment which says in effect that the content is of interest only insofar as it remains susceptible to transformation by means of stylization. What counts in one's view of Sternberg's films as camp, then, is the perception of an underlying emotional autobiography—a disguise of self and obsessions by means of the artificial. One does not need to see these disguises in a strictly literal way. It is enough to sense the irony in the tensions that arise from Sternberg's anguish and cynicism, and his predilection for the most outrageous sexual symbolism as a means of objectifying personal fantasies [Babuscio in Dyer 1977, 50–51].

Walter Holland writes:

I intuited even then that I felt little attraction to women, but I knew Dietrich wouldn't care. She would recognize me, shrug me off with just a stare and a knowing smile. It made no difference in the game of survival and hers had been a life of live-and-let-live. [...] She [reminds] me of that unique relationship between gay men and female actresses as well as the female characters they have created to represent their innermost desires and thoughts [Holland in Montlack 2009: 48].

In many ways, in fact, such actresses become to many gays something rather similar to what imaginary friends are to some children.

Dietrich will remain forever the ultimate femme fatale, the idol of many gay boys who identify with her and see her as a sort of elder sister, notably those who wish they were "fatale," but, in the immortal words of gay icon Liza Minnelli as Sally Bowles in *Cabaret* (Bob Fosse, 1972), are "about as 'fatale' as an after-dinner mint." What is problematic for some stars is that when they begin playing femmes fatales, they risk getting typecast, though such typecasting does not necessarily displease their gay fans, who love seeing their icons as femmes fatales, on and off screen.

As Stevie Simkin reminds us, before the Hays Code, "the femme fatale was one of several powerful female personae that dominated the screen. A number of female stars took on [Theda] Bara's mantle, including [...] Greta Garbo." Garbo was to complain about the great number of vamp roles she was made to play. "Perhaps it is inherent in the power of the role of the vamp and the femme fatale that actresses playing it subsequently find it difficult to avoid typecasting." I thoroughly agree, and personally never tire of the power of such roles. Simkin continues: "It is certainly evidence of another kind of blurring of the real and the imaginary. In this respect, Kathleen Turner (*Body Heat*), Sharon Stone (*Basic Instinct*) and

Linda Fiorentino (*The Last Seduction*) are good examples to set alongside Greta Garbo" (Simkin 2014: 38). Surely John Waters remembered that when he cast gay favorite Kathleen Turner in *Serial Mom* (John Waters, 1994).

Céline Dion (1968–)

It is really hard to decide just how naïve Céline Dion is. She seems oblivious in so many ways. She never seems to do anything tongue-in-cheek (what the French call *second degré*), every word she utters in interviews seems to be meant to be taken entirely at face value (what the French call *premier degré*). The *second degré* is equally absent from her singing. She's always sobbing, on and off stage, and you cannot help but believe in her tears. Now that she is a widow, she is bound to do even more crying. Of course, the gay men who love her do not mind, because they can do the *second degré* for her. They can take her every sentimental declaration with a pinch of salt, they can sing with her, yelling their lungs out, while marveling at her apparent lack of distance from her lyrics. Her gay public tends to attribute those characteristics to her being French Canadian, and that might be a valid hypothesis—however much of an insulting sweeping generalization linked to xenophobic stereotyping it is. Whatever the explanation, even if Dion could not be more different from, say, Cher, who does little at face value these days, even though Dion is a constant fashion disaster and rarely sports a decent hairdo, even though she has no idea what a glory hole is, unlike Madonna (to pick an example at random), she does yell and scream and yodels as convincingly as Barbra Streisand, with no sense of irony.[63] Indeed she even graced us in 1997 with a charmingly syrupy duet with Streisand, "Tell Him," thus grabbing a bit of the elder singer's gay iconicity to reinforce hers. In the same way and with the same results, Donna Summer recorded "No More Tears" with Streisand (1979).

Her husband and manager, René Angélil, was 26 years older. He and Dion were very often in the tabloids, and not only because she was his third wife. His own early efforts at pop singing, in the 1960s band Les

Baronets, are intriguing pieces of curio that can be found on YouTube. She released a single entitled "Lolita (trop jeune pour aimer)" in 1987 and to this day I wonder if she knew what she was doing, considering she was already dating Angélil, whom she would marry seven years later. Has she read Vladimir Nabokov? From 1981 onward she inundated the French-speaking market with records, often extremely successful. She had to wait until 1990, after careful planning, to launch her conquest of the English-speaking market. After that her ascension was continuous, in spite of pauses due to her efforts at reproduction (she has three sons) and her husband's health issues (he died in 2016). Finally, and fittingly, she became a permanent fixture in Las Vegas. Many gay icons have done Vegas: you cannot get more artificial, glitzy, kitschy, and campy. Dion has often voiced her support for gays, as in *Billboard* magazine in June 2017 when she said:

> I've been fortunate to be surrounded by so many beautiful people from the LGBTQ community throughout my entire career ... from talented performers, musicians, producers and songwriters, to colleagues who have contributed significantly to my success, and last but not least, to so many of my loyal fans who have stood by me, in the name of love.[64]

In the fall of 2016 she agreed to appear on the extremely gay Tyler Oakley show (ellentube.com) and even kissed Tyler.

When gay men went to see *Titanic* (James Cameron, 1997) and identified with Rose DeWitt Bukater (Kate Winslet), wanting to be grabbed by the waist by a young and vivacious Jack Dawson (Leonardo DiCaprio) while shrieking, "I'm the Queen of the World," they were accompanied by Dion's song "My Heart Will Go On" (and on and on). Some have not yet completely recovered. Indeed, funnily enough, gay men seem to be divided into two camps when it comes to this. Scott Dagostino writes in *Fab: The Gay Scene Magazine*:

> Yes, Celine Dion has a lot to answer for but my own longstanding grudge against her is purely personal: years ago, while I was soft putty in the grip of young love, I dated a Céline fan. Romance curdled into something terrifying as he would turn the lights down low, place [her CD] in the CD tray and lean in for a kiss while his diva wailed [...].

He goes on to say that, for many, "that's when you run for the door."[65] Talking about romance, it would seem that, perhaps, Dion found male companionship again, at least for the summer. In August 2017, she was often photographed at the arm of sexy model and dancer Pepe Muñoz, who is certain to obtain the gay fans' blessing.

Divine (1945–1988)

Wayne Koestenbaum writes: "Bitchiness is reputed to be a gay mode. Repartee, cat-fights, and one-liners are staples of works embodying one kind of gay taste: Oscar Wilde's plays, Ivy Compton-Burnett's novels, George Cukor's *The Women*. These cadences aren't limited to 'high' art; they show up in drag shows, in John Waters films, in bar argot" (Koestenbaum 2001: 113–114). Divine is the immortal star of the cult films of John Waters, Divine is bitchiness incarnate.

Divine was born Harris Glenn Milstead in Baltimore and rose to fame in drag in the films of number one decadent Baltimorean, John Waters. In *Pink Flamingos* (John Waters, 1972), as IMDb describes, "Notorious Baltimore criminal and underground figure Divine goes up against a sleazy married couple who make a passionate attempt to humiliate her and seize her tabloid-given title as 'The Filthiest Person Alive.'" Few people have embodied as fascinatingly as the Waters/Divine holy pair the practice of trash aesthetics. Gays do often like their cinema with a healthy dose of tongue-in-cheek fun and/or social critique. Divine was trash camp at its best. Outrageous in every way, she notably exaggerated in her makeup even the exaggerations of ordinary drag queens, drawing emphatic eyebrows halfway up her forehead.

Divine owed her name both to Greta Garbo, nicknamed Divine since *The Divine Woman* (Victor Seastrom, 1928), and to Jean Genet's novel *Notre-Dame-des-Fleurs* (1943), which tells the story of a gorgeous 16-year-old murderer and his relationship with a transvestite named Divine. Neither pantomime dame nor straightforward glamorous drag queen, Divine practically invented a new form of drag that was both comic and subversive. Sadly, she died very early, notably before she had a chance to record the song "Cha-Cha Heels." The song alludes to one of the most famous lines in the John Waters/Divine pantheon, spoken by Dawn Davenport's father in *Female Trouble* (John Waters, 1974), "Nice girls don't wear cha-cha heels!" Eartha Kitt released it in 1989, featuring the very gay band Bronski Beat, and it was a hit in gay clubs (more about that below).

In his book *Nice Girls Don't Wear Cha-Cha Heels! Camp Lines from Classic Films* (1999), Leigh Rutledge quotes many lines spoken by gay icons in their most iconic movies, and the choice of this one makes perfect sense. The movie *Grease* (Randal Kleiser, 1978) incorporates that line in its diegesis without actually speaking it, when bad girl Cha-Cha DiGregorio (Annette Charles) is opposed to good girl Sandy Olsson (Olivia Newton John) and dances in a "sluttish" manner at the school dance.[66] Brilliantly, the whole spirit of that cultish line presides over both *Hairspray* (John Waters, 1988) and *Cry-Baby* (John Waters, 1990). Divine is memorable in two parts in *Hairspray*, that of Edna Turnblad and that of Arvin Hodgepile; the latter is out of drag, some say. I would say instead that he is in male drag.

In 1981 I went to see Divine perform at Heroes, in Manchester, England. I was lucky enough to talk to her at some length after she sang a couple of dance tracks and I cherish the memory of our conversation. She was extremely funny in such conversations, which helped her gay iconicity. Millions of us cried when she died, apparently of causes related to her extreme weight. She was undoubtedly the most famous drag queen in the world. These days RuPaul is the reigning queen, but has yet to inspire a Disney character, the way Divine inspired Ursula the Sea Witch in *The Little Mermaid* (1989).

What made Divine such a success is that her star quality and performance rested on two seemingly conflicting levels. As Richard Dyer puts it, she "is an enormous drag queen [...] full of energy, fun and lust for life. 'She' (Glenn Milstead) always plays definitely female characters in the films, yet every viewer must know she is a man" (Dyer 1990: 170). Like all true female stars, Divine was a walking contradiction (Guilbert 2002: 91–110). "In sex scenes, the scraggy or self-obsessed quality of her partners evokes joyless heterosexual screwing, but Divine's magnificent lust is a paean to gay desire" (Dyer 1990: 170). Is it any wonder she is a huge gay icon in every sense of the word?

Agnetha Fältskog (1950–)

Agnetha Fältskog is one-quarter of the Swedish band Abba: the quarter that gays like best. Even though her face is pink, wholesome and slightly "corny," unlike the sculpted faces of most of the gay icons featured in this book, she is much loved. Many would declare her cheekbones not pronounced enough.[67] In the gay cult movie *The Adventures of Priscilla, Queen of the Desert* (Stephan Elliott, 1994), the most classically aesthetic character, a beautiful young man named Adam (played by a young and muscular Guy Pearce) makes a living as a drag queen on the stages of Australian clubs. He never goes anywhere without a sacred relic: a piece of turd left by Agnetha Fältskog in the ladies' room. So this is how far the devotion of a gay man to a gay icon can go, with a lot of camp humor verging on trash humor.

Abba reigned over the pop world from 1974 to 1980 with six of their eight albums. Their outfits, perfectly fashionable in the 1970s and marvelously kitsch, account for some of their popularity with the gays: flares, flowery tunics and fringed suede jackets, nothing was too colorful or too tawdry. Their songs function as the exact definition of what the purest pop should be, and the purest pop has often enchanted gays. When it is pure, pop music can be consumed at face value; when it borders on easy listening, it can delight people who often resort to tongue-in-cheek appreciation. The song that propelled Abba to fame was "Waterloo," which they performed at the Eurovision Song Contest, a rather camp competition that is very much a gay favorite.[68] But of the 4 band members, only Agnetha became a gay icon. The song "Dancing Queen," deliciously polysemic and marvelous to dance to, accounts for much of their appeal (Guilbert in Fitzgerald & Williams 2013: 177–188). It is featured on the album *Arrival*, which came out in 1976.[69]

Agnetha is atypical as a gay icon because she is not a diva in any sense of the term. In the 1970s she was blond, but she never really managed to sport a decent hairdo, multiplying the most horrendous capillary mistakes. She looked too healthy and her smile was too "natural" and too good-natured, but gays wanted to go out for coffee with her, to discuss her marital issues and their constant attempts at scoring. When asked by *Out* magazine in 2013 why she thought Abba had such a loyal gay fanbase, she replied: "I think it partly comes from how ABBA was presented from the start—with high heels, spectacular costumes, and music you wanted to dance to."[70] Indeed, that is a start.

The musical *Mamma Mia!* (1999), based on Abba songs, renewed the band's gay favor, notably with young men who bought the best-ofs after they had seen the show. Then the phenomenon became global and much more accessible when the musical was filmed as *Mamma Mia!* (Phyllida Lloyd, 2008), a rather camp movie with gay icon Meryl Strep as Donna.

On a mainstream French primetime news program, I recently heard this about gay parenting: "Just because their parents listen to Abba and George Michael doesn't mean that they're going to be raised badly."[71] It needs no comment. In March 2006, Abba delighted many fans around the world when they reunited, quite exceptionally, to sign souvenirs to be auctioned for Fundacja Rownosci, a Polish gay rights organization. Agnetha usually stays away from her old colleagues, notably because the two men pocket all the Abba money, but she was motivated by the horrendous situations of LGBTQ+ people in Poland.

Agnetha might be a little bit too sincere, and we have known since Oscar Wilde that sincerity is vastly overrated, but she will forever remain every gay boy's dancing queen.

Mylène Farmer (1961–)

It might seem strange to include this French performer here, but my decision was validated when I read David Halperin's indispensable book *How to Be Gay* (2012) and was thrilled to see that he mentions both her and Dalida. Like Madonna, Farmer has an ambiguous rapport with Catholicism, which fuels her creation. In many ways she has become "the Madonna of French gays" in every possible sense of the phrase. The my-gay-paris.com website calls her "France's biggest gay icon."[72] Like Madonna, she concentrated on the production of powerful videos very early on. Indeed, many of her videos were released in two formats, the long one functioning exactly like a short movie, with a coherent diegesis and costing a great deal of money.

When she sings "Sans contrefaçon" (1987), Farmer makes a forceful point about the construction of gender, basically advertising that you can be anything you like. With no counterfeiting, she is a boy, she claims. How many singers are brave enough to sing a song entitled "Fuck Them All" (2005), which turns into an instant gay anthem? She actually sings those three words, in English, and it is easy to see how they can constitute a rallying cry against homophobia. Her first hit was actually a lesbian song, "Maman a tort" (1984); a first-person narrative, it dealt with a young girl, very possibly underage, who fell in love with a nurse.

Farmer writes some of her own material and often makes inspired choices of fashion designers, choreographers and dancers. She does not, however, always make the gayest choices as far as her musical collaborators are concerned: Moby, Sting, or Seal, rather than, say, Mirwais, Justin Timberlake, or Nicki Minaj. For one season, however, she did recruit RedOne, who had worked with Lady Gaga.

Farmer is the Sylvia Plath of French pop. If you are about to commit suicide, reading a Sylvia Plath book and listening to a Farmer album is the best way to finish yourself off gloriously. Her lyrics are often all about feeling down, feeling low, feeling dejected—but oh-so-gorgeous in her despair. And that despair is a cheerful despair, as it were, similar to that of Japan's gay favorite David Sylvian, as notably expressed in the song "Despair" from the *Quiet Life* album (1979), in which he sang about a cheerful form of despair, as it were (in French in the text). Lana Del Rey does very much the same; some of her songs are quite depressing, and gays listen to them with masochistic glee. Farmer's fans love being depressed with her. In every one of her concerts, there comes a moment when she interrupts the fast tunes and the energetic dancing with the sexy dancers to launch the sad section of the show, alone in a ray of light with her faithful pianist collaborator, who grows fatter and greyer every tour, whereas she remains plastic and flawless. She sings a couple of heartbreaking slow songs, heartbreakingly, and actually cries, real tears, magnified a thousand-fold on the gigantic video screens above the stage. Needless to say, all of the gay boys in the audience cry with her. This is the stuff gay icons are made of. When she is asked why she is a gay icon, she surmises that it is because, like gays, she is different and acutely aware of it.[73]

Indeed, Farmer could merely walk on stage and stand there, doing nothing special, and the crowd would still be delirious. You only need to watch her concert DVDs to be convinced. What matters, both for her and for some of the other women in this book, is her star performance.

Zsa Zsa Gabor (1917–2016)

Zsa Zsa Gabor, who lived nearly a century, had nine husbands, an extraordinary record even by Hollywood standards. Jean-Noël Liaut writes:

Once upon a time there were four Hungarian vamps named Jolie, Magda, Zsa Zsa and Eva Gabor. The four of them put together, mother and daughters, married 23 times, catching in their nets men such as the founder of the Hilton hotel chain, a German prince, one of the creators of the Barbie doll and the actor George Sanders, who married two of them [Liaut 2013: 75, my translation].

Indeed, George Sanders married Zsa Zsa in 1949 and then divorced her; in 1970 he married her sister Magda (1915–1997). There was one other wife in between. Although her sister Eva Gabor (1919–1995) is a gay favorite herself, she never became quite as iconic as Zsa Zsa.

Her many magnificent quotes, very camp ones, are now common knowledge:

"How many husbands have you had?" "You mean, other than my own?"[74]
"I'm a wonderful housekeeper. Every time I get divorced, I keep the house" [Zsa Zsa Gabor in Warren 2000: 51].
"I haven't known any open marriages, although quite a few have been ajar" [Zsa Zsa Gabor in Warren 2000: 72].
"A girl must marry for love, and keep on marrying until she finds it" [Zsa Zsa Gabor in Warren 2000: 72].
"I want a man who's kind and understanding. Is that too much to ask of a millionaire?" [Zsa Zsa Gabor in Warren 2000: 76].
"Macho does not prove mucho" [Zsa Zsa Gabor in Warren 2000: 78].

Tom Teicholz remembers:

Over the last several decades, Zsa Zsa appeared in a wide variety of movies, from camp to trash, and in later years poked fun at herself but continued to be at her best as a talk show guest. Here are some more of her one-liners: "Husbands are like fire. They go out when unattended." [...] "I believe in large families: Every woman should have at least three husbands." [...] Although famous, Zsa Zsa attained notoriety in 1989 when she went on trial for slapping a Beverly Hills police officer. It was not the first time she had behaved poorly, just the first time she crossed the line with an officer of the court. She received a sentence of three days in jail—and plenty of publicity. Finally, it should be noted that the Gabors were all successful businesswomen.[75]

More than anything else, Gabor is a remarkable example of overblown, entirely woman-made femininity, screaming its artificiality: "I wasn't born,

I was ordered from room service," she declared. Her hyperfemininity was used for survival. The most splendid camp is often the one that comes from despair. The originally Jewish Gabors had rather show off their blondness and cleavage and jewels than reminisce about their flight from the Nazis in Budapest (Liaut 2013: 76).

Zsa Zsa Gabor did stage work, film, television, books, everything. What many gays particularly remember are perhaps her parts as Jane Avril in *Moulin Rouge* (John Huston, 1952), Talleah in *Queen of Outer Space* (Edward Bernds, 1958), Minerva in the *Batman* television series (1968), and her many talk-show appearances. But, as Richard Dyer claims, even people who are fascinated by her are not interested primarily in her films, "Zsa Zsa Gabor is a film star whose films only a dedicated buff could name" (Dyer 1979: 61).

She occasionally expressed homophobic sentiments, but gays tended to forgive her. When she died, *Attitude* magazine wrote: "Essentially, she was *Sex and the City*'s Samantha Jones [...], and like that character, Zsa Zsa's every-girl-for-herself attitude to life and love earned her legions of gay fans."[76]

Lady Gaga (1986–)

Lady Gaga is a self-proclaimed gay icon.[77] This might have been counterproductive, but apart from a little Internet trolling, the self-proclamation was widely accepted. It did not work quite so well for Katy Perry, who unsubtly courted LGBTQ+ audiences with her songs "Ur So Gay" (2008) and "I Kissed a Girl" (2008). Usually, "calling oneself a gay icon does not a gay icon make."[78] Beside declaring her immense gay-friendliness/bisexuality/whatever in the most public of arenas (and she must be commended for not hesitating to risk losing many buyers, being so vocal about it all), Lady Gaga has done everything it takes to deserve the label. Basically, she occasionally rewrites David Bowie, she constantly rewrites the 1980–1985 Grace Jones and the 1984–1993 Madonna. In those years, postmodern Madonna rewrote all sorts of gay icons of yesteryear, notably Mae

West, Marlene Dietrich and Greta Garbo. In her palimpsestuous writing, you could see them under the ink, as it were. When you examine Gaga, you can see Madonna under the ink, and under Madonna, you can see those previous gay icons. How vertiginously postmodern can you get? Some might even be tempted to call Gaga post-postmodern, but that is not very helpful in this context (nor is the label "hypermodern"). Whereas Madonna reinvented herself every two years or so, Gaga reinvents herself every week, which might be seen as unfortunate. Indeed, venomous observers might be tempted to see it all as a mere succession of meaningless disguises, as opposed to the clever, meaningful drag of Madonna (and David Bowie before her).

To please the young gays, Gaga also provides perfectly calibrated dance music. She wears as many wigs as drag queens and Nicki Minaj do. To please older gays, she sings old ballads with Tony Bennett.

In matters of sexual orientation, Gaga is terribly essentialist, singing as she does "Born This Way" (2011). It is a rare feat to decide in advance that a song will be a gay anthem—competing with "Over the Rainbow" and "I Will Survive"—and then laugh all the way to the bank, in spite of *some* gay discontent. In other words, in political terms, she is in the modern assimilationist gay camp. Fortunately, in matters of gender, she is constructionist, looking and sounding postmodern and queer. The way she handles fashion in and out of her videos and concerts, although often unnerving, provides a permanent commentary not only on gender but also on the sartorial practices of the well-to-do of Paris, London, New York and Los Angeles.

In 2015 she became a hit on the television screen when she appeared in the fifth season of *American Horror Story*. Naturally, she had previously appeared in tremendous videos that craftily pleased even the most demanding of postmodern critics, third-wave constructionist feminists and queer theorists—especially "Paparazzi" (2009), "Bad Romance" (2009), "Alejandro" (2010), and "Telephone" (with Beyoncé, 2010). She had also been featured in the metacinema of Robert Rodriguez. However, it was in *American Horror Story: Hotel* that she found the role her gay fans had been waiting for. Ryan Murphy, casting her as an ancient vampire, knew exactly what he was doing. He had repeatedly shown in *Glee* that he had mastered the art of gay-icon-mongering,[79] and he was perfectly aware of the direct filiation between the Lilith legends, vampire lore, old Hollywood vamps and femmes fatales and Gaga (via Madonna).[80] There is even a bit of the *Hunger* Deneuve in that Gaga vampire. Gaga notoriously calls her fans "little monsters." There are many gay boys among them (although, as evidenced on Facebook by writer Matthew Rettenmund, the monsters also paradoxically count among their ranks homophobes who troll well-meaning bloggers, spewing hatred in the most vulgar vocabulary complete with grammatical mistakes and appalling spelling).

Finally, Lady Gaga, aka Mother Monster, has been paid tons of tributes by drag queens across the globe, and has been known to mix with some of RuPaul's drag queens,[81] the last accolade she needed to be the definitive gay icon of the 21st century she very possibly aspires to be.

Greta Garbo (1905–1990)

It is rumored that in 1925, Greta Garbo had an affair with her fellow gay icon and number-one competitor Marlene Dietrich. Part of Garbo's appeal rested on her androgyny and low throaty voice. Strangely enough, when critics speak of androgyny in pop-culture icons, they generally mean aesthetically appealing androgyny, i.e., people who are beautiful whether they are women or men. No one ever speaks of unattractive androgynous people, who are quite numerous but outside the scope of this book.

Susan Sontag finds camp in Garbo's very face, speaking of "the haunting androgynous vacancy behind the perfect beauty of Greta Garbo" (Sontag 1969: 281). Later she notes, with respect to "the great serious idol of camp taste," Greta Garbo, that her "incompetence (at the least, lack of depth) as an actress enhances her beauty. She's always herself" (Sontag 1969: 287). As we have seen, for worshippers of gay icons, it is no problem at all for a Crawford or a Dietrich or a Garbo to be herself. The word "herself" in such pronouncements should be inserted between inverted commas, anyway, given that we are really talking about the intermediary (star) persona between the forever-unknown *realitatis femina* and the *dramatis personae* she incarnates in fictional works, such as the divine[82] Queen Christina in the case of Garbo.

Greta Garbo

Roland Barthes was one of the first scholars to enthuse about Garbo's extremely beautiful face:

> It is indeed an admirable face-object. In *Queen Christina* [...] the makeup has the snowy thickness of a mask: it is not a painted face, but one set in plaster, protected by the surface of the color, not by its lineaments. Amid all this snow at once fragile and compact, the eyes alone, black like strange soft flesh, but not in the least expressive, are two faintly tremulous wounds [Barthes 1993: 56–57].

Precisely. The experimental short movie *Meeting of Two Queens* (Cecilia Barriga, 1993) proposes a queer reading of the filmography of Greta Garbo and Marlene Dietrich. Which of the two was the last word in vamps remains to be determined.

Diva magazine concentrates more on biographical data, which complete the work and contribute to the gay iconicity of Garbo—although many have firmly chosen sides.

> Noted for her reclusive later years and for uttering those infamous words "I want to be alone" (*Grand Hotel*, 1932), Greta Garbo was another of Hollywood's leading bisexual ladies. Unlike Dietrich, Garbo never married, had no children and for the majority of her life, lived alone. She had public affairs with fashion designer George Schlee and conductor Leopold Stokowski, as well as more private relationships with actresses Lilyan Tashman, Louise Brooks and Mercedes de Acosta (Hollywood's original "hub"). However, it seems that Garbo's soulmate was Swedish actress Mimi Pollak, who back in 2005 released their private correspondence, including poetry Garbo wrote about Pollack and a letter from 1928 where, writing to the now-married Pollak she says, "I dream of seeing you and discovering whether you still care as much about your old bachelor. I love you, little Mimosa."[83]

Antoni Gronowicz quotes her in *Garbo: Her Story* (1990): "As far back as I can reach into my memory, I have always wanted to be like Sarah Bernhardt" (Gronowicz 1991: 266). Bernhardt, something of a gay icon, sometimes performed in drag, believing herself so talented that no part—whether feminine or masculine—was beyond her reach (she thought no man could play Hamlet as well as she did). Perhaps Garbo was not quite so talented, but she was equally interesting in drag, and much more glamorous, to the delight of millions of gays worldwide. Besides, her star persona, linked to her early retirement (before her beauty faded), is what delights gays, possibly more than her movies. In a paragraph that is relevant to much of this book, Richard Dyer writes: "The deaths of Montgomery Clift, James Dean, Marilyn Monroe and Judy Garland (and the premature retirement of Greta Garbo) may be as significant as the films they made, while Lana Turner's later films were largely a mere illustration of her life" (Dyer 1979: 61). For the record, the cult gay porn star of yester-year, Peter Berlin, was nicknamed "the Garbo of gay porn."

Judy Garland (1922–1969)

Many deem that no one should even consider being iconoclastic enough to even dream of disputing that Judy Garland is the number one gay icon ever, taking in every century and every country (admittedly, with Bette Davis, Joan Crawford, Cher and Madonna close behind). Simon Gage *et al.* call her "movie star and gay icon extraordinaire" and explain that "as much as her talent, it was the way she embodied both vulnerability and strength which had gay men hooked" (Gage *et al.* 2002: 46). Steven Cohan confirms: "This view of Garland as the phoenix-like diva of suffering, often used to account for her strong, cultish appeal to gay fans, dominates how her stardom is now remembered" (Cohan in Tinkcom & Villarejo 2001: 120).

Hayden Manders explains:

> The icon becomes a voice for the gay man, allowing him to express himself indirectly. The likes of Donna Summer, Barbra Streisand, Whitney Houston, and Judy Garland are lifeblood. He aligns himself with them, because they identify with his quest to succeed in the face of adversity [...]. [B]eing a woman is rather indispensable for the title. [...] [T]he majority of past gay icons were women, but they were *glamorous women*—women who were larger than life, but plagued by self-doubt. Judy Garland is, by and large, the definition of gay icon [Manders 2013].[84]

Garland began her movie career at the age of eight. As she often reminded us in song, she was born in a trunk, i.e., a show business trunk, full of lace dresses and shiny accessories. At the age of 16 she played Dorothy in *The Wizard of Oz* (Victor Fleming, 1939). In 1939, when the movie came out, she was 17. In that movie, she rules. She leads the dance. She gives hope and trust back to three individuals who doubt terribly and dislike themselves: the Scarecrow who thinks he is brainless, the Tin Man who is sorry he has no heart, and the Cowardly Lion who worries about his lack of courage. It is not hard to spot the metaphor for homosexuality. The pitch is that Dorothy helps them accept themselves with their differences.

Judy Garland officially became the number-one gay cult with that role, the official fag hag of the Western world. However, as endearing as the aging Cowardly Lion might be with his bow in this mane, Dorothy's three companions alone do not account for the film's cult appeal: there are also the oh-so-famous ruby slippers, full of sequins and magic. At least one rare pair of the surviving historic shoes, which were worn on-set, can be admired at the Smithsonian in Washington, D.C. They are drag shoes, quite simply.[85] Dorothy's utterly adorable little dog, Toto, clearly does nothing to heterosexualize the movie. When she confides in him that they are not in Kansas anymore, one can only fall for them.[86] *The Wizard of Oz* is arguably the most important hypotext of American culture, far above the Bible and Shakespeare. The movie is constantly quoted in other movies, in television series, comic books and elsewhere—whether one is confronted by a yellow brick road to be followed, evokes a melting Wicked Witch of the West, or wonders about what there could possibly be on the other side of the rainbow. The answer, as it happens, is clear for gays, fans of the song "Over the Rainbow": on the other side there are the multicolored gays and their multicolored life, there is a kingdom without homophobia and without strict gender rules and gender roles. Gays, as the whole world knows, made Dorothy's rainbow their flag[87]: it contains all the colors of all of the sexualities and all of the alternative lifestyles, it incorporates all the colors of Dorothy in Oz.

Indeed, gay fans of Oz often choose to forget that Dorothy ludicrously intends to return to her sad, boring, black-and-white native Kansas, whereas Oz is gorgeous, colorful and gay. Obviously, in the non-censored version, somewhere in an alternative universe (over the rainbow?), Dorothy never goes back to her farming Aunt Em, electing to stay with her adoptive aunts such as Glinda, the Good Witch of the South. My reading of every element of the movie is queer. Alexander Doty has a totally lesbian reading of it, which is not necessarily incompatible.[88] Golden-age Hollywood musicals and movies such as *The Wizard of Oz* have always lent themselves particularly well to transgressive—and notably, queer—readings. Clearly, there is a strong equation between the realitatis femina Frances Ethel Gumm, the star persona Judy Garland and the dramatis persona Dorothy.

Indeed, the outmoded expression "a friend of Dorothy" means a homosexual, as described in the Tallulah Bankhead section. It refers to

Judy Garland and the writer Dorothy Parker.[89] Garland was the singer of musicals par excellence. She delighted her gay aficionados not only in movies such as *Meet Me in St Louis* (Vincente Minnelli, 1944), *Ziegfeld Follies* (Vincente Minnelli *et al.* 1945), *Easter Parade* (Charles Walters, 1948), *A Star Is Born* (George Cukor, 1954), but also in her concerts. When she sang torch songs, she set women's and gay men's hearts on fire with her endless, sentimental notes. Her father Frank Gumm was gay: indeed, he took the family to California to flee Minnesota, where he had "gotten into trouble" due to his sexuality (Clarke 2002, 14, 23). When Garland started going out unchaperoned, whether in California or elsewhere, she became a regular patron of gay bars, where she went with gay friends. Garland always had a tendency to fall in love with, if not to marry, more-or-less closeted gay men such as Vincente Minnelli and Mark Herron. At best she fell in love with married men, often very famous ones.

She was very fragile. From her very early days she was fed handfuls of amphetamines so that she would remain thin and work hard. Of course, she then had to resort to barbiturates when night fell, if she wanted to sleep at all. She spent most of her adult life doing drugs and drinking. Gays often identify with all that. On the outside, Judy Garland was a magnificent star, a stupendous actress and thrilling singer, a man-eater with five husbands. Like many women in this book, she is even rumored to have had an affair with Jack Kennedy. Inside, she was a brittle little girl who really only ever wanted one thing: a man, a "real man," with broad shoulders, who would take her in his strong arms as she cried and who would promise her that everything was going to be all right and then keep his promise. Gays understand those things.

Michael Abernethy writes: "You've gone over to meet the new neighbor and introduce yourself. [...] Left alone for a moment in his living room while he takes a phone call, you do a quick scan of his CD collection for clues as to which "team" he plays for. [...] You find the damning evidence: copies of *Judy at Carnegie Hall*, the soundtrack of *Funny Girl*, and the extended play version of Madonna's *Vogue*. Yep, he's a queer."[90]

The June 1969 Stonewall riots in New York, which most of us view as the real start of modern gay activism, closely followed Garland's death from a barbiturate overdose. There was a cause-and-effect relationship, we say: the LGBT people who were victimized yet again by a police raid while mourning Garland were too saddened by her demise to put up with yet more police persecution. "When drag queens fought back at Stonewall, chances are that what they had on their minds was the shameless chutzpah of their film icons, whose bravura displays of gutsiness they were reenacting [...]" (Harris 1997: 14). Garland is an integral part of gay culture to this day—and no doubt, she will continue to be. Take, for instance, the way Rufus Wainwright has appropriated her (a move that was frowned upon by some, almost on moral grounds). Marvelous levels of camp were reached in 2006 when Wainwright covered the entire *Judy at Carnegie Hall* concert (not just "Over the Rainbow"). Garland was camp incarnate herself, I find, although not all agree, and the fact that Wainwright is singing every single one of her torch songs without changing the pronouns suffices to take it up a notch. I don't know that I can follow Michael Bronski, who writes: "A great deal of gay humor is based upon camp: irony and distancing. However, Judy Garland was revered because she was the antithesis of camp: she was utterly serious" (Bronksi 1984: 104). I guess it all depends what you mean by "camp" and by "serious"; indeed, it depends on whether you believe one can do serious camp, seriously do camp, or do camp seriously. The Carnegie Hall website says: "For two nights in 2006, Rufus Wainwright performed a love letter to Judy Garland's *Judy at Carnegie Hall* concert with a tribute of his own, *Rufus Does Judy at Carnegie Hall*. Backed by a 36-piece orchestra, he performed Judy's epic 1961 Carnegie Hall performance in its entirety."[91] Wainwright's love letter to Garland was very serious.

Naturally, it is hard to say anything really new or really interesting to say on the subject after having read Richard Dyer's indispensable chapter, "Judy Garland and Gay Men," in his 1986 book *Heavenly Bodies: Film Stars and Society*, which is a must for anyone interested in the mechanisms of Garland's stardom, notably among gays. Dyer was intent both on "picking up on the camp elements in her image" (Dyer 2004: 156) and on discussing "the androgyny of her image and her camp humor, the former at odds with the sex role norms of the films, the latter tending to denaturalize their normality," among other splendid insights (Dyer 2004: 158). Looking at that androgyny, Dyer speaks of the tramp image (in the sense of being a bum, not in the other sense) and writes: "If in the vamp gay men could identify with someone whose sexuality is accepted by the boys, in the tramp we could identify with someone who has left questions of sexuality behind in an androgyny that is not so much in-between (marked as both feminine and masculine) as without gender" (Dyer 2004: 175).

Even straights know that Garland is a gay icon. Judith A. Peraino quotes a 1967 *Time* article as saying: "A disproportionate part of her nightly claque seems to be homosexual. The boys in the tight trousers roll their eyes, tear at their hair and practically levitate from their seats, particularly when Judy sings ['Over the Rainbow']." As Peraino reminds us, that article even quoted psychiatrists' opinions about gay Garland worship (Peraino 2005: 125–126).

Gloria Gaynor (1949–)

Even if she had only ever recorded one song—"I Will Survive" (1978)—Gloria Gaynor would have become a gay icon. As it happens, she recorded other gay favorites, including "Never Can Say Goodbye" (1974) and her cover of the Four Tops' 1966 classic "Reach Out, I'll Be There" (1975). She has the sort of voice employed with the sort of tunes that delight gay men. I feel almost embarrassed writing this entry, because this is so obviously in the realm of clichés. Who does not know that just like "Over the Rainbow," "I Will Survive" is a gay anthem?

Well, come to think of it, an entire soccer organization didn't. The cover of the song by the uninspiring Hermes House Band (a Dutch formation) became the official hymn of the French national team in 1998. It seems France won the World Cup that year. Maybe they knew and did not care. Or worse, they were homophobic and decided to try and steal the song from gays out of spite. Unless, more interestingly, someone inside was actually gay, and thought it would be a great joke to thus queer the soccer championship. We will never know. On the other hand, Régine, feted by many Frenchmen as a gay icon, covered the song in French, as (unsurprisingly) "Je survivrai" (1979).[92] The song has been used all over the world by many filmmakers. Perhaps the most inspired use of "I Will Survive" was made by Stephan Elliott in *Priscilla, Queen of the Desert*. I have seen dozens of drag queens on three continents lip-sync to the song over the decades, and *Priscilla* presents it as such, a drag routine, seen a zillion times, but, precisely, always and forever hugely enjoyable. The end-of-the-movie mix of Gaynor's song with traditional aboriginal music was delightfully original.

Mexican gay favorite Gloria Trevi also, and rather successfully, covered the song. Diana Ross covered it in 1995, making a video that clearly presents the song as a gay anthem (more about this in the Diana Ross entry below). Why is this song a gay anthem? Because it is pure disco music of the sort that is hard to resist, magically dragging the shyest of gays to the dance floor. Additionally, it tells a typical gay icon/gay story: what Gage *et al.* call a "my man done me wrong" narrative. Except it is also a recovery story! Think of "Surabaya Johnny" by Bertold Brecht and Kurt Weill. When sung by Bette Midler it is a totally gay-iconic torch song: her man has treated her appallingly, and she has never recovered, to the point that she is now an absolute wreck, let her cry in the arms of sympathetic gay men who have suffered similarly (more about this in the Bette Midler entry below). In "I Will Survive," the man has mistreated Gloria, who really thought she could not possibly exist without his company. But then she picked herself up, she changed, and she is telling him to get out for good. She has become a strong, independent woman.

Naturally, with the onset of AIDS, "I Will Survive" became a entirely new song; suddenly it dealt with surviving the AIDS epidemic. In spite of what some gays might claim, there *are* gay hymns, all over the place, and this one is particularly central to gay culture.[93] Maeve Walsh writes: "becoming a gay anthem in an era of Aids and prejudice, and a feminist anthem for women left by, or leaving, their men. In 1996, Naomi Wolf hailed Gaynor as "one of the most casually influential political figures in the popular culture of the 1970s and 1980s."[94]

Like other African American performers, Gloria Gaynor has often been said to owe part of her gay iconicity and popularity with white disco boys to the color of her skin. This poses a serious political problem, as white gay men have often been accused of cultural appropriation in the sense that millions of white gays in the U.S. love the demeanor and especially the vernacular of black women. I realize this claim is terribly risky in its generalization. Indeed, I have met a great many gay men who consciously imitate (in a way that I find funny but that some of my friends find offensive) what they see as the "sassy black woman." Although I offer no solution to the dilemma, in the interests of intellectual and political honesty, I had to mention it. RuPaul, as an African American drag queen, is, one supposes, a bit more entitled than a white one to appropriate the clichéd sassiness of the clichéd African American woman, but then RuPaul is hugely popular with white gays who learn to speak in the same manner.... Unsurprisingly, RuPaul has a personal history with "I Will Survive." "Mama Ru" was interviewed by *Vulture* in March 2016:

> Last week on Drag Race, you eliminated both queens, Laila McQueen and Dax Exclamationpoint. This has only happened one other time in Drag Race history. What was disappointing about their Gloria Gaynor, "I Will Survive," lip-sync battle?
> Because Drag 101, the first song you learn to lip-sync to is Gloria Gaynor's "I Will Survive." And every human alive knows the words to that song, just by default, because they play it so motherfucking much. And it was like, "What the fuck? You don't know the words to "I Will Survive"? Then both you bitches need to go. I've heard these theories of, "Oh, they planned that." Bitch, we didn't plan that. Did you see the performance? It was absolutely awful.[95]

Françoise Hardy (1944–)

Beautiful Françoise Hardy is a French fashion icon and gay icon. She is one of the original yé-yé singers (Sontag 1969: 280). Unlike many of her contemporaries, she survived the yé-yé craze and quickly evolved into a "cool" singer, singing both her own and other people's songs while hip musicians and lyricists fought over the honor of writing songs for her. She has a hunky singer/actor estranged husband, Jacques Dutronc. She has a gorgeous singer/actor son, Thomas Dutronc. She has been the friend and/ or muse of a great number of impressive performers over the decades, including Serge Gainsbourg, Brigitte Fontaine, Bob Dylan, Paul McCartney, Mick Jagger,[96] David Bowie, Iggy Pop, Étienne Daho, Damon Albarn, Benjamin Biolay, etc. Fans like imagining that these were often more than friends.

In various respects Hardy is a French version of Marianne Faithfull. Her songs "Tous les garçons et les filles" (1962), "Le temps de l'amour" (1962) and "Mon amie la rose" (1964),[97] international classics, have been covered by various people, including the Eurythmics[98] and fellow gay icon Vanessa Paradis. Many English speakers find the song "Find Me a Boy," Hardy's own English version of "Tous les garcons et les filles," rather endearing, notably because of her accent. Originally shy and introverted, Hardy had to fight her most visceral temptation, which was to hide in her room reading novels and listening to other people's music. In 1968 she made headlines posing in Paco Rabanne mini dresses, becoming more iconic than ever before. Those pictures are now legendary and inspired Lizzy Gardiner's design both of the costumes for *Priscilla Queen of the Desert* (Stephan Elliott, 1994) and of her own Oscars dress, a tremendous creation made of credit cards.

In the 1970s Hardy broke away from yé-yé to make what she saw as more "serious" music. Three albums are particular gay favorites: *Message personnel* (1973), *Musique saoule* (1978) and *Gin Tonic* (1980). They were released in France and a dozen other countries, mostly Spanish-speaking and English-speaking. One of the elements of the Françoise Hardy reluctant star persona that gays enjoy is the mixture of agonizing doubt, worry, nostalgia and the "cheerful despair" that later gay icon Mylène Farmer made her trademark (see above), except that Hardy's persona is mixed with a naïveté that paradoxically endures. She has repeatedly declared that her most devoted friends and fans are gay.[99]

In recent years Hardy has repeatedly disappointed her gay fans, at least to a degree, as she became increasingly right-wing (and very outspoken about it),[100] and increasingly convinced that she is a talented astrologer (she even writes odd books about it). Her father was gay, killed by a rent boy, as she revealed,[101] and one of her best friends is French gay favorite "Schizophrenia" singer Armande Altaï. Hardy ages rather gracefully, although she has been facing successive bouts of serious diseases: she's a survivor. But perhaps the principal reason she remains a gay icon is that she personifies "French cool" like no other, albeit with some competition from Vanessa Paradis.

Jean Harlow (1911–1937)

It is undeniable that gay men like their tragic diva stories (and no, I do not think that is inherently misogynistic). Jean Harlow is a case in point. Gay men like rumors. Back in the 1930s, instead of acknowledging that Harlow died of kidney failure, they actually preferred to believe in all of the train-wreck rumors about the reasons for her untimely demise at the age of 26: booze, drugs, a botched abortion, and the best one of all, peroxide poisoning (a rumor that dogged other blondes throughout the history of entertainment). This rumor was cleverly alluded to in *Priscilla, Queen of the Desert.*

I partially disagree with Quentin Crisp when he writes: "As a rule, it is a great advantage for movie actresses to die young, but in Miss Harlow's case, this was not so. In spite of her platinum hair, her appeal was not glamorous—still less exotic or mysterious. She was sexy in the coarsest way. This quality could have lasted into middle age or even old age."[102] I do believe that dying young helped make Harlow an icon, gay or otherwise—even though it is possible that she might have aged well. But I agree that she was coarse, in the best sense of the word, as it were. Crisp reminds us that the press often referred to her "effortless vulgarity" and bitchily tells us that in her early publicity pictures "her hair is chalky white, her lips, boot black, and her eyebrows are two penciled lines, varying neither in thickness nor in emphasis." He also judges that Harlow's "postures, frequently with her terrible knees on view for all the world to see, are so awkward that they seem like parodies of glamorous attitudes. Her dresses, neither elegant nor daring, look like part of the wardrobe of a barman's daughter who has just won a lottery. Furthermore, they are rumpled [...]."[103] Precisely. It is those parodic aspects that made Harlow a gay icon. She was exactly like an inexpensive drag queen from her native Missouri or somewhere like it. According to Crisp, she was delightfully vulgar, coarse like a man. People saw her as a laughing vamp, a blonde bombshell, she appealed to straight men's most basic desires the way many gay men dream of crassly appealing to straight men. James Ursini and Dominique Mainon call her a "proletarian femme fatale" (Ursini & Mainon 2009: 115).

Carroll Baker starred in a marvelously bad biopic, *Harlow* (Gordon Douglas, 1965), mythical for some of us, which added to the "gay points" she had already scored with *Baby Doll* (Elia Kazan, 1956). It was one of the two poor biopics, both entitled *Harlow*, that came out in 1965. In this movie, Baker appropriated some of Harlow's iconicity in this movie—although not as spectacularly as Dunaway appropriated Crawford's iconicity in *Mommie Dearest.*

Rita Hayworth (1918–1987)

Philip French writes:

> She was one of the world's most beautiful women and became an icon long before that word entered the lexicon of celebrity. Her image was inscribed on the first post-war atom bomb, tested in 1946 on the atoll that gave its name to the bikini. A poster for her most celebrated movie, the noir classic *Gilda*, was being put up on a wall in Rome by the hero of the Italian neo-realist film, *Bicycle Thieves* (1948), when his bike was stolen.[104]

It is slightly embarrassing to discuss the "Put the Blame on Mame" scene in *Gilda* (Charles Vidor, 1946), as entire books have been written on the subject. It is basically a song and dance number that ends with a striptease, except that all Hayworth takes off is her gloves. However, the way she takes them off can still be seen as more erotic than many forms of nudity, many forms of dance, etc.[105] A true seductress never needs to take off all her clothes to get her men. Hayworth is the original pin-up girl. The darling of the GIs. "It may be as pinups that Betty Grable and Rita Hayworth are really important [...]" (Dyer 1979: 61).

Gilda notoriously lends itself rather well to queer readings (cf. Dyer 2002: 104–108). In some ways, Hayworth (like Elizabeth Taylor in several movies, as we'll see) functions as queer bait or a straight (translucent) screen. And Glenn Ford is offered to the desiring gaze of whoever might be interested. "The film underscores the similarity between them as covetable items. One hardly needs to go into Rita Hayworth's screen goddess glamour in this, her most famous role, but this is complemented by a glamorization of Glenn Ford as Johnny" (Dyer 2002: 107). In spite of herself, Hayworth was involved in what *The New Yorker* calls "nuclear kitsch." During atomic testing in the Marshall Islands, one Bikini bomb was christened "Gilda." It bore a picture of Hayworth.[106]

She was married (and divorced) five times, to Edward C. Judson, Orson Welles, Prince Aly Khan, Dick Haymes, and James Hill. In 1937, her first husband helped transform her from dark-haired half Spanish Margarita Carmen Cansino to flamboyant red-headed Rita Hayworth, the embodiment of American sexiness—after she had been featured in several movies as Rita Cansino. She had a string of lovers, prompting her to reveal that "men go to bed with Gilda, but wake up with me," which is as funny as it is sad. Gay fans pay as much attention to the marriages of their heroines as to their movies, if not more. Edward Field remembers:

> I grew up during the era when the movie studios built up their movie stars into gods and goddesses—but especially, for me, the goddesses, figures like Bette Davis, Joan Crawford, Rita Hayworth, Ava Gardner, Ingrid Bergman, Greta Garbo, and of course, Judy—a pantheon that dominated the fantasy lives of the whole country. The plots of their movies were inextricably part of the legends of these ladies, as well as their social and love lives, including their marriages, most of which were largely invented for them by the studios' publicity departments. It was a world of supreme fiction that engaged the imagination totally [Field in Montlack 2009: 43].

Fiction is boring when there is no drama, no brutal breakup and little suffering. Hayworth's fiction delivered both on- and off-screen. Trevor Martin writes: "The most noted and revered of gay men's icons are inevitably quirky or uncommonly beautiful and always talented." But that is not all: "They portray a vulnerability that is often wrapped up in strength in the face of adversity. Lurking behind the glitz they may have troubled personal lives—perhaps their lives are tainted by emotional turbulence—and sometimes a subtle sense of pathos filters out from just behind the eyes."[107] For the interesting mirror effects between her life, her movies and the media's take on them, the following movies are particularly recommended: *Only Angels Have Wings* (Howard Hawks, 1939); *Angels Over Broadway* (Ben Hecht & Lee Garmes, 1940); *The Lady from Shanghai* (Orson Welles, 1947), for which Welles legendarily forced her to go blonde; and *Miss Sadie Thompson* (Curtis Bernhardt, 1953).

Like many of the women in this book, Hayworth had at least one illegal abortion, as all the biographies document. Then, however, she had two children: Rebecca Welles and Yasmin Aga Khan. Remarkably, in the late 1940s she was the target of many high-profile moralists who criticized her behavior, something that could only endear her to gays. She spent much of her life feeling miserable, suffering from alcoholism, and (at the end) stricken by Alzheimer's disease. But we'll always have Gilda.

Audrey Hepburn (1929–1993)

It might be argued that Audrey Hepburn was too sweet, too natural, too fresh to be a gay icon. Gays like their icons to strut on vertiginous heels and wear copious amounts of makeup, not walk like a boy on flat ballerinas and look like a wide-eyed teenage boy—or do they? Maybe Audrey Hepburn satisfies the occasional need for a return to innocence lost. Or maybe they like her androgyny. At a time when Hollywood women were curvy and voluptuous, Hepburn was a bit of a stick figure, offering a sort of European sensibility and charm that were often seen as waif-like. She was indeed European (Dutch, English and Irish), but American gays are still grateful she crossed the Atlantic Ocean.

Her big break came with *Roman Holiday* (William Wyler, 1953), in which she plays an overprotected princess who falls for an American reporter in the Eternal City. Watching this movie, every gay boy who feels like a princess can dream of falling into the strong arms of Gregory Peck. To concentrate on the gay favorites in her filmography, we then move on to *Sabrina* (Billy Wilder, 1954), with the massively attractive Humphrey Bogart and William Holden; *Funny Face* (Stanley Donen, 1957), with Fred Astaire, set in the fashion world; *Breakfast at Tiffany's* (Blake Edwards, 1961), detailed below; *Charade* (Stanley Donen, 1963), a Parisian intrigue; and the masterpiece *My Fair Lady* (George Cukor, 1964), which was all about changing one's accent and behavior to be a real princess—and gays know a few things about that.

Needless to say, *Breakfast at Tiffany's* is a totally gay movie, and not only because it is adapted from a very gay novella by the very gay Truman Capote (1958). Hepburn was never as iconic before or after as she was playing Holly Golightly in this ultra-camp fest. Dressed by Hubert de Givenchy (who also designed Hepburn's memorable off-screen clothes) with the assistance of Edith Head, Holly moves in an inimitable way, with her hairdo and her hat and her cigarette holder, but which precisely everyone has constantly tried to imitate everywhere since. Perhaps the best imitation, visually speaking, was achieved by the late Brittany Murphy in *Love and Other Disasters* (Alek Keshishian, 2006), whatever else one might think of her and the movie. Around the world there are thousands of artifacts with Holly Golightly prints, mostly in cheap decoration stores, and I personally know many a gay man guilty of owning a Holly Golightly cushion. The sugar-babying character is a gorgeous mistress of reinvention, she is glamorous, she is flippant, she is funny. Of course, she is also sad and vulnerable. She is every drag queen's dream. And even if they de-gayed the narrator/Paul Varjak character for the movie, the whole thing is still queer.

Hepburn's private life also defies the usual patterns of gay iconicity: she was not particularly scandalous, nor heart-crushingly unhappy in spectacularly disastrous love affairs. She suffered many miscarriages, divorced first husband, actor Mel Ferrer (with whom she had son Sean), after 14 years, and divorced second husband, psychiatrist Andrea Dotti (with whom she had son Luca), after 13 years. She had a couple of lovers. In her final years she did a great deal of laudable humanitarian work, notably for UNICEF—but iconic Holly Golightly is what she will be remembered for forever, even by people who haven't seen the film and do not necessarily remember her name.

Katharine Hepburn (1907–2003)

In her fourth movie, Louisa May Alcott's *Little Women* (George Cukor, 1933), Katharine Hepburn played Jo the tomboy. In her ninth movie, *Sylvia Scarlett* (George Cukor, 1935), she played Sylvia, aka Sylvester. An actress who dons boy drag runs a serious risk of reinforcing her popularity with gays—even if she isn't really credible in drag and one has to seriously stretch one's willing suspension of disbelief. George Cukor was gay, as everyone knows, and was an expert at bolstering female gay iconicity, as his movies repeatedly demonstrated, notably his Hepburn vehicles. In many of those she performed within the performance (gays loved her histrionics), allowing Cukor to indulge in clever *mises en abyme.* Hepburn was very cagy about the issue of Cukor's sexuality in her book *Me: Stories of My Life* (1991), but she does reveal that Cukor was not very "macho" (Hepburn 1991: 156) and that what he was most interested in was highlighting the talent and beauty of his casts as opposed to seeking praise for his own aesthetic talents (Hepburn 1991: 154). In *Mary of Scotland* (John Ford, 1936) Hepburn played Mary Stuart, and gays love conflicted queens who go through hell. Her subsequent gay favorites include *Bringing Up Baby* (Howard Hawks, 1938), with sexy Cary Grant (whom everyone now knows was gay); *The Philadelphia Story* (George Cukor, 1940), again with Cary Grant; *The African Queen* (John Huston, 1951), with super-butch

Humphrey Bogart; *Summertime* (David Lean, 1955), during the shooting of which she contracted her lifelong eye infection in the canals of Venice; and *Suddenly Last Summer* (Joseph L. Mankiewicz, 1959), with fellow gay icon Elizabeth Taylor. She also did a lot of television and theater, and those of us who were lucky enough to see her on stage feel distinctly privileged.

Some biographies now claim that she herself was either bisexual or a lesbian (and that Spencer Tracy was either bisexual or gay). In particular, the Scotty Bowers book *Full Service: My Adventures in Hollywood and the Secret Sex Lives of the Stars* (2012) caused quite a stir, with its "revelations" about Hepburn and other stars. Larry Kramer and Gore Vidal also went around telling people Hepburn was a lesbian. But Hepburn's gay iconicity did not require this. Sometimes gay icons are crypto-lesbians, period. Her much publicized devotion to Spencer Tracy becomes in no way less impressive if it was the support and loyalty of a very close friend rather than traditional monogamous wifely devotion. She had one husband, a Philadelphia businessman (the marriage lasted 6 years), many lovers, notoriously including Howard Hughes (who was linked to many of the icons in this book) and who knows who else. She deliberately refrained from having children, which may be seen as a feminist choice. She was an outspoken supporter of birth control and legal abortion. She was strong, powerful, self-assured, independent. She said, "If you obey all the rules you miss all the fun" (Warren 2000: 101). Hepburn disapproved of fellow gay icon Meryl Streep (see below), whom she saw as an overly intellectual actress; she felt you could see the cogs going "click-click-click" as she acted. Hepburn claimed that she herself was a more instinctive actress.[108] This is surprising, as it is well-known that just like Streep, she rehearsed a great deal, learned her partners' lines as well as her own, and learned all sorts of skills to help her play a part.

Billie Holiday (1915–1959)

During his gayest period, Lou Reed, something of an authority on drug addiction, wrote a very poignant song entitled "Lady Day" (1973), which was a tribute to Billie Holiday. Its lyrics are now legendary. In her autobiography, *Lady Sings the Blues* (1956) Holiday's only mention of fellow gay icon Tallulah Bankhead is that "my step-mother is Tallulah Bankhead's maid" (Holiday 2006: 55). Pity, when we have heard all the juicy gossip about their passionate affair and their bitter bickering afterward. She claims in that book that women such as her and her mother, who did menial jobs, were mistaken by the police and everyone else for prostitutes. Many biographies claim she and her mother did resort to prostitution at one time or another, which in a queer perspective is seen as sex work, i.e., something that is not morally reprehensible, at least not on their part. This kind of "detail" makes Holiday all the more lovable in the eyes of her gay fans, who vibrate intensely with every tragic aspect of her life, from cradle to grave: illegitimate musician father, extreme poverty, sexual assault, housekeeping in brothels as a child, reform school, prison, loneliness, etc. Even when the story seems to get better, with the teenager singing in Harlem nightclubs, meeting all the "right" musicians, there are always sad elements. At 18, she started making records with the greatest musicians, and soon she sang lead vocals for tremendous bands such as the Count Basie Band and the Artie Shaw Band. Then she became a star, basically, and performed in countless concerts.

The Holiday recordings that gays cherish most include "Summertime" (1936), "Fine Romance" (1936), "The Way You Look Tonight" (1936), "They Can't Take That Away from Me" (1937), "You Go to My Head" (1938), "Strange Fruit" (1939) (which we can choose to read as polysemic), and "God Bless the Child" (1941). These tracks are to be found in the record collections of every gay men who is aware that people recorded music before Sonny and Cher's *Look at Us* (1965). Seeing her in *New Orleans* (Arthur Lubin, 1947), holding on to the side of the piano, alongside Louis Armstrong, is a moving experience.

Holiday married jazz musician Jimmy Monroe. She then divorced Monroe and married a Mafioso, Louis McKay. In addition, she had affairs with both men and women, notably Hollywood denizens. She always found herself drawn to abusive people who treated her miserably. By the 1950s, Holiday was an irredeemable alcoholic and a junkie. Both her health and her voice had seriously deteriorated. Holiday died penniless at the age of 44, a train-wreck story to make us all cry as we play her records. The lady sang the blues and gays listened. They still do.

Whitney Houston (1963–2012)

When vacationing in Sydney in July and August 1996, I dragged my traveling companion to drag pubs and drag clubs every single evening. Australian drag has, after all, become a staple of tourist menus, notably thanks to *Priscilla, Queen of the Desert*. Nowadays, there are even bus tours that drive foreign visitors from one drag hotspot to another. Although my companion was good enough to comply, he complained about one feature of the shows: there were, he noted, far too many Whitney Houston numbers. Houston, he judged, did not sing: she yelled. Or, as he alternately put it, she yodeled. I myself am particularly fond of Houston's "yoo hoo ooh ooh oohs." Some say that Houston invented the modern pop diva genre. Although my companion bravely endured the Houston numbers, he cheered the drag queens much more when they lip-synced to other singers. One of my favorite haunts was a pub on Oxford Street called The Albury. Last time I checked, it had become a Puma store. On the eve of our departure from the country, we made our way up the street to the pub, which boasted a huge banner advertising a politically incorrect special night, "Dreaming of a White Whitney." Indeed, every single white drag queen that night did a Whitney Houston number or two, and nothing else. Some of them even actually sang rather than lip-synced, standing on the counter while the audience roared with joy.

I do not think anyone would dispute Houston's gay iconicity. She was beautiful, she was black, she was fierce (sometimes), she sang dance music. In 1985, she first made the gays snivel to "Saving All My Love for You," and then she made them work out quite a sweat to "How Will I Know."

The song "I Will Always Love You" (1992), from *The Bodyguard* (Mick Jackson, 1992) soundtrack, was originally sung by Dolly Parton, who wrote it herself and released it in 1974. Here again, what is at stake is a splendid transmission from gay icon to gay icon, with the iconicity of both being reinforced rather than dissipated. Moreover, remember (as discussed earlier) that Miley Cyrus' godmother is Dolly Parton. Similarly, Aretha Franklin was Whitney Houston's "honorary" godmother, and Dionne Warwick was her cousin. Both women are gay favorites to be reckoned with.

In 1987, Houston sang "I Wanna Dance with Somebody." The gays could relate to that disco feeling. And, like her in the song, they are interested in being made aware of the change in temperature of the body of their partner, who preferably falls for them. Gays shed a tear of identificatory compassion when they learned that Bobby Brown was an abusive husband.[109] They bitched about her acting abilities while feeling sorry that she won a Razzie Award for worst actress in *The Bodyguard*. She was arguably better in *Waiting to Exhale* (Forest Whitaker, 1995)—a movie that would certainly not pass the Bechdel test—but she suffered from comparison to the sublime Angela Bassett. Gays worried about her when they found out about the drugs—and the gays who did a lot of drugs felt vaguely guilty. Like Garland and other gay icons and so many gay men, Houston was an addict.[110] When she died so tragically, multitudes of gay men the world over were devastated.

Grace Jones (1948–)

Paul Burston claims that gay men "invented the 1970s. Or at the very least they made the decade's finest moments happen." He goes on to explain that they were "behind the scenes when Ziggy had his first moonage daydream in stack heels and lip gloss, and they were out on the dance floor when Grace Jones first sang about needing a man to make her dreams come true. Without gay men there would have been no stardust, no glam drag and no disco" (Burston 1995: 175).

Grace Jones was born in Jamaica. At the age of 12 she emigrated to the U.S. Her family is largely made up of Protestant preachers, which immediately leads one to imagine that her career is the adverse result of her upbringing (much in the way Madonna is the product of her virulent reaction to the Catholicism she was force-fed as a child). When she was a mere model (not yet a singer and actress), Jones posed for the cover of Billy Paul's album *Ebony Woman* (1970). That record sleeve, now legendary, shows a superb Grace Jones who already had a strong personality. In New York she became more or less an actress, and then mostly a singer, not by exhausting herself in search of opportunities but instead by letting chance encounters guide her. People often believe that graphic designer/

photographer/director Jean Paul Goude launched her career, but she was already on the way up when she met him—having notably covered gay favorite Edith Piaf's "La Vie en Rose" (1977). It is, however, to Goude that gays owe the best pictures of and around Grace Jones, potent images of unapologetic androgyny.

In Jean-Paul Goude's videos of her songs, he and Grace Jones constantly tell us about gender, sexuality and race. When he shoots her as a lamp, he is staging centuries of objectification of the colonized by the colonizers, he is staging slavery, *Art nègre*, the exotic Other, etc. When he puts her on all fours in a cage as an angry panther, he is pointing to the most basic racism. Black people, some racists still think (in the 1970s as today), are closer to animals than white people, they have the jungle within them. Jones and Goude even tell us, decades before the concept became fashionable, that to a large degree, even race is the product of a more or less conscious construction, notably by painting Jones' body different shades from mahogany to violet. When Goude photographs Jones standing naked with a man of the same skin color, the man has Jones' face. Although this picture even launched a rumor that Jones had a twin brother, it was simply her face pasted onto the body of a man. Such practices can very well be called queering.

In Jones' 1982 *One Man Show* (note the queer title), she enters the stage in a full gorilla suit. The public is not really surprised to see her face emerge when she takes off her animal head, and many of them already liked Marlene Dietrich in *Blonde Venus* doing the same thing. However, although von Sternberg and Dietrich were well intentioned, their message was ambiguous. Here it is not ambiguous, and it is clearly anti-racist. Even better, Jones links the savagery of the gorilla to the masculinity of the black man, as fantasized and feared by the white racist man. She rewrites Liza Minnelli in *Cabaret* (Bob Fosse, 1972)—through association, as it were, even though the gorilla in *Cabaret* wasn't Minnelli (but could have been).

Even when Jones disported herself in magazine spreads and beaches with her nine-years-younger Swedish lover, Dolph Lundgren,[111] following her split with Goude, it could only reinforce her gay iconicity: Dolph is Aryan and gorgeous to the point of caricature, he is extremely muscular and extremely tall. Their famous black-and-white pictures in *Playboy* reflect the purest biracial fantasies.

In Jones' fourth album, *Warm Leatherette* (1980), she covered "Pars," a song by French singer Jacques Higelin. This cover was trashed by many critics who tended to find it useless, at best; I myself find it quite interesting. From a gay iconicity point of view, the song is perfect for a drama queen. Go on, the song intimates, go away, and don't turn back, leave me alone with your child who is so like you. She half speaks, half yells those words in her unique Jonesian androgynous rendition and you shiver with the pathos of it all. The song "Warm Leatherette" was first released in 1978 by The Normal. It is a summary of J.G. Ballard's novel *Crash* (1973), about sex in car crashes (complete with Elizabeth Taylor obsession). It works much better when covered by Grace Jones. Indeed, Jones' song encapsulates the novel in a few minutes much more convincingly than the disappointing movie *Crash* (David Cronenberg, 1996).

In *Nightclubbing* (1981), her fifth album, she encourages us to dance the night away, in a totally nihilistic way, after David Bowie and Iggy Pop (1976). Here, she is a bit like Franco-Uruguayan gay favorite Elli Medeiros singing (with a post-punk Jacno) "L'Âge atomique" (1980), a tongue-in-cheek electro track about welcoming the atomic age and cheering the impending explosion of the planet. This album also offers her most potent single, particularly loved by the promiscuous disco-dancing gays of those days, "I've Seen That Face Before (Libertango)." It echoes the gloomier aspects of Parisian nightclubbing. She raps in French, asking the addressee of the song if s/he is suffering from megalomania and if s/he is attempting to find death. Grace Jones does it better than anyone else. She slays.

Smith Galtney remembers that when he was 14, he knew exactly what present he wanted to get, although he was afraid it might signal him as gay to his schoolmates. The present was *Slave to the Rhythm* by Grace Jones, "one of the most gay-identified artists of the twentieth century."

> Not that I even know Grace Jones is a humongous gay icon. I don't know she's a former model who kicked off her singing career by performing for throngs of homosexuals in discos around the world. All I know is what I've seen on MTV: this towering, hulking, mannish woman with skin so black it looks blue, with lips so heavily painted they look plastic, and a flattop Afro so sleek and stylized it looks like a pillbox hat [Galtney in Andreoli 2004: 38].

There are a few camp gems in Jones' autobiography that can only delight her gay readers, including the following:

> This was where disco became more full-on, and ballooned into the outrageous and, ultimately, the camp. I suppose I arrived naked so many times it was partly my fault [Jones 2015: 156].

> There was a surprise party at one of those drag clubs [in LA] where one of the drag queens does me very well [Jones 2015: 341].
>
> If there were ever an orgy—or love-in—in my vicinity, I wouldn't be hosting it. I would be at the center. I'd be the queen bee, darling [Jones 2015: 320].

Obviously, Jones is acutely aware of her gay icon status. She was the original Queen B(ee), long before Beyoncé was even born, and in 1986, when Lady Gaga was born, Jones was already almost 40. Every outrageous hat ever worn by Gaga resembles one that Jones wore before—to cite but one example for the time being.

Jones is fearless, Jones is fierce, she lashes out at interviewers who annoy her; she will always be loved by the gays, who will continue treasuring her 1982 *One Man Show*, as well as her performances in gay favorites *Conan the Destroyer* (Richard Fleischer, 1984), *A View to a Kill* (John Glen, 1985), and the terrible *Vamp* (Richard Wenk, 1986).

Eartha Kitt (1927–2008)

Orson Welles (who more or less "discovered" her in Europe) called Eartha Kitt "the most exciting woman in the world." Peter Shapiro calls her "camp sex kitten chanteuse" in his book *Turn the Beat Around: The Secret History of Disco* (Shapiro 2006: 59). Gay actor John Fraser remembers that people thought she looked like a frog, but "Eartha Kitt was so scabrously sexy, so witty, so naughty and so talented that she challenged the concept of beauty" (Fraser 2004: 69).

Kitt was of mixed heritage: African American, Caucasian and Native American. Various versions of her circumstances have circulated along the years, some of them her own. Her father might have been a plantation owner who raped her mother in the Deep South. Or he might have been the local doctor. Her mother gave her away, or perhaps things were not so simple. Apparently she only learned her real date of birth at age 71 (Williams 2013: 8–30). She often said she knew how it felt to belong to a minority, to be destitute and to be alone and to be picked on, notably when she supported gay rights. She danced her way up from Harlem to Paris and then in various countries around the world, from nightclubs to concert halls, before finally hitting Broadway in 1952, the year she began making records. The singles we remember especially well are "C'est Si Bon" (1953), "Let's Do It" (1954), "Where Is My Man?" (1983), "I Love Men" (1984), "This Is My Life" (1986), and "Cha-Cha Heels" (1989). We saw in the Divine entry that "Cha-Cha Heels" was originally supposed to be sung by Divine, but how fitting is it that Eartha Kitt finally recorded it? Divine was a male female impersonator, Kitt a female female impersonator. The kind of femininity they peddled was equally constructed, equally overblown, and equally tongue-in-cheek. It is thanks to gay clubs that she sold records again in the 1980s, with a few well-chosen dance music tunes. In those years she very much parodied her own Catwoman days star persona, to the intense delight of her gay audiences, who purred right along with her.

Indeed, she replaced Julie Newmar in the role of Catwoman in Season 3 of the television series *Batman* (1966), and she will always be cherished by gays for that. Her Catwoman outcamped even Batman and Robin, which for this series is saying a lot. In *Batman* as in her records and elsewhere, the "purr-fect" diva came up with her own brand of purring, really halfway between purring and growling—and it is those sounds alone that make her worth the effort. She played in many other television series, some better than others.

Kitt had a daughter with a white businessman husband whom she later divorced. She was a feminist, an anti–Vietnam war activist (so much so that she had to work outside the U.S. between 1968 and 1974), and then (like other gay icons such as Elizabeth Taylor) both an ardent supporter of gay rights and an AIDS activist. She was watched by the CIA for years (Williams 2013: 274). She was a hard worker and always spoke her mind, even if it got her into trouble. Gays love straight talkers.

Beyoncé Knowles (1981–)

So much has been written in the media about Beyoncé Knowles (notably on her feminism or lack thereof, but also on her gay iconicity) that it is difficult to know where to start and how to avoid clichés. Hardly a day goes by without an "in-depth" article or two being published by some newspaper or magazine. Besides, she fascinates many academics, is taught at some universities (I plead guilty), and even luminaries such as the great bell hooks have things to say about her. Some see her as a throwback to slavery and an antifeminist, others see her as the number one heroine of the African American cause and a feminist heroine. No one disputes she is a gay icon, though.

When still a member of Destiny's Child, she co-wrote "Survivor" (2001), which was clearly a wink-wink tribute to Gloria Gaynor's "I Will Survive," with similar lines. Gay men love it when a gay icon consolidates her gay iconicity by referencing an elder gay icon, especially when using the theme of survival.

In November 2016 Beyoncé performed "Daddy Lessons" at the Country Music Association Awards with the Dixie Chicks. She decided long ago that however dear she was to her black and gay audiences, she was going to be mainstream, i.e., she would please white heterosexuals. How better to demonstrate that than by singing country music with the Dixie Chicks?

On February 1, 2017, the first day of Black History Month, Beyoncé posted beautiful photographs of herself—pregnant and surrounded by flowers—on the Internet. The pictures established clearly, with an unsubtle but terribly effective sense of semiotics, that she was a new Madonna, a black Madonna (in every sense of the word "Madonna"). The photographs were by artist Awol Erizku, a political choice considering his African and African American subjects, although they were also a little in the style of white gay-icon-mongers Pierre et Gilles.

On February 12, 2017, Beyoncé sang at the Grammys. She was nominated for nine awards, more than anybody else in 2017, and she performed while pregnant with twins. Everything about the general *mise en scène* screamed reigning queen, and very cleverly. A regal diva if ever there was any, Beyoncé was even paid a respectful homage by Adele, who broke her award in two as a sign of allegiance to the queen, saying "the artist of my life is Beyoncé." Indeed, most of the articles that discussed the event in the Anglophone press used words such as "queen," "regal," "reign" and "royal." Clearly, when Beyoncé performatively declared, possibly in 2006 after Destiny's Child disbanded, that she would be queen, Queen Bey, or

Queen Bee, or Queen B., it worked. She has become a mistress of story-telling, and she influences the very vocabulary that the media use—like a politician or a spin doctor. She decided she was going to be a feminist, displayed the word in big white letters on a black background behind her in her shows, filmed a dozen marvelously controversial videos, and bam, some of us use her as a viable example of black feminism. The particularly relevant ones are: "Single Ladies (Put a Ring on It)" (2008), "Telephone" (2010, with fellow gay icon Lady Gaga), "Party" (2011), "Run the World (Girls)" (2011), the very Madonnesque "Haunted" (2013), "Partition" (2013), and obviously all of *Lemonade* (2016). She decided that she would keep us guessing about which brand of feminism she had chosen, construc-tionist or essentialist. Although we continue to wonder, her latest *mise en scène* of Marian motherhood seems terribly essentialist.

Who "Run the World (Girls)"? This particular girl does.

Amanda Lear (1939–)

Whether Amanda Lear was really born a French boy and then changed sex and nationality will prudently not be discussed here. There are quite a few books and a thousand websites that address these issues, notably the books of Ian Gibson,[112] Coccinelle[113] and Lady Ashley.[114] Most biogra-phers believe she was born in 1939, whatever she might declare to the contrary, according to her mood of the day (1949, 1950, 1959…). Linguists observe that she has a French accent when she speaks (and sings in) English. She is, admittedly, absolutely fluent in French, English, German, Italian and Spanish. Her Italian is particularly excellent. The fact of the matter is that the rumors of her sex change did little to dispel her gay iconicity, as she is well aware. "I hate to spread rumors—but what else can one do with them?," Lear once said (Amanda Lear in Warren 2000: 47). She even released a song called "La Rumeur" (2016).

Lear is a model, singer, movie and theater actress, painter, sculptor, writer, TV host and muse (not necessarily in that order). Notably, she was Salvador Dalí's muse for a number of years. Indeed, she wrote a fascinating book about those legendary days, which she published three times, each time with a different title, changing a word here and there. I suspect many gay men knowingly bought the three versions, if only for the different jackets and pictures. She had Dalí's wife Gala's blessing to pose as often as needed for the genius and to escort him and babysit him in his outings in Spain, France, or elsewhere, however decadent. This is abundantly documented in various biographies of Dalí.

She claims that she has had affairs with the likes of Brian Jones, David Bowie, Roxy Music's Bryan Ferry,[115] Jimmy Page, and several other rock 'n' rollers.[116] She was their muse as well as Dalí's. Indeed, she also inspired fashion designers and various artists in various domains throughout the decades (but mostly in the 1960s). Many websites claim she is the "Amanda Jones" of the Rolling Stones (album *Between the Buttons*, 1967), which is a pleasant thought, and some say she inspired the creation of *Absolutely Fabulous'* Patsy Stone.[117] She hung out with everyone from Kirk Douglas to royalty, including Mary Quant, Andy Warhol and the Factory people. She was even decorated by the French government in January 2007, becoming Chevalier des Arts et des Lettres for services rendered to culture.

A little bit of Googling will rapidly get you pictures of her throughout the 1960s and 1970s, notably in London, mixing with the coolest people. She modeled for every important UK fashion designer in the 1960s. In the 1980s and 1990s the pictures tend to be more Italian, whereas they are more French thereafter. Perhaps the most iconic of all of her endeavors is when she performed with David Bowie in *The 1980 Floor Show*, recorded in October 1973 at London's Marquee Club. In the 1970s she became the ultimate disco queen, Eurotrash at its best, finding stimulation for her looks in comics such as *Vampirella*, *Barbarella*,[118] or *Pravda la Survireuse*...

So what if some observe that she is not a particularly good singer? What if she is often said to talk her way through her lyrics? That is entirely beside the point. She has a very, very deep voice—dare I say masculine? Indeed, she sounds like Marlene Dietrich, and milks it for all it is worth (as we have established, gay icons are often wont to rewrite other gay icons).

At the beginning of her singing career, Lear recorded a few singles that had a moderate impact. A cover version of Elvis Presley's "Trouble" in various languages (1975) indicates that she is unafraid of fighting. She knows how to use her fists and will not hesitate to punch you in the face if you annoy her. If you're trying to provoke a fight, she sings, you will indeed get one. How feminist is that? "Alphabet" (1977) has also been recorded in several languages, allowing Lear to express various viewpoints about what is important to her. In her first album, *I Am a Photograph* (1977), Amanda Lear shows that she knows everything there is to know about the value of appearances, pure surface. In the eponymous single she sings about being (nothing but) a shiny picture. Her second album, *Sweet Revenge* (1978), is all about S&M, leather fetishism and whipping bad boys. It is her most successful ever, boasting the disco classic "Follow Me," to which millions of gay boys danced joyfully. On the back sleeve she poses in her underwear, with a feather boa and a top hat à la Dietrich, and—what do you know—one of the tracks is a cover of "Lili Marlen." Her third album is entitled *Never Trust a Pretty Face* (1979), signaling Lear's continued decision to tell us that we must not trust her: she is a fake, she is plastic, she is an aesthetic construction—entirely artificial. What is there not to like? Nothing here is done at face value, all the lyrics are tongue-in-cheek, all the outfits. Lear has read Oscar Wilde, frequented David Bowie, Lear is an aesthete. On the cover of *Never Trust a Pretty Face* she is a sphinx[119] in a superbly kitsch painting by F.J. Rogner (shades of Keats and Doctor Who). She is a mysterious, enigmatic, mythological creature, a hybrid, part-human, part-animal, the way some might be part-male, part-female: her bottom half is reptilian, her back, arms and face human. It is impossible to determine if she has breasts, as her arms, resting on (grabbing?) planet Earth, or a planet very much like it, hide her chest. A pair of blue wings grows out of her back. She is in a science-fictional décor, with a desert and neo-classical columns, clearly out to conquer not just the world but the universe—if not the universes.

In the song "Miroir," she explains that she is made of plastic, she is a blowup doll, so she will never become wrinkled, she will never age, unlike the addressee of the song, a mere human, and unlike her listeners, who must accept the onset of old age. The (rare) English version is not as interesting, and basically contradicts the original lyrics. So Amanda Lear is a monster, a freak, and she is actually warning us. But that is exactly why we adore her. She has repeatedly commented upon her plastic image, starting with her first album. In her book *Je ne suis pas du tout celle que vous croyez* (2009) she discusses Marilyn Monroe's claim that she switched "Marilyn Monroe" on at will, claiming that she does the same thing (Lear

2009: 19). Celluloid dolls don't eat, she says, but she does (Lear 2009: 21). Affirming her affiliation with other stars, she tells taxi drivers who ask if she is Amanda Lear: "Depends, sometimes, not always" (Lear 2009: 22, translation mine). She wears masks, she tells us, tempting the reader to respond, "Well, duh" (Lear 2009: 27).

Her subsequent albums are less impressive. She continued recording all sorts of songs in all sorts of languages through the next four decades (more than 20 studio albums, plus a series of best-of compilations), with varied commercial success, but none that were as impressive or catchy or gay-iconish as the songs of those first three albums.

As Lear herself has repeatedly pointed out, in the 1970s she did every-thing Madonna would do later in terms of sexual and religious provoca-tion, notably with leather, nun outfits and whips. With a wink at Bettie Page, she brought the dominatrix into the mainstream decades before anybody else.

Many believe she married a Scotsman called Paul Morgan Lear in 1965 and kept his name. One likes to suppose she chose him strictly for his British nationality and surname.[120]

She married Alain-Philippe Malagnac d'Argens de Villèle in 1979. Malagnac, a night owl and reckless entrepreneur, was adopted by the gay writer Roger Peyrefitte, who fell in love with him, as he himself documents notably in two novels, *Notre Amour* (1967) and *L'Enfant de Coeur* (1978).[121] Peyrefitte became an intimate of Lear.[122] Malagnac was widely perceived as gay, notably because he officially owned and managed an openly gay club in the rue Sainte Anne in Paris,[123] but that never seemed to faze Lear.[124]

By the 1980s she had become a household name in France (though slightly less so than in Italy) as a TV personality. When I taught high school in the 1980s, I once took a party of school children to Spain on a school trip. At the Salvador Dalí museum in Figueres I pointed to an enormous painting in the middle of the central foyer, *Roger Freeing Angelica* (*St. George and the Damsel*, 1970), and asked them if they knew who had posed for the nude figure. Only one did, a 15-year-old boy who set my gaydar to ringing loudly when he yelled, "Amanda Lear!" The other kids refused to believe us until we showed them Yul Brynner's famous 1971 photograph of Dalí painting and Lear posing, entitled "Salvador Dalí painting Amanda Lear." One of the reasons they refused to believe it is that they knew a later version of her, yet another incarnation, and because she has had constant recourse to plastic surgery (as her pictures clearly indicate) and gives different birth years in different interviews (as YouTube will confirm), they calculated that she could not have been more than a little girl at the time of the painting. As far as cinema is concerned, Lear never really did anything interesting in any country. This is rather unfortunate, because many of us are convinced she could have done wonders, being such a bucketload of concentrated glamour.

In the animated movie *The Incredibles* (Bard Bird, 2004), Lear dubs the voice of Edna E. Mode for the French version that Brad Bird did himself in the original American version (i.e., a male voice). Considering the character, this was obviously a perfect choice. She appeared in all sorts of movies and TV movies, but nothing to write home about. More interestingly, she nearly played the part of Octobriana in a movie that would have become an instant camp classic. Octobriana is a 1971 comic book super-heroine Russian spy, the creation of Peter Sadecky. David Bowie was very much in favor of the project and tried to promote it, but it never got made. However, some marvelous pictures of Lear in Octobriana garb survive and can be easily found on the Internet.

Always a mistress of reinvention, in 2009 she became huge on the Parisian *théâtre de boulevard* circuit, playing powerful, cougarish women and delighting old Parisian *bourgeoises* and young gays equally. Following the logic developed above of how the iconization process is well-served by the conflation between the (supposed) private life of the actress and the dramatis personae she plays, the fact that she is widely perceived as a cougar serves her cult. Since her husband's death she has only ever been seen with very young and very beautiful men, who occasionally grace red carpets with her. They are generally Italian, and generally (more or less) work as fashion models. "My attraction to young bodies stems from my fierce—and totally desperate—refusal of the degrading body. The boys who surround me are beautiful, young, athletic. I like people who look after themselves" (Lear 2009: 161, my translation).

Adding to the legend, the death of Lear's husband did little to lift part of the mystery. In 2000, their house in the South of France burnt. As *The Guardian* presented it: "[H]er house in southern France, which contained a number of works by Salvador Dalí [...] burnt down. The house also contained her husband, Alain-Philippe Malagnac d'Argens and his 20-year-old friend, Didier Dieufis, a cat breeder." *The Guardian* goes on to point out that "in the reports the deaths of these two men seemed almost incidental, merely the surreal background to the main tragedy, the damage to a few surrealist paintings." The house also contained several cats at the time of the fire, sadly.[125]

In 2016 Lear announced her retirement, but one can be quite certain we have not heard the last of her—although her plastic surgery is probably becoming more and more of a challenge. She shares many characteristics with the heroine of her novel *L'Immortelle* (1987), Zorah Zorkan, aka Erica Glamour, but perhaps not quite all of them.

Madonna (1958–)

During the "Madonna Carpool Karaoke" (*The Late Show with James Corden*) in early December 2016, Madonna said that she was the rebellious Madonna onstage, but not offstage. "I'm quite square. I have a very predictable life." She declared: "And then I go home and I'm Julie Andrews. And that's the crux of the matter. I mean, give me a nun's habit." However much of that is true, Madonna is definitely both a sexual icon and a gay icon. She even prompted Madonna studies in the late 1990s. Chuck Kosterman writes: "Whenever I hear intellectuals talk about sexual icons of the present day, the name mentioned most is Madonna. That seems like a good answer, and it's the kind of answer Madonna has worked very hard to perpetuate" (Klosterman 2003: 83).

In 2002 I published a whole book on Madonna that was translated into several languages. I actually owe her my career. So when I write that she was not a particularly good singer to begin with, it is with immense love. And when I claim that her face and body were not traditionally appealing to begin with, it is with utmost respect. What made Madonna such an astonishing gay icon is precisely—among other things—the fact that she built herself from scratch, deciding in a performative way that she was going to be a huge star. Her beauty was constructed and depended on many factors, notably the photographers who shot her. The aforementioned Catherine Deneuve, to use but one example, was always equally and universally beautiful throughout the 1960s and 1970s, regardless of which famous photographer took her picture (and every one of them did). In the 1980s and 1990s, Madonna used massive amounts of makeup. The recourse to makeup in the construction of stardom has been analyzed often in the past eight decades, but its specificity in pop—as opposed to cinema—has been less commented upon. Madonna's thick makeup was basically the same as that of Golden Age glamorous Hollywood icons and that of yesteryear's slapstick actors. If the effect was different, the strategy was identical. Her makeup also recalled European theater before the improvement of lighting, traditional Japanese theater, etc. But it was first and foremost similar to those of drag queens: it's all about pancake and foundation. Madonna's metamorphoses were inscribed in that tradition. Depending on photographers, her face in the 1980s and 1990s changed in stupefying ways. Always palimpsestuous, it sometimes looked like Dietrich's, Garbo's, Turner's or Monroe's—among others. It was the result of an extremely coordinated artistic production, it was always ephemeral, for it was but one of the ever-changing face(t)s she showed the public. Just like drag queens. For the researcher, drag culture constitutes a most interesting subculture within gay subculture. Madonna shares with drag queens a sense of exhibitionism, provocation and camp. She very much rewrote Mae West in the 1980s and 1990s, West who was suspected of being a drag queen, because no woman could possibly behave that way, as we will see below.

"Madonna, because she is a textual persona, can never become a flesh and blood person. She is a representation that imparts meaning through the readers' interpretation" (Lewis 1990: 206). One of the main points I made in my book was that hers was postmodern cosmetic writing, but that it worked exactly in the same way as the postmodern literary writing of some novelists—and very much in the same way as particularly talented semiologist drag queens.

Super control freak and megadiva Madonna has been universally hailed as a gay icon for all the usual reasons, plus the fact that she has spent her life borrowing from gay culture and the gay subculture of drag. There is a synergy between her and gays that is very similar to the one that exists between Cher and gays. Cathy Schwichtenberg writes that Madonna "becomes king when she behaves like a queen; she is a woman playing a man playing a woman" (Schwichtenberg in Dion 1994: 10).

Madonna

Like the glamorous drag queens who informed Madonna's work (and Dietrich's before her), Madonna plays with every signifier of femininity. Her femininity, as overblown as that of drag queens, is as much of a mask (persona) as theirs, obviously. In her work she has paid tributes to many previous gay icons (her predecessors), mostly through visuals, but in "Vogue," in many ways her gayest song, she pays tribute to them in her visuals *and* lyrics (Guilbert 2002: 123–131). "Vogue" notoriously plunders/ pays tribute to the drag culture of the Harlem balls. Having encouraged her listeners to take poses and disport themselves on the dance floor, she lists Greta Garbo, Marilyn Monroe, Marlene Dietrich, Grace Kelly, Jean Harlow, Ginger Rogers, Lauren Bacall, Katharine Hepburn, Lana Turner, Bette Davis and Rita Hayworth as people who knew what to do with their looks. I often quote Cindy Patton, who writes:

> Where some critics have viewed *Vogue* and Madonna's work in general as para-
> sitic on, variously, black and gay culture and even on feminism, I will suggest
> that she reroutes through mass culture quotidian critiques of dominant cultures
> (in this case, voguing's critique of whiteness and of gender), making them more
> available as places of resistance, although this may come at some cost [Patton in
> Schwichtenberg 1993: 83].

The video of "Vogue" is fascinating, but every subsequent *mise en scène* of the song (on television or on the stages of the world) adds layers and layers of meaning, constantly reinforcing Madonna's gay iconicity, like half the things she does (or did in the 1980s and 1990s, anyway). She is perfectly aware of the political implications of "Vogue." Of course, when Madonna sings about the photographs of "beauty queens," she is *au fait* of the polysemy of the words. It is all about "[giving] good face" as she sings, pilfering the expression from Harlem drag queens. Thus, Madonna is "actively participating in gay culture," as the British gay magazine *Attitude* claims.[126]

David Van Leer discusses gay men's camping through their (ironic) discourse:

> Generalizations about verbal structures, rhetorics, and syntaxes characteristic
> of gay language tend to treat as identical all statements about the kindness of
> strangers or not being in Kansas anymore. Yet even within a clearly gay tradi-
> tion of camp quotation, what is striking is the variety of uses to which camp is
> put. [...] The exact character of that irony depends considerably on the author's
> tone, degree of self-consciousness, and relation to the original context of the
> line [Van Leer 1995: 60].

Madonna has done little else in her career, camping like a gay man, quoting like a gay man, alluding to Tennessee Williams and *The Wizard of Oz* and whatnot. She has always been exceedingly self-conscious in that enterprise and has always mastered the "gay" texts she was using, texts such as those of the aforementioned divas, etc. That is (among other things) what we mean by her actively participating in gay culture, surely, even if she has occasionally defended Eminem's homophobia. She has often remarked that gay men deal with women on an intellectual and emotional level, without wanting to own them or belittle them as straight men do (Guilbert 2002: 62).

Madonna is strong, sassy, rebellious, provocative, bitchy, unapologetic, independent, funny, powerful (she has huge star power), empowering, and an LGBTQ+ ally. She is unafraid of her sexuality. She tells it like it is, sister. And she encourages us to do the same. "Express Yourself," she tells us. And naturally, even Madonna, who always seems so strong, so much the control freak, has a terrible love life, like so many of us. Her long-standing relationships read like so many successive disasters.

Susanna Danuta Walters writes:

> Feminist work on spectatorship has also focuses on the phenomena of stars and the fans who identify, imitate, adore, and revile them. Critics such as Richard Dyer and Christine Gledhill have asserted that a female gaze is activated or encouraged by the presence of certain kinds of female icons, such as Bette Davis, Katharine Hepburn, Marlene Dietrich, and, of course, Madonna. In her recent work on music videos, Lisa Lewis suggests that both Madonna and Cyndi Lauper "address girl audiences by textually making reference to consumer girl culture" in such a way that, in their mimicking of the rock stars, young girls play out "the stars' subversive stance against the femininity discourse and the privileging of male adolescence" [Walters 1995: 96].

Replace "female" and "girl" by "gay" everywhere and this works perfectly well for gay icons and their public.

Many have been too quick to dismiss Madonna as irrelevant in recent years. However, isn't it undeniable that she is aging relatively well (plastic surgery or not) and continues to make music that even very young gays can dance to? She is still very much a gay icon. In *Gay Times*, the anonymous reviewer of Madonna's album *MDNA* (2012) calls the song "Gang Bang" "the campest thing she's done since 'Hanky Panky.'" The reviewer adds:

> Bizarre and faintly terrifying German techno update of Nancy Sinatra's "Bang Bang (My Baby Shot Me Down)." Madonna channels Gaga's "Telephone" video as she screeches around a post-apocalyptic landscape calling violent revenge on a no-good boyfriend. "Now drive bitch! Now die bitch!" will soon be in the homosexual catchphrase lexicon forevermore. Brilliant.[127]

There are other Madonna quotes that have become part of "the homosexual catchphrase lexicon," if not forevermore, then at least for a couple of decades. In addition to attending Madonna concerts, gays love going to the cinema. And in the 20th century they loved it when Madonna delivered a good performance as an actress in the traditional sense of the word, which was the exception rather than the rule. Julie Lobalzo Wright writes: "[A] handful of films are often mentioned as positive examples of music stars as film stars: Madonna in *Desperately Seeking Susan* (1985), Prince in *Purple Rain* (1984), Eminem in *8 Mile* (2002), Mick Jagger in *Performance* (1970) and David Bowie in *The Man Who Fell to Earth* (1976)." She uses the notion of "perfect fit" between star image and character that Richard Dyer develops in the "Stars and 'Character'" chapter of his 1979 book *Stars* (Wright in Devereux et al 2015: 230) What Dyer calls "traces" or "residues" of the realitatis femina are notoriously abundant in *Desperately Seeking Susan*. Gays love it when the biographical intrudes on the diegesis—and vice versa.

Jayne Mansfield (1933–1967)

Bette Davis famously said about Jayne Mansfield that "dramatic art in her opinion is knowing how to fill a sweater" (Parish 2002: 208). In 2011, Mansfield was the subject of French novelist Simon Liberati's book *Jayne Mansfield 1967*, possibly the most interesting text she ever inspired. In many ways Marilyn Monroe was a pastiche of femininity, and from 1953 to 1962 she largely pastiched herself from one movie to the next. This is obviously no reproach: I believe that aspect is one of the elements that make her so interesting. Right down to her voice, Jayne Mansfield was a pastiche of Marilyn Monroe. When drag queens pastiche her, they have to go to extremes, otherwise it does not always work. Jaymes Mansfield was cast in Season 9 of *RuPaul's Drag Race* and was the first queen to be eliminated. She does have thousands of fans worldwide, though.[128]

In the end what do people remember? I know for a fact that not every one of her admirers has actually watched Jayne Mansfield's movies more than once, as I have—mostly *The Girl Can't Help It* (Frank Tashlin, 1956) and *The Loves of Hercules* (*Gli amori di Ercole*, Carlo Ludovico Bragaglia, 1960). People remember her photographs, her figure, her breasts, her clothes. They vaguely remember her body-building husband Mickey Hargitay. And mostly, they know she died in an extremely famous "tragic" car accident. People also remember the cover of Kenneth Anger's infamous book *Hollywood Babylon* (1965/1975), even if they have never read it. On the picture she is bent forward and her skimpy dress shows off her naked breasts. At the end of the book, Anger went so far as to publish a shot of one of her dead dogs (two of her dogs died in her car crash) amid various debris.

People sometimes also remember that extraordinary photograph of Sophia Loren apparently ogling Mansfield's breasts at a restaurant. In her autobiography the Italian star finally explained: she was attending her first big Hollywood event, a cocktail party thrown by Paramount at Mike Romanoff's celebrated restaurant.

> She knew everyone was looking at her, and indeed it was impossible to look away from her more than generous cleavage. It was as if she were somehow saying: "Here comes Jayne Mansfield. The Blond Bombshell!" She sat next to me and started talking, like a volcano erupting. As she got worked up, I suddenly saw one of her breasts on my plate. [...] One particularly quick reporter pressed the button on his camera, and the image went around the world [Loren 2014: 141, my translation].

Some of us celebrity studies people spend years wondering about blondeness, researching blondeness, deconstructing blondeness. We write about peroxide blondes and dumb blondes and blond bombshells and blondes who have more fun, but we continue speculating. Many of the gay icons featured in this book were blond at one time or another, very few of them natural blondes. Susan Brownmiller writes:

> Of all the wonders Hollywood has created, nothing can match the pantheon of celebrated blondes who have fed the fantasies of men and fueled the aspirations of women ever since the flickering image began to move across the giant screen. Did Hollywood create the American cult of blondness, or did it merely magnify the collective dreams of a melting pot that despite democratic intentions placed the highest value in feminine beauty on Nordic fairness and flaxen hair? Surely the dark-haired immigrant entrepreneurs from Eastern Europe and their first-generation sons who abandoned the steamy garment center of New York to pioneer a motion picture empire in the sunshine of the West were fully aware that the visions of blonde loveliness they projected onto the screen bore no resemblance to their mothers and sisters, or to the women they might have been expected to marry. Those who hand-cranked the dream machine spun their own fantasies of

California gold, angel-haired virgins and peroxide sirens who had never seen the inside of a ghetto [Brownmiller 1986: 46].

Without going back to Ancient Greece and Ancient Rome (remember the Roman ladies who dunked their hair in horse's urine to bleach it), it is well-known that every corner of the Western world has favored blondes for centuries, either seeing them as virginal flowers or burning hot vixens (or a combination of the two), especially in places where natural blondes are rare. The first totally peroxide blonde in Hollywood was Jean Harlow, and there have been a few in between, but obviously Jayne Mansfield pushed the vision to its furthest limits. She was crowned Miss Tomato, Miss Lobster, Miss Negligee, but also Queen of the Chihuahua, Queen of the Palm Spring Rodeo, Nylon Sweater Queen, as well as the Cleavage Queen (Stern 1990: 203). She became a walking fantasy with little concern for reality or realism. In the end she was a concept. And she died a very conceptual death. Gays love concepts who die conceptual deaths—especially after they've had a rich sex life and are rumored to have had flings with the likes of Jack Kennedy.

Ethel Merman (1908–1984)

In 2014 Genna Rivieccio argued that there would never be a better gay icon than Ethel Merman—even Judy Garland could not compete: "Why, you ask? Well, chiefly because of the musical theater element of Merman's career. While younger gay men (read: twinks) might have trouble seeing the value in this, they can, if nothing else, see how camp and esoteric musical theater in general is." Rivieccio goes on to say that the flamboyant Merman owes her gay iconicity notably to her parts in George and Ira Gershwin and Cole Porter musicals. Obviously, the double entendres of classic songs such as "I Get a Kick Out of You," "You're the Top," and "Blow Gabriel Blow" delight the dirty-minded gays. Merman had an occasionally trashy sense of humor that delighted gays: she was ballsy and often bossy. Rivieccio writes: "Moreover, Merman's ability to make fun of her larger than life, grandiose stature is also part of what contributes to her being a goddess of camp, ergo a goddess of gay. This much is apparent in her cameo in *Airplane!*, wherein she plays a traumatized soldier convinced he's Ethel Merman."[129]

Other Merman productions that might be enjoyed by gay men who were too young or too poor (or not yet born) to see her on stage include *Anything Goes* (Lewis Milestone, 1936), (with Bing Crosby), *There's No Business Like Show Business* (Walter Lang, 1954), or even the six episodes of the TV series *The Love Boat* (ABC, 1979–1982) that she graced with her presence.

It seems Merman turned on the charm full blast whenever there was an attractive man around, and if he did not seem enraptured, she declared him a "faggot." Weirdly, she even sounded homophobic on occasions, although she was constantly surrounded by gays. Brian Kellow writes: "[I]f she had to attend a social gathering, she was often hoping to find romantic male companionship. She had gay friends galore; what she craved was a lover [...]. And as is the case for many other gay icons [...], there was a part of her that resented the homosexuals who held her in such high esteem" (Kellow 2007: 271). Her tragic life story fascinated gays: she got married four times and got divorced four times. Bafflingly, her last husband was Ernest Borgnine; their marriage lasted a few weeks. Her daughter died of a drug overdose at the age of 25, a tragedy that did nothing to diminish her gay iconicity.

A quick YouTube search will allow you to see and hear Merman sing all sorts of vital show tunes. I especially recommend her singing with Judy Garland or Lucille Ball: two gay icons for the price of one. Ethel Merman pleases gay men because she embodies Broadway, she embodies musical comedy, "a classic site of camp culture [...], whose visions of nostalgic sanctuaries frequently strive to offer the comforts of a better world of make-believe" (Lassen 2011: 42).

Bette Midler (1945–)

David Serlin writes:

In a 2002 episode of the popular television program *Will & Grace*, the character Jack falls asleep and dreams that he has died and gone to heaven, only to

113

> encounter Cher, played by the performer herself. Shaking with anticipation, he
> asks her, "Are you God?" The pop diva's pithy reply? "It depends on what bath-
> house you pray at." Cher's playful comment is an inside joke that conjures up
> the heyday of bathhouse culture during the 1970s, when popular gay icons like
> Bette Midler, Barry Manilow, and the Village People performed at gay bath-
> houses in New York and San Francisco. But as Cher's witty reference suggests,
> bathhouses continue to occupy an important place in the gay male imagination
> even into the twenty-first century [Serlin in Stein 2004: 122].

The song "Surabaya Johnny" was mentioned in the Gloria Gaynor
entry above. Sontag writes that camp emphasizes style and believes that
"to emphasize style is to slight content." (Sontag 1969: 279) If you watch
a video of Bette Midler singing the melodramatic song by Bertolt Brecht
and Kurt Weil "Surabaya Johnny"—in any of her camp public renditions
of it—you cannot fail to see that style is extremely emphasized here: The
Divine Miss M. (as she used to like calling herself) is camp to the nth
degree, she piles up layer after layer of stylization (her voice modulations,
her moves, her attire, her facial expressions); and yet the content of the
song is in no way slighted. Quite the contrary: it's a history lesson, it's a
series of edifying comments on class, gender, and sexuality, etc. Midler
most certainly does not "introduce an attitude which is neutral with
respect to content" (Sontag 1969: 279) in that rendition. This is true even
if it admittedly might seem to some that the song has been transformed
into a mere torch song as opposed to a "serious" excerpt from *Happy End*
(1929), which was written by the very intense Brecht, a man who once
wrote *Mother Courage and Her Children* (1938) and who probably turns
in his grave every time he hears anyone establish a connection between
any aspect of his work and camp, notably Bathhouse Betty herself.[130] I
wonder if it is at all possible for the camp practitioner to ever be completely
"neutral with respect to content." One would have to be clueless to completely disregard content, and camp is many things but it is never clueless.
Clearly, when Ute Lemper and then Marianne Faithfull[131] cover "Surabaya
Johnny," they add more (new and different) layers of camp to it—although
admittedly they are not as classically camp as Midler. Then, of course,
when Rufus Wainwright starts singing it, yet another level of camp is
added, one that is queerer, because he is a man singing about how Johnny
mistreats him. Any man singing "Like a Virgin" or "Over the Rainbow,"
for instance, is automatically saying something about gender and sexuality,
and there are splendid examples. But men are not the subject of this book.

Midler is talented in every domain: she can act, sing, and dance, and she is extremely funny, blessed with a superb sense of timing. Half-jocularly calling herself "divine" in the 1970s was a very camp thing to do. It incorporated Jean Genet's *Notre Dame des Fleurs*, Greta Garbo, and John Waters' Divine. It signaled a great deal of irony. Calling her 1979 concert movie *Divine Madness* (Michael Ritchie, 1980) took it all a step further. Gays all over the Western world flocked to see it, whether or not they had been lucky enough to see her live during the tour. One of her personae, Delores DeLago, the Toast of Chicago, is a mermaid who moves around in a wheelchair. She is absolutely hilarious and nods to gays in more ways than one. Depending on city and date, at one point Midler starts singing the gay anthem "I Will Survive" (cf. Gloria Gaynor entry) crawling on the stage, then heaving herself onto her electric wheelchair and singing with her DeLago sisters (who are singing along in their own electric wheelchairs) with an elaborate, politically incorrect choreography. As a gay icon paying tribute to an older gay icon, Lady Gaga did the exact same thing in 2011, donning a green wig and a long fishtail and moving around the stage in a wheelchair. Three decades after Midler, the camp homage worked exceedingly well as postmodern pop, but it enraged many disability groups, notably in Australia and the U.S.

David Bianco writes:

> Her popularity at the Continental helped her land a guest spot on the *Tonight Show*, and Midler was soon starring in feature films, including *The Rose* (1978), in which she did a lesbian scene. Midler also performed at gay and lesbian celebrations [...] but Midler has had a mixed relationship with the gay and lesbian community. [...] Still, Midler has performed at a number of AIDS fund-raising events and is widely considered a gay icon for her campy sensibility. She remains one of the most popular targets for impersonation by drag performers [Bianco 1999: 223–224].

It seems Midler grew a bit tired at some point of constantly hearing about her gay-bathhouse past, and some gays even got the impression that she no longer cared for them. When she went mainstream, many prominent gay New Yorkers resented her for what they saw as being dropped by the idol they felt they had created. I suppose her weariness with her past was understandable in that it diverted public attention from her other achievements. She did, after all, engineer a major career change when she veered toward Disney productions in the late 1980s. This does not mean that she turned against gays, as some have excessively claimed. As Vito Russo rightly reminded us: "Bette Midler owes her audience one thing: a good show. She does not have to acknowledge Gay Pride Week; she does not have to *thank* gay people for their support; she does not have to be into the movement to be acceptable" (Schiavi 2011: 107). She still occasionally claims to be proud of her flamboyant Bathhouse Betty past (Schiavi 2011: 105). The author of *The Celluloid Closet*, the late Vito Russo, went around for a while with a bootleg copy of Midler performing at the Continental Baths in 1971. Midler's people made him stop screening it (Schiavi 2011: 134). Many of us wish they had seen her show at the Continental Baths, or at least that bootleg film.

In a November 1999 episode of the television series *Will & Grace*, "Homo for the Holidays" (season 2, episode 7), Will remembers hiding Midler albums in Led Zeppelin sleeves when he was a teenager, because he was closeted—a story that is reminiscent of the Streisand stigma in *In & Out* mentioned in my Introduction. What is particularly enjoyable in Midler (at least the pre–1982 Midler) is that she is as entertaining as the most outrageous drag queens, in very similar ways indeed. Roberta Mock presents Midler as a camp heteroqueer lady and reminds us of the fact that Michael Bronski described Midler as a "female female impersonator" (Bronski 1984: 107). I do not know if Bronski was the first to write this, but it is something I heard in cabaret clubs in the 1970s, a term I myself have always used—at any rate, I spoke of females in female drag. And how could I not? The notion is indispensable to anyone who has always suspected, like many LGBT people throughout history even before the advent of gender studies, that femininity and masculinity are not all that natural. Nope, sorry, ladies, you did not come out of your mother's womb pouting seductively and wiggling your bottom in that sexy high-heel-wearing way. Mock looks at how Midler plies her trade like a drag queen:

> Midler learned how to be a "lady" from gay men and their appreciation of ironic distancing, camp connoisseurship, and parodic appropriation of the notion of a stable gender identity were studied as part of the lesson. As a result of this transaction, she acts as if she has balls under her dress, despite (or because of?) the fact that she emphasizes her full physical attributes and is explicit in presenting her own heterosexuality [Mock 2003: 27].

How can one not agree with that? Indeed, it is true not only of Midler (especially the pre–1982 Midler) but also of a majority of the gay icons featured in this book. A great many show-business genetic female performers are "female female impersonators." It is easy to declare, *à la* Judith Butler, that every woman is a female impersonator. So let us not forget that in the case of performers like Midler, we are talking about women who know that this is exactly what they are doing, and who actually make a career of it. The differences between them is the degree of amusement they and their audience derive from it, the quantity of comic relief that is infused in it all. One of the keys to Midler's early success was her rewriting of the Andrews Sisters (well-liked by the gays in their day).

Many of Midler's songs are gay favorites and reinforce her iconicity, such as "When a Man Loves a Woman" or Cole Porter's "Miss Otis Regrets," a monument of highly allusive camp. Those who still need convincing should visit YouTube and watch her 1975 "Trashy Ladies" medley with fellow gay icon Cher, before going to Facebook to watch five-year-old Alfie Shields from Stockport, UK, perform Midler's *Hocus Pocus* "I Put a Spell on You" in drag. He did it so well that Midler herself actually shared the video on her page.[132]

Nicki Minaj (1982–)

Nicki Minaj, aka Nicki Lewinski, the Mistress, or the Baddest Bitch, took the popular music industry by surprise when she released her debut album *Pink Friday* (2010). Even though she had already reached a certain level of notoriety, thanks to three moderately successful mixtapes between 2007 and 2009, it is really *Pink Friday* that launched her to international fame. Abandoning her underground pursuits for the mainstream stage, Onika Maraj, the little Trinidadian girl from Queens, became Nicki Minaj, hip-hop/pop monster. She gained the greater part of her gay fanbase at that early stage, already on her way to gay iconicity.

The Nicki Minaj star persona may appear scattered and chaotic to the uninitiated, but in reality, this apparent mayhem is exquisitely controlled. Like some other prominent pop figures in this book, Minaj succeeded in creating the foundations of a legend around herself, with her every move and appearance surrounded by mystery and contradictory expectations. Her fashion sense is, to put it mildly, acute. Wearing the most prestigious designers, she swings from chic outfits to totally out-of-the-box getups that some call horrendous and back again. Bright and shiny colors, sparkly fabrics, the least that can be said is that she is original and rarely repeats herself. Her often-extreme clothing is usually paired with unsubtle accessories and makeup, but most importantly with wigs. Wigs are part and parcel of the aesthetics of the rapper. She uses them unlike any other female MC before (with the possible exception of Lil' Kim in the 1990s). Lady Gaga also resorts to wigs constantly, but in different ways. Electric blue, bubblegum pink, long, short, wavy, straight, animal printed, she has tried them all. These wigs contribute greatly to her flamboyance and have everything to do with the practices of drag queens.

Beyond the aesthetics and the music, Minaj has relied on a multiplicity of alter egos that she has created over time to give herself a wider range. Some of her endeavors in this domain evoke the practices of David Bowie and Madonna. These alter egos vary greatly, from Harajuku Barbie, the manga-inspired persona from which Nicki Minaj evolved, as it were, to Martha Zolanski, an old British lady with a strong accent. The one that particularly interests us here is Roman Zolanksi, described by Minaj herself as the reflection of her masculine and violent self—and, most importantly, as gay. This alter ego is mostly used in songs in which Minaj "throws shade," as the now classic African American (and Latino) gay phrase goes ("Want Some More," 2014).

Even though she bloomed in a hip-hop environment—a hotbed of sexism and homophobia—from the beginning of her career, Minaj was not shy about putting forward discussions around sexuality and gender. From her graphic videos to her explicit lyrics, she is unafraid of pushing buttons, discussing women's sexuality, rapping about pausing exclusively for pedestrians or particularly interesting lesbians ("Go Hard," 2009). Admittedly, she is not the first female MC who has sexualized women's bodies, but she is the first one to use lesbian themes. Offstage, Minaj is less outspoken when it comes to her sexuality, which does little to dissipate the mystery (yes, it is possible to remain mysterious even as you abundantly display your body). Never clearly acknowledging either lesbian tendencies or a bisexual identity, she nevertheless gives a few crumbs to interviewers. In December 2010, during an interview with the magazine *Details,* she did not react when she was addressed by a journalist as an "openly bisexual rapper." A few months later, however, she responded, arguing with no hesitation that she was not bisexual. Nevertheless, she remained vocal about the rampant homophobia in hip-hop, hoping to help change the situation.

By labeling her fans "Barbz," she generated a gender divide between a LGBTQ-friendly pop audience who readily embraced the title and a hip-hop and rap public who was more reluctant to accept the feminized denomination. As far as her ever-changing appearance is concerned, since the beginning of her career Minaj has been compared to female pop moguls such as Madonna and Lady Gaga. Although she rejected the comparison with Gaga, she more than embraced her similarities to Madonna, notably but not exclusively with respect to their bossy businesswoman aspects. Her raps in Madonna's tracks "Give Me All Your Luvin'" (2012), "I Don't Give A" (2012), and "Bitch I'm Madonna" (2015) are particularly relevant. She is basically acknowledging Madonna's supreme regal diva and savvy entrepreneur status. She was onstage next to Madonna at prestigious events such as the 2012 Super Bowl halftime show.

Such is the synergy of gay icons that Minaj truly benefited from the aura of already well-established gay icons such as Beyoncé or Mariah Carey by collaborating with them. Some see those "featurings" as mere epiphenomena in her musical career, but I believe they are most significant.

Minaj has been playing with her own antagonistic personae. On the one hand, there is the bubbly and eccentric Barbie doll with resolutely more pop, and even electro tracks. On the other hand, her rap persona is equally elaborate as a construction, and more explicit in her discourse. This does not always work, and she ends up alienating part of her audience.

Although I draw links between Minaj and white performers, one must not forget that things are more complicated for her. As an African American woman, Minaj's performance in out and of drag, as it were, must be viewed through the lens of a racially conflicted America. Restricted by the hypersexualization and exoticism traditionally associated with the African American female body, Minaj never held back in her performances, but the backlash that ensued was usually stronger for her than for her white counterparts. However, I would like to think that her gay audience saw this racial identity as yet another marker of identification because race, just like gender and sexuality, can be associated with some sort of oppression.

119

All in all, the flamboyant Minaj has everything it takes to be seen as a legitimate gay icon. Yet with her latest album, *The Pinkprint* (2014), she seemed to have opted for a more "stripped-down" persona. In addition, her recent non-involvement in the LGBTQ+ cause disappointed many of her gay fans, most notably when she did not express her support after the 2016 Orlando nightclub shooting. However, as established above, voicing support for LGBTQ+ concerns is not a prerequisite of gay iconicity. In 2010, though, she had told MTV: "I would encourage my gay fans to be fighters and to be brave. People face difficulties, no matter who you are. I faced difficulties with a lot of things. I face opposition every day, but I didn't kill myself and now, thank God, I'm here. So I want my life to be a testimony to my fans and my gay fans."[133]

Liza Minnelli (1946–)

Is there a cinematic pre–*Cabaret* Liza Minnelli, as far as gays are concerned? Not really. Perhaps the Minnelli of *The Sterile Cuckoo* (Alan J. Pakula, 1969), to a moderate degree. But there is certainly a musical pre–*Cabaret* Liza Minnelli, going back to the 1960s. She performed with her mother and fellow gay icon Judy Garland, most notably in 1964 at the London Palladium.

In 1972, the immense gay icon Liza Minnelli, singer, dancer and actress, shot *Cabaret* (Bob Fosse, 1972), the movie that definitively placed her in the pantheon of gay-friendly stars. Never mind the complicated processes of rewriting the Sally Bowles story from real life to literature to theater to musical theater, from Christopher Isherwood to John Van Druten to Joe Masteroff to Jay Allen—here we consider Minnelli and what she makes of Sally Bowles ... a character tailor-made to delight gay men around the world. Surely everyone knows the songs, so perfectly sung by Minnelli in the movie: "Maybe This Time," "Mein Herr," and "Cabaret," principally, all of them glorious camp classics.

Since then, every drag club in the Western world has featured a *Cabaret* number at one point or another, and many gay icons have paid more-

or-less subtle tributes to the Liza Minnelli of *Cabaret* (such as Madonna and Kylie Minogue), sometimes via the Joel Grey and gorilla characters. As both Mark Booth and Linda Mizejewski (among others) remind us, *Cabaret* comes after the Marlene Dietrich movies of the 1930s, and it comes after *The Damned* (*La caduta degli dei*, Luchino Visconti, 1969), with its celebrated scene in which Helmet Berger dons Dietrich drag (Booth 1983: 12; Mizejewski 1992: 201–202). Obviously, it incorporates it all, and in more ways than one, Minnelli does Dietrich drag herself (remembering that Dietrich did little but Dietrich drag in her seven Josef von Sternberg movies to begin with—and had largely learned her trade in drag clubs).

After *Cabaret*, Minnelli was mostly appreciated by gays for her live shows, television appearances and records (notably her 1989 album *Results*, produced by the Pet Shop Boys, who are good at fanning the flames of gay iconicity). In *New York, New York* (Martin Scorsese, 1977) she is good but perhaps not as stupendous as in *Cabaret*. In the appalling movie *Sex and the City 2* (Michael Patrick King, 2010) she is pathetic in a camp way. Or is it camp in a pathetic way?

Liza Minnelli is very much her mother's daughter. If one did not happily reject most essentialist and deterministic narratives, one would be awfully tempted to say that Minnelli could only become a gay icon, given her parents and her education. She is the astonishing daughter of the amazing Vincente Minnelli (1903–1969). Vincente Minnelli was notoriously gay before leaving New York for Los Angeles (Levy 2009: 66). What is less certain is whether he totally changed his sexual practices when he settled in Hollywood in 1940 and married Garland in 1945 (the first of his four wives). It is said that Garland's first suicide attempt occurred after she found her husband in bed with a man.[134] Minnelli was flamboyant and flighty. Many of his films are gay hymns in pictures, such as *Meet Me in Saint Louis* (1944), *An American in Paris* (1951), *The Band Wagon* (1953), or even *Gigi* (1958). The affinity of gays for musicals (especially those of the 1940s and 1950s) has long been documented and is a funny cliché—and those of Vincente Minnelli are particularly sparkly.

Judy Garland, Liza Minnelli's mother, tended to marry men who liked men (she had 5 husbands). Liza shares this tendency (she has had 4 husbands). Sometimes their husbands even had sex together—for example, Mark Herron and Peter Allen, as Gerald Clarke reports (Clarke 2002:

406). Judy's father Frank Gumm was homosexual, as we saw (Clarke 2002: *passim*), so Liza had a grandfather, a father and husbands who liked men.[135] Some might find that excessive, others might read too much into it. Like her mother, Liza is a bit of a train-wreck diva, Liza has had problematic relationships with drugs and alcohol, covered by thousands of media all over the globe. Like her mother, her health is shaky, and gays tremble for her. Liza Minnelli embodies "divine decadence," and they do not want to lose such a splendid monument.

Kylie Minogue (1968–)

Simon Gage *et al.* write: "Having wrestled with comparisons to Madonna throughout her [...] career, diminutive Australian disco-pop diva Kylie Minogue is [...] the ultimate in kitsch gay icons." (Gage *et al.* 2002, 26) When I went to Kylie Minogue's concert in Paris in 2011 (*Aphrodite World Tour*), there was an intermission, just like old times. I swiftly made my way down to the men's room and witnessed something I had never seen before (or since) at a concert: outside the ladies' room next door, there were two women standing in line; outside the men's room, there were 17 men standing in line. Thus alerted to an opportunity for anthropological research, I spent the rest of the evening looking around me almost as much as I looked toward the stage (sorry, Kylie) and counted an overwhelming majority of men, most of whom my gaydar identified as gay.

Minogue's gay iconicity developed gradually after *Neighbours*. She started acting professionally as a child in the Australian television series *The Sullivans* (Nine, 1976–1983). Later, she was featured in four other series before finally landing the part of Charlene Mitchell in *Neighbours* (Seven, then Ten, then Eleven 1985–2017). She left the show in 1989 to concentrate on her pop singing career. In 1998, when she covered Abba's "Dancing Queen" (itself a gay anthem if ever there was any, as established earlier) in Sydney (during her *Intimate and Live Tour* on her own turf), one of the gayest gay capitals in the world, she reached terrific levels of camp. She wore Parisian Lido musical review feathers with a bustier and danced down a staircase with a pair of very beautiful, rather muscular waxed men, who danced in a very queeny manner. Their costume consisted of a pair of pink shorts draped over their groins and a pair of pink wings attached to their bodies with an S&M harness. Even Madonna and Mylène Farmer had never given so much to their gay fans—and Goddess knows they have given them a lot. However, when she sang "Dancing Queen" in 2000 at the Sydney Olympic Games, she straightened it, de-gayed it, and whitewashed it appallingly. Her dancers were more numerous, totally dressed, and dancing to a more subdued choreography. I guess it's called catering to one's audience.

Generally speaking, her live shows are particularly enjoyed by gay men because of the inordinate amount of utterly gorgeous male dancers with to-die-for bodies who surround her, carry her, and generally mock-woo her, their muscular flesh sheathed in glittery sweat. Other singers do that, notably Madonna and Mylène Farmer, and many female performers now make sure that the writhing bodies of their male dancers are as scantily clad as possible—which is clearly feminist, after decades of men surrounded by women in bikinis. When one of the men in a gay couple worships a diva, forcing the other one to go to a show, the latter can always find consolation in the abundant eye candy. But where Kylie goes further than her contemporaries is that her dancers seem even more clearly coded as gay (admittedly, it sounds hardly possible). There are always a few female dancers as well, generally chosen in all of our divas' concerts for their physical contrast with the diva. This is the way of divas who delight in their gay iconicity. There are those who say the Communards' cover of "Dancing Queen" is gayer, but it is hard to believe anything can be as gay as Minogue's 1998 rendition of it. David Halperin says that Minogue is more of a gay icon in the UK and Australia than in the U.S. That may well be, but she is certainly one in France, and I have yet to meet a gay American who has nothing to say about her.

To publicize her support for marriage equality and hopefully influence decision-makers in Oz, Kylie Minogue declared in October 2016 that she would not get married to fiancé British actor Joshua Sasse until gay marriage became legal in Australia. In February 2017 she announced their separation.[136] Her sister Dannii Minogue, if not quite a full-fledged gay icon, is also much favored by gay men, especially in Australia and the UK.

Her career, whatever its actual merits, is largely eclipsed by Kylie's (although it was the other way around for a while). Moreover, Kylie always picks gorgeous European boyfriends (models/actors) who delight her gay fans, such as Olivier Martinez and Andrés Velencoso.[137] David Browne debates Kylie's gay iconicity and writes: "As fabulous as Kylie is, what has she actually done for the gays? Apart from [releasing] numerous pop gems to dance [...] to [...]?"[138] This is easy to dispute. What has she done for gay men? She has created those tremendous dance tracks that men have danced to, cried to, fornicated to—and that is quite a lot. Even if you don't take the visuals of her videos and concerts into account. Those visuals reached marvelous heights during her *Aphrodite World Tour* when she sat on a huge glittery skull on stage, affirming her victory over breast cancer in a splendidly unsubtle way.

In 1999, she sang "Diamonds Are a Girl's Best Friend" upon the occasion of the opening of 20th Century–Fox's Australian Studios. She was wearing a Marilyn Monroe hairdo and sporting Marilyn Monroe makeup. Obviously, she was also wearing the same dress as worn by Monroe when she sang the same number and danced to the same choreography in *Gentlemen Prefer Blondes* (Howard Hawks, 1953). In other words, she was in Monroe drag. Quite frankly, it was easy to be disappointed. Or maybe one needed to be really very refined, to intellectualize her performance and understand it as the musical equivalent of Gus Van Sant's remake of *Psycho* (1998). So many drag queens have done this exact same thing over the years all over the world (Jimmy James, most impressively), with the point being a faithful—sometimes uncannily so—reproduction. If one compares this to Madonna's much-discussed rewrite of "Diamonds Are a Girl's Best Friend" in her "Material Girl" (1984) video, one cannot but feel that Madonna is actually saying something worthwhile, making all sorts of feminist (more or less intellectualized) statements. Perhaps the point that Kylie Minogue is making is that anyone can do Marilyn Monroe, and this is a perfectly valid point. As we'll see in the next entry, "Marilyn Monroe" is mostly a concept, a pure construction, Marilyn Monroe herself was in Marilyn Monroe drag, basically. As important as "Material Girl" was to Madonna's career, Kylie Minogue has recorded numerous songs that will be remembered: "Locomotion" (1987), "I Should Be So Lucky" (1987), "Confide in Me" (1994), "Where the Wild Roses Grow" (1995, with Nick Cave), "Can't Get You Out of My Head" (2001). But gay fans will buy anything she releases.[139] As far as her movies are concerned, it seems that no one was ever willing to give her a chance by offering her a real part in a good film. She has made many cameo appearances, which are actively pursued by her most devoted fans. Her (unwittingly) funniest part is that of soldier Cammy in the Jean-Claude Van Damme vehicle *Street Fighter* (Steven E. de Souza, 1994), an absolute must for gay lovers of tackiness.

Marilyn Monroe (1926–1962)

Admittedly, Monroe's gay icon status is contested, but surely it would have been criminal to leave her out of this book. Perhaps before going into her gay iconicity it might be helpful to remember that Marilyn Monroe is an icon, period. This is true of other actresses in this book, but even more so of her. She is much more than an actress (some would say much less). She died in 1962 and yet her image is everywhere. From cheap ashtrays to expensive paintings, her face travels through time, space and media. There is even a winemaker selling Marilyn Wines. Everyone knows Marilyn Monroe, even the young.

Well, as it happens, most young people have seen between zero and two Monroe movies (as shown by repeated surveys on both sides of the Atlantic), which tends to make one think that her actual work as an actress has little responsibility for her iconicity. Perhaps it is a question of degree. In addition to the countless biographies that continue turning up, she is featured in novels (including science fiction and uchronian novels) and comic books. Many songs talk about her. Even if one has a soft spot for unpretentious rom-coms such as *Bus Stop* (Joshua Logan, 1956), only five of her movies can be said to really matter, with their interesting discourse on class, gender, and desire: *Gentlemen Prefer Blondes* (Howard Hawks 1953), *The Seven Year Itch* (Billy Wilder, 1955), *Some Like It Hot* (Billy Wilder, 1959), *Let's Make Love* (George Cukor, 1960), and *The Misfits* (John Huston, 1961). Of those five, only two are *entirely* the stuff that gay icons are made of: *Gentlemen Prefer Blondes* and *Some Like It Hot*.

Those who dispute Monroe's gay iconicity might object, reminding us of her sex symbol status, her number-one bombshell status. If she is the ultimate object of desire for straight men (think of the historic white-dress subway-grate scene in *The Seven Year Itch*), how can she also be a gay icon? The answer is that those categories have never been mutually exclusive, and one mustn't forget the identification process. In the same way, feminist scholars are practically under obligation to form—and often formulate—an opinion on Marilyn Monroe, and feminist opinions often clash with one another, notably in this field (Steinem 2013: *passim*). When you spend a substantial part of your career deconstructing blondeness, you see that in the case of gay icons Harlow and Monroe, extreme platinum blondeness obviously signifies sex; however, it also signifies purity or even childhood, depending on the scene and movie. According to its place and epoch, blondeness has been equaled with desirability or purity or, para-doxically, both.

> Clairol's ingenious question, "Is it true blondes have more fun?" was answered by Hollywood legend with an unfortunate twist. America's most tragic blondes, Jean Harlow and Marilyn Monroe, were patently false and celebrated as such—good-time girls (as long as they lasted) of no identifiable background, no parent-age and no pedigree except for American blondeness and the egalitarian dream [Brownmiller 1986: 49].

Monroe is a woman-child (*femme enfant* in French works much bet-ter). Heterosexual pornography, so easily accessible today at any age on the Internet, is filled with images of entirely hairless women, i.e., women with prepubescent bodies, little girls' bodies, in a way. This is so much the case that young girls now consider all-over waxing "normal," as sociolog-ical surveys have shown. Without getting much further into male domi-nation and its horrors at this stage, what can one make of a society—which we know to be ageist anyway—that deems a little girl to be the number-one model of desirability? Without going back to the days when our ances-tors traded fertile young girls for cattle, it is clear that this is one of the keys to Monroe's iconicity: she is a monster, a freak, a little girl with a little girl's voice in a hypersexualized body, at the same time fragile, inno-cent, vulnerable and super "hot." Indeed when you read books and arti-cles about Monroe between the 1950s and today, you often find in the same paragraph notions of the childlike Monroe and the bombshell Mon-roe.

That is why her part in *Let's Make Love* is relevant here. The most important song of the movie, "My Heart Belongs to Daddy," is intradiegetic because the character played by Monroe, Amanda, sings it on stage. However, like all the best intradiegetic songs it also comments upon the diegesis, in the sense that the lyrics reflect the type of relationship that Amanda is going to have with millionaire Jean-Marc Clément (played by an aging Yves Montand), Monroe's usual persona, and some of her real-life relationships. In the movie, Clément is about to become her sugar daddy. And Arthur Miller was Monroe's intellectual daddy, as it were. Monroe's list of (alleged) glamorous lovers and husbands is the stuff that can make many a gay man dream: prominent sportsmen, intellectuals, politicians (the Kennedy brothers), Mafiosi, etc. The dress that Marilyn Monroe wore to sing "Happy Birthday, Mr. President" to President Kennedy in 1962 was sold (for the second time) in November 2016. It was auctioned in Los Angeles for $4,800,000.[140]

As far as gender politics is concerned, some think that Marilyn Monroe knew exactly what she was doing, whereas others believe she had little clue. We now have five decades of biographies and investigations to help us decide. It seems that Monroe did discern some of the mechanisms of the construction of her stardom and her star persona, intimating as she did that she switched on "Marilyn Monroe" when she decided it was required, as seen above, but that otherwise she could walk down a busy street without being recognized. But that does not mean she was a quasi-Butlerian constructionist 40 years ahead of her time (as Dietrich had been 60 years ahead of hers); it does not mean she felt that her femininity itself owed little to nature. Just how "intellectual" was Monroe in her final years? "[A] star as profoundly contradictory as Monroe was also at the same time the 'ultimate' dumb blonde," writes Richard Dyer (Dyer 1979/1998: 99). Bimbos and dumb blondes may have more fun, but surely Monroe was quite intelligent, and at the end, quite cultivated (see her reading and fragmentary writings).

The first victim of the 60s in a way, Monroe is defined as a pinnacle of glamour. The word "glamour" is etymologically linked to "grimoire," i.e., to magic. If almost everyone agrees to attribute so much power of attraction to her, perhaps it is more because she embodies her times culturally and politically than because of magic.

Monroe very much took her cues from Jean Harlow, Hollywood's first platinum blonde bombshell. When she started shooting the unfinished

Something's Got to Give (George Cukor, 1962), she hired hairdresser Pearl Porterfield, who had done the hair of Jean Harlow and Mae West. But then, she herself was and is constantly rewritten, paid tribute to, parodied, pastiched, imitated, copied, plagiarized, etc. Indeed, a handful of her contemporaries were trying to out–Monroe her, including Mamie Van Doren and Jayne Mansfield. Even some European actresses attempted to compete, including Diana Dors in the UK and Virna Lisi in Italy.

Later, in addition to the famous rewrites of Monroe by Kylie Minogue and Madonna, a great many performers have done Monroe at one point or another, if only for a photo shoot: Boy George's onetime boyfriend Marilyn, Christina Aguilera, Britney Spears, Lindsay Lohan (photographed by Bert Stern like Monroe in her famous "Last Sitting"), Gwen Stefani, Lady Gaga, Amanda Lepore (obsessed with Monroe), Lisa Marie Presley (with makeup by Kevin Aucoin), Miley Cyrus, Scarlett Johansen, etc. Monroe is everywhere, she is Baudrillardesque in her ubiquitous hyperreality, she is everything to everyone—or rather anything to anyone. How could she not also be a gay icon to gays, who cannot not find fascinating the manner in which people are able to project all of their fantasies onto her—and not only sexual? Veronica Slater calls Warhol's Marilyn Monroe "an icon of heterosexuality" (Slater in Horne & Lewis 1996: 131). That is extremely debatable. Monroe herself might, if one must, be called an icon of heterosexuality (even if she is a gay icon), if only because so many straight men around the planet dreamed of bedding her. But to say that Warhol's Marilyn Monroe is an icon of heterosexuality is extremely reductive. I guess one should speak in the plural, to begin with. Warhol's Monroes are precisely this: plural. Monroe is infinite, Monroe is a simulacrum, she's ubiquitous, she's a Warholian myth and a supermarket product, like laundry soap. Monroe is queered by Warhol, who it can be argued queered everything he touched.[141]

Even more so than *Let's Make Love*, *Gentlemen Prefer Blondes* is about sugar-babying, but there are also possible lesbian readings. Alexander Doty writes of the gays who might "find a form of queer pleasure in the alternately tender and boisterous rapport between Lorelei/Marilyn Monroe and Dorothy/Jane Russell in *Gentlemen Prefer Blondes*" (Doty 1993: 8). Doty speaks of "Russell being the 'gentleman' who preferred blonde Monroe, who looked out for her best interests, who protected her against men, and who enjoyed performing with her" (Doty 1993: 9). He tells us about Lucie Arbuthnot and Gail Seneca's article "Pre-text and Text in *Gentlemen Prefer Blondes*" (Arbuthnot & Gail, 1982), recalling that it is "perhaps the best-known lesbian-positioned piece on the musical," even if the word "lesbian" is never encountered (Doty 1993: 12). Doty does know that speaking of bisexuality when dealing with "a mainstream text like *Gentlemen Prefer Blondes* is always done within the context of definitional and ideological debates that are themselves complicated by the fact that heterocentrism makes the queer erotics of mainstream films invisible or 'subtextual' for most people in the first place." (Doty 2000: 132) Still, the argument is quite convincing. Naturally, that is what ferretting the queer out of cultural products and/or queering cultural products is all about. Gays in general and gay scholars in particular excel at undertaking subtextual readings and spotting queer erotics. And Doty did a great deal of that in his invaluable critical writing.

In 2003, Chuck Klosterman boldly compared Pamela Anderson (who has said she loves gays) to Marilyn Monroe. Monroe was the most important woman of the 20th century, he tells us. And he claims that Pamela Anderson is "the most crucial woman of her generation, partially because we hate to think about what Pam Anderson's heaving bosom means to our culture" (Klosterman 2003: 72). He then establishes striking parallels between the two women, writing: "Men in the fifties wanted Monroe because she made love to the men they respected, modern men want Anderson because she makes love to the concept of celebrity" (Klosterman 2003: 78). Pamela Anderson is a Barbie doll, he says, and intellectual men desire her "because she can be appreciated lecherously *and* ironically" (Klosterman 2003: 80). It is true, at any rate, that many gay men love the unspeakably bad movie *Barb Wire* (David Hogan, 1996), both a loose adaptation of the eponymous Dark Horse comic book and a loose remake of *Casablanca* (Michael Curtiz, 1942), and wrong on so many levels, notably because of her terribly low camp performance.

Gay magazines are fond of regularly reminding us of the fact that Monroe "hung out" with gays such as Milton Greene, Montgomery Clift, and Truman Capote.[142] She was even prone to doing light camp now and again, notably in interviews, with lines such as "It's not true I had nothing on, I had the radio on," or "What do I wear in bed? Why, Chanel No. 5, of course." Edgar Morin, author of *Les Stars*, famously declared that her death marked the end of the star system (Morin 1957: 26). Maybe she killed herself, maybe she committed suicide; maybe her death is related to the Kennedys, or the FBI, or the CIA, or to anti–Castro Cubans, or to pro–Castro Cubans, or to the Italian-American Mafia... Fascinating as all those speculations might be, if she is a gay icon, remembering the Chanel No. 5 line is more to the point.

María Montez (1912–1951)

Spanish/Dominican cult actress María Montez was nicknamed the Queen of Technicolor after she appeared in *White Savage* (Arthur Lubin, 1943). In fact, the moniker was even used in the trailers of her next movies. Maureen O'Hara (1920–2015) was also called the Queen of Technicolor, but she was no gay icon to speak of.

Montez appeared in more than 20 movies before her untimely death, becoming truly famous with *Arabian Nights* (John Rawlins, 1942). Her movies tend to be kitschy, schmaltzy and are definitely colorful. They have wildly evocative titles such as *Gipsy Wildcat* (Roy William Neill, 1944) and *Siren of Atlantis* (Gregg G. Tallas, 1949). Her headdress in *Cobra Woman* (Robert Siodmak, 1944) alone is worthy of camp worship. She was not remarkably talented as an actress (some say she was atrocious), but that was totally beside the point. The point was to watch her be exotic in exotic garb in purely escapist Hollywood fantasy movies. Her publicity pictures are occasionally used on the covers of novels.

With a very keen sense of marketing, Montez courted every form of publicity and largely participated in the organization of her own cult. Gays love that—look at Madonna. Seeing her image in *Arabian Nights* inspired her to deliver her most famous quote: "When I look at myself, I am so beautiful I scream with joy!" Apparently, after seeing herself in *The Invisible Woman* (A. Edward Sutherland, 1940), she had already declared: "When I see myself on the screen, I am so beautiful, I jump for joy!" What is there not to love in such a woman? Who needs demure, modest, innocent actresses who doubt their powers of attraction?

After her marriage to William McFeeters, she married French actor Jean-Pierre Aumont. They had a daughter, actress Tina Aumont, who married actor/director Christian Marquand and occasionally went by Tina Marquand. Montez drowned in her bath in Paris at age 39 after a heart attack. Gays love it when their icons never age.

And if gays love mistresses of reinvention such as Madonna, they also love a diva who knows the side on which her bread is buttered and peddles the same schmaltz over and over again. Why change a winning formula? María Montez went from kitsch to camp and back again all the time, to the delight of her fans and the satisfaction of Universal Studios. "Universal's stars would play a specialty over and over again. María Montez, queen of sarong-and-volcano melodrama, was one such, a distinctly '40s figure whose vehicles would nevertheless not have been out of place in the silent period" (Mordden 1988: 353–354).

Gay icons always inspire gay men. Sometimes that inspiration leads to singular creations. María Montez inspired a member of Andy Warhol's Factory, drag queen Mario Montez, born René Rivera. He was one of Jack Smith's *Flaming Creatures* (1963) and appeared in a dozen Warhol films— what more is there to say? Perhaps simply that Smith's film is, among other things, "a satire of Hollywood B movies and a tribute to the actress María Montez, who starred in such pictures" (Levy 2015: 275). Smith famously adored Montez, and wrote about his cult actress, whom he defended against her detractors (Smith 2008: 25–35).

Sara Montiel (1928–2013)

Mexican-Spanish singer and actress Sara Montiel (aka Sarita Montiel), a ravishing brunette, began to act in movies at a rather young age. Her first movie was *Te quiero para mí* (Ladislao Vajda, 1944). A few years later she soared through the stars, simultaneously transforming herself into a feminist icon and a gay icon (it often goes together) in Franco's suffocating Spain, when the clueless fascist censors were incapable of reading the subtext of *El Último cuplé* (*Valencia*, Juan de Orduña, 1957), a marvelous musical melodrama in which she shines more than ever. That being said, by 1948 she had already reached peaks of eroticism in *Locura de amor* (*Madness for Love/The Mad Queen*, Juan de Orduña, 1948), in which she moves particularly well, wearing very little. I also recommend *La Violetera* (Luis César Amadori, 1958), to complete your familiarity with the woman if you are not yet a fan. Montiel was a free woman, a liberated woman who let no man dictate her conduct, even in an era in which Catholic/Francoist morals were imposed on everyone. She made films abroad, she was cosmopolitan and daring. She sang as well as she acted and all the Spanish drag queens still imitate her, as can be witnessed in *La mala educación* (*Bad Education*, Pedro Almodóvar, 2004). This movie is a gay favorite which boasts the sexy Gael García Bernal in a sheath dress and blond wig lip-syncing to Montiel's immortal "Quizas, quizas, quizas," confirming her gay icon status. Her interpretations of "La Paloma," "Besame mucho," "La vida en rosa," and "Es mi hombre" (in a red dress and black ostrich feather boa) are unforgettably camp. They can all be found on YouTube.

Many saw her as a camp diva back then, and it seems many more do retrospectively. In *La Violetera* she was seen as a Latin Elizabeth Taylor. She even managed to retain some control over the songs, the costumes and the décor.

During her short Hollywood period, she made films many of us treasure. In the masterpiece *Vera Cruz* (Robert Aldrich, 1954), which takes place during the Franco-Mexican war, she plays Nina, and she acts opposite Burt Lancaster and Gary Cooper. Denise Darcel plays the Countess Marie Duvarre—Montiel called her "la francesa"—whereas Montiel plays a spy. In the tremendous musical drama *Serenade* (Anthony Mann, 1956), with the great Mario Lanza, she plays a Mexican bullfighter's daughter. In *Run of the Arrow* (Samuel Fuller, 1957) she plays a Native American (dubbed by Angie Dickinson!).

In 2009 she and Spanish gay icon (and Movida[143] survivor) Alaska (1963–)[144] released a duet, "Absolutamente," with a video calculated to delight the gays of the Chueca district in Madrid: leopard prints galore, schlock decor and *mises en abyme*, with the two women posing à la Mae West and trying to outcamp each other while evoking candles lit for Saint Sebastian[145] (Alaska is half of the band Fangoria).

Agnes Moorehead (1900–1974)

Actress Agnes Moorehead starred in dozens of movies, including *Magnificent Obsession* (Douglas Sirk, 1954), *Dark Passage* (Delmer Daves, 1947) and *Citizen Kane* (Orson Welles, 1941), mostly in supporting roles, but she is known worldwide for playing Endora in the television series *Bewitched* (ABC, 1964–1972). *Bewitched* (forget the unspeakably bad movie with Nicole Kidman) stars Elizabeth Montgomery as Samantha the witch, daughter of Endora the witch. It is easy to see how it may please feminists—or does it? Some even see it as antifeminist (all about hiding girl power). *I Dream of Jeannie* (NBC, 1965–1970) is another gay favorite, although not as cult as *Bewitched.* This is how Andi Zeisler sees these shows:

> [A] surreal dyad of anxiety about female rebellion against gender roles. They embodied the contradictions facing real women at the time, both offering a winking facet of wish fulfillment (what housewife wouldn't want to take care of the housework merely by wiggling her nose?) and a warning of what might happen to a woman whose feminine power can be uncorked at will. With a knowing wink, they hinted at the push toward female emancipation that was to come while simultaneously affirming the conventional wisdom that women were most fulfilled when they were assisting their male partners and assuring their success [Zeisler 2008: 41].

So here is a person, Samantha, who is very different from the others, and she has to hide it because of the pressure of society and of those close to her. Does that ring a bell? Samantha is a closeted witch: no wonder gay men like the show. Plus, she is blonde and gorgeous and has a sense of humor. With only a little stretch, one could even see her as a drag queen or a transwoman who passes and has a "straight" husband, Darrin, who is terrified at the idea of her being found out. Indeed, Samantha is actually a queen: as some episodes show, she is the queen of the witchy people. And of course, only one letter differentiates "witch" from "bitch."

Would it not be wonderful to twitch our noses like her and get what we want? Just like that? Twitch, no more homophobia! Twitch, the neighbor's son suddenly realizes what a catch we are! Twitch, our dad stops trying to butch us up with some compulsory sport!

Samantha, as played by Elizabeth Montgomery, spends a lot of time manipulating husband Darrin (played first by Dick York then by Dick Sargent), with or without magic. But Samantha's mother, Endora, is much more manipulative, and is a much more interesting character from our point of view. She is immensely camp in every possible sense of the word. With a shiny mass of unsubtle red hair piled up on her head, she is always wearing the most flamboyant getups and joyfully overacting, plus she is fiercely independent. She has a sort of husband, Samantha's father Maurice, but they most certainly do not live together, and both are very attached to their independence. One must admit that warlock Maurice is rather queeny in his deportment, although apparently in the service of heterosexual pursuits. The most enjoyable characteristic of Endora, undoubtedly, one that forever enshrined Agnes Moorehead in the heart of gays, is how she puts down Darrin at all times. She constantly bitches about him, forgets his name, and is prepared to turn him into objects or animals (if not to cast a much worse spell) using wide emphatic gestures. Sometimes even Samantha cannot help finding her mother's shenanigans a little bit funny. The show also appeals to our countercultural hippyish side, considering that it timidly showcases the evolution of American society from 1964 to 1972, notably in terms of gender and sexuality and at the very least, in its sartorial endeavors.

Patricia White writes: "Moorehead is a prime candidate for gay hagiography. Her best-known incarnation, Endora, is a camp icon; she passes even the cinephile test, having been featured in films by auteurs such as Welles, Sirk, Ray, and Aldrich." White then mentions the many negative roles Moorehead played, establishing that "although the ideological stake in subordinating female difference is apparent, this negativity may also be Moorehead's most subversive edge" (White in Creekmur & Doty 1995: 92–93).

Walter Metz sums up:

> Nothing establishes the adult sensibility of *Bewitched* more than its queer theoretical subtext. The show, it turns out, was populated with the major figures of popular gay American culture of the 1960s. The analysis of these figures has concentrated on Agnes Moorehead, the flamboyant matriarch of the show, and Paul Lynde, who played Arthur, Samantha's gay (in both the naïve and cosmopolitan sense), wise-cracking, beloved uncle. The second actor to play Darrin, Dick Sargent, while closeted at the time of the show, outed himself in the late 1980s. In retrospect, it is clear that Sargent played the role of Darrin, the "normal" husband and father on *Bewitched*, with an angry, sardonic edge not

brought to the role by his predecessor Dick York, who offered a more genial, beleaguered interpretation [Metz 2007: 6].

Even though the feminism of the show on the whole is disputed, Endora can easily be read as a feminist. As Metz points out, she even uses Betty Friedan's ideas (Metz 2007: 18), as does Serena, Samantha's lookalike cousin.

Moorehead married John Griffith Lee in 1930 and divorced him in 1952. Then she married Robert Gist in 1954; they divorced in 1958. However, she was reportedly considered by everyone in Hollywood to be a lesbian. According to Betty Wood, when asked about her sexuality in an interview Moorehead once replied: "You apparently have your own informants. I don't know what you've heard, and I don't want to hear, and some of it may be true."[146] Many of her friends have claimed it was all nothing but rumors, though. Whatever her own sexuality, she will always remain a gay icon, and reruns of *Bewitched* have a bright future ahead.

Sharon Needles (1981–)

I picked Sharon Needles, who won Season 4 of *RuPaul's Drag Race*, but I might well have chosen any of the winners from Season 1 to Season 9, as they have always become more-or-less important gay icons. Admittedly, their shelf life as such might be a little short, clashing slightly with the definitional attempts of my Introduction, but in the Internet age they become huge worldwide, making up for their short duration in their degree of worldwide fame. Scholars who hail the death of camp and drag and gay iconicity, claiming that they are irrelevant to the young, need only attend a *RuPaul's Drag Race Battle of the Seasons* show in any Western city to see how wrong they are. The theaters are packed with roaring young people aged 16 to 29—plus a couple of old gender studies academics.

Admittedly, one could also argue that biological woman Michelle Visage is a gay icon, appearing as she does in most of RuPaul's televised efforts and embodying the "gay man trapped in a straight woman's body" to perfection.

Postmodern drag queen Sharon Needles won in 2012, performatively becoming "America's Next Drag Superstar." Happily ghoulish Needles certainly became a cult, on television, in clubs and theaters and in cyberspace. What allowed her to thrive so convincingly is her methodical rewrite of different types of female glamour, always done tongue-in-cheek and with a degree of cheerful morbidity. This is linked to her deep knowledge of U.S. pop culture, notably science fiction and horror movies. In her palimpsestuous shows, Needles plays with genders, genres and subgenres, troubling the viewers and getting richer.

As they say on *RuPaul's Drag Race*, Needles serves B-horror-movie realness. She does Freddy Krueger, Marilyn Manson, Vampira, Elvira; she can do Disney heroines, she can even do Cher if she must. In addition to pleasing the more and more mainstream public of drag, Needles caters to minorities within the minority, i.e., gays who like hard rock, heavy metal, or punk rock. The songs she records reflect that. She can even sound convincing when she imitates a British punk rocker, complete with appropriate accent. In this she is similar to some of the show's other minority drag queens, whose origins and cultures obviously rated highly in the casting process. *RuPaul's Drag Race* means to be totally intersectional, and the queens' stories of growing up in adversity often make for very entertaining television, as well as food for thought.

Needles is from Pittsburgh, and Pittsburgh is grateful for Needles. The Pittsburgh City Council officially declared that June 12, 2012, was "Sharon Needles Day." She used to be Alaska Thunderfuck's lover. Thunderfuck is also from Pittsburgh and was the winner of Season 2 of *RuPaul's Drag Race All Stars* in 2016. Like Needles, she benefits from quite a cult following.

Vanessa Paradis (1972–)

Beautiful singer and actress Vanessa Paradis is huge in France. In the U.S., many know her only as Johnny Depp's ex, but many others have listened at least to her album *Vanessa Paradis* (1992), produced by her then-boyfriend Lenny Kravitz, and understood what she was doing when she covered Lou Reed's "I'm Waiting for the Man." In 1990 she had already covered Lou Reed's "Walk on the Wild Side" in an album, *Variations sur le meme t'aime*, whose lyrics were otherwise written by Serge Gainsbourg. The late Gainsbourg was undoubtedly the most iconogenic of all French musicians and songwriters, writing for a great many stars—Brigitte Bardot, Régine, Jane Birkin, Catherine Deneuve, Charlotte Gainsbourg, Isabelle Adjani, Françoise Hardy, etc.—some of whom are gay icons.

Paradis began singing in public at age eight. In 1987, aged 14, she had a huge hit with "Joe le taxi," which topped the French charts for 11 weeks. She even reached number 3 in the UK, which had not happened to a French performer since Serge Gainsbourg and Jane Birkin's sexy and controversial "Je t'aime ... moi non plus" (1969). She sold records in 15 countries. After that, she kept recording, acting in more-or-less arty movies and touring. She evolved in a very classy way, from the Lolita many mocked to uber-cool sophisticate. In 1991, Grace Jones' Jean Paul Goude shot a cult commercial for Coco by Chanel that featured Paradis in a cage as an *oiseau de paradis* (a bird of paradise).

Among her movies, we will remember in particular *Noce Blanche* (Jean-Claude Brisseau, 1989), *Élisa* (Jean Becker, 1995), and *L'Arnacoeur* (*Heartbreaker*, Pascal Chaumeil, 2010), with Romain Duris. The latter is one of a handful of successful French romantic comedies, with an actual rom-com pace. Most impressive of all, her performance in the odd *Fading Gigolo* (John Turturro, 2013) as Avigal, a Hasidic Jewish widow, will remain a high point of her career. For those not yet familiar with all her songs, her live albums offer a lovely introduction and include splendid covers other than the aforementioned Lou Reed tracks, including "Les cactus" (1994), "As Tears Go By" (1994), "Requiem pour un con" (2001), "Le tourbillon de la vie" (2008), and "Le temps de l'amour" (2010).

In her private life, Paradis kept upgrading, moving up the ladder of glamour: first the French singer Florent Pagny, then Lenny Kravitz, then Johnny Depp. Unfortunately, her story with Depp did not last. He went on to make a fool of himself in unworthy productions and delight every tabloid with his doomed relationship with a much younger actress, Amber Heard, as every entertainment and tabloid magazine on the planet reported. Paradis and Depp have two children, one of whom, Lily-Rose Depp, is already an actress and Chanel model like her mother before her. According to the Brangelina or Bennifer logic, the glamour of Paradis added to the glamour of Depp was more than the sum of its parts, and gay fans of Paradis could also both drool over Depp and fantasize about their real estate empire. Now they will have to wait and see who she dates after singer Benjamin Biolay and (since November 2016) writer and filmmaker Samuel Benchetrit, which makes every single French tabloid speculate.

Marisa Paredes (1946–)

Spanish actress Marisa Paredes was once something of a teen idol, but it took her two decades to mutate into a shiny gay icon, mostly thanks to gay Spanish filmmaker Pedro Almodóvar. Her face, ordinarily good-looking in her youth, acquired gravitas in the 1980s. Hopefully the few paragraphs that follow, dedicated to Almodóvar, will be forgiven; they might seem out of place but they are not, when you consider that he is both a lifelong gay-icon worshipper and a gay-icon-monger.

In *Tacones lejanos* (*High Heels*, Pedro Almodóvar, 1991), he pays his customary attention to the colorful décor, but he pays even more attention than usual to the clothing. The outfits of his two stars, Victoria Abril and Marisa Paredes, are stupendous. Paredes plays hyper-glamorous star Becky del Páramo, who returns to Spain after a long absence. She sings two songs to her adoring public. It apparently was Almodóvar who convinced singer Luz Casal to record them both. One, "Piensa en mi," is marvelously schmaltzy. The other, "Un año de amor," is a terrific camp masterpiece that can only make you happy you're alive. Except that it was not always camp.

The French singer (of Italian origin) Nino Ferrer recorded his first single in 1963. The B-side contained a pleasant song entitled "C'est irreparable." How do you make camp from something that is not camp? In 1965 "C'est irréparable" was covered by gay icon Dalida in French, acquiring a few degrees of camp. Until 1991 and its Almodóvarization, the song was mostly famous in Italian as the even-camper "Un anno d'amore," sung by gay icon Mina (who recorded it in 1965 in Italian, Spanish, Japanese, Turkish, and perhaps other languages). Then comes Luz Casal's Spanish version, "Un año de amor." Casal herself has everything it takes as far as her voice is concerned: the range, the pathos, the power.

However, she has an indifferent look and moderately interesting looks. However famous in Spain, Casal never became a proper gay icon, though some Spanish fans of hers would disagree. When Marisa Paredes lip-syncs to "Un año de amor," she adds supplementary degrees of camp to the monument. The song is intradiegetic and comments upon the diegesis; the viewer knows that within the diegesis, singer Becky del Páramo sings it. But he also knows and never forgets that this is really Marisa Paredes miming the lyrics to perfection, i.e., behaving like a cabaret drag queen.

The viewer is meant to understand that Becky del Páramo is a gay icon. When she goes to the Villa Rosa club, she finds drag queen Letal doing her in what is clearly a classic drag number. This tremendous *mise en abyme* performance by actor and singer Miguel Bosé obviously adds a final handful of degrees of camp to the song.[147] Irony, distance, aestheticism, artificiality, theatricality, incongruity, what is there to complain about? Becky has Warholian portraits of herself in her apartment (among other allusions to Warhol), and when she sings "Piensa en mi," she kisses the floor of the theater, leaving lipstick traces on the wood. Need one say more?

In *Todo sobre mi madre* (*All About My Mother*, 1999), charismatic Paredes plays a show-woman again, Bette Davis style. The title signals a rewrite of the gay cult movie *All About Eve*, discussed above. Huma is an actress who plays Blanche DuBois in Tennessee Williams' *A Streetcar Named Desire* (1947). Manuela (Cecilia Roth) works in the transplant unit of a Madrid hospital. She has a teenage son, Esteban, who is very attached to her and is a fan of Huma's. He is clearly gay: he's a writer, a voracious reader, he's sensitive, he likes Tennessee Williams and Truman Capote, he likes classic movies that are gay favorites, such as *All About Eve*—and he makes the viewer think of a young Pedro Almodóvar, obviously. *Todo sobre mi madre* is all about women, loving women and women loving, it is all about mothers, and it is all about performance (notably but not exclusively the performance of gender). Manuela, like Eve, becomes an assistant to the diva and then an understudy, though in the case of Manuela, without calculation. *Todo sobre mi madre* is also all about theater, and women who act replacing other women who act, in every sense of the verb.

It takes a larger-than-life actress to play Blanche Dubois: Jessica Tandy, Vivien Leigh, Cate Blanchett in 2009, Huma/Marisa Paredes (bringing her glamorous iconic star power to it all, literally larger than life on the huge posters of *Un tranvía llamado Deseo* in the streets of Madrid.

Leo Bersani and Ulysse Dutoit call all of these women "campy actresses." (Bersani & Dutoit in Epps & Kakoudaki 2009: 245) Pedro Almodóvar adored actresses Bette Davis and Joan Crawford, discovering their great movie roles through post-synchronized versions, horribly dubbed into Spanish—he had to wait years before he could watch them in English with Spanish subtitles. Every Pedro Almodóvar film is (to a more or less large extent) a rewrite of classic Hollywood; every one of his films alludes to classic Hollywood in postmodern tributes or pastiches. He constantly plays transtextual games, winking notably at 1950s Hitchcock movies or Douglas Sirk melodramas. In Huma's dressing room there are pictures of Elizabeth Taylor (as Cleopatra) and Marilyn Monroe. At some point Huma explains why she goes by this pseudonym: "huma" means "inhale," and she smokes like Bette Davis.

Before *Todo sobre mi madre*, Almodóvar had iconized Carmen Maura and "discovered" transwoman Bibi Andersen. Gorgeous Bibi Andersen, a gay icon in Spain, was born Manuel Fernández Chica in Tangier in 1954. A few years later, Manuel Fernández Chica became Bibiana Fernández. After four minor roles she was given a small part in *Matador* (Pedro Almodóvar, 1986), having become Bibi Andersen. Let us note the singular, very postmodern onomastic approach. The cult Swedish actress of *Persona* (Ingmar Bergman, 1966) is called Bibi Andersson. Andersson and Andersen mean etymologically "son of man." Bibi Andersen is her own offspring, as it were, after surgical intervention, and appropriates the cinematic legend of her choice. Andersen is also the name of Danish writer Hans Christian Andersen, the author of fairy tales. Manuel Fernández Chica was the ugly duckling, Bibi Andersen is the swan. Almodóvar could only approve.

Almodóvar loves women, and he loves actresses. He enjoys portraying strong female characters, fierce mothers, such as Manuela, or Raimunda in *Volver* (2006). He declared in British gay magazine *Attitude*: "I grew up surrounded by incredibly strong women who were a lot less prejudiced than the men. This had a great influence on my work."[148] He sometimes presents them in essentialist ways, implying that these women are typically, naturally feminine. However, when it comes to drag queens, transvestites and transgender people, his cinematic discourse becomes more constructionist. In *La ley del deseo* (*Law of Desire*, 1987), the femininity of Tina, with its stereotypical traits of a Spanish housewife (red dress and dishwashing gloves) is subtly opposed to the "masculinity" embodied by the Grace Jones photograph repeatedly displayed on the wall of Pablo's kitchen. Clearly, Almodóvar is also constructionist regarding sexuality and sexual orientation. His characters often move from one object of desire to another in a way that further exposes the rich fluidity of desire rather than any simplistic notion of some basic bisexuality in everyone.

Carmen Maura and the sublime Penelope Cruz are Almodóvarian heroines, iconized like Paredes, except the latter (who has a lesbian affair as Huma in *Todo sobre mi madre*) is much more of a gay icon.

Dolly Parton (1946–)

"I'm not offended by all the dumb-blonde jokes because I know that I'm not dumb. I also know I'm not blonde" (Parton in Warren 2000: 12). Dolly Parton is the only country music gay icon featured in this book (Taylor Swift started in country music before turning altogether mainstream, but however delicious, she is not as universally accepted as a gay icon as Parton). One does not usually associate country music with gays; indeed, there is quite a bit of homophobia in country-music circles, and every male country singer seems to thrive on presenting butch behavior as unequivocally as he can (the costumes are another matter, but this is not the place to develop that notion[149]). The television show *Nashville* (ABC then CMT 2012–2017) recently addressed this issue. Women in country music have more leeway.

Parton practically invented big hair, evoking the wigs of Queen Marie-Antoinette and the exaggerated wigs of drag queens. It is only in the 21st century that she started sporting less voluminous hairdos. All she needed, really, to reach instant gay icon status, was to utter those celebrated words, her ubiquitously quoted catchphrase: "You'd be surprised how much it costs to look this cheap." Surely few stars have reached such high points of camp with one simple sentence. There are several versions of the line. Drag queens all over the U.S. quote it all the time, like Alaska Thunderfuck in her song "Hieee" (2015). Who cares if Parton did not come up with it first? It fits her like a glove. The love of the exaggerated is clearly an element of camp. No camp object can ever be played down or understated. Camp is excessive, camp is over-emphasized, camp is the opposite of moderation. If Dolly Parton had moderately sized breasts, moderately blonde and moderately voluminous hair, moderately ornate boots and moderate makeup, she would not be quite as camp. As she is, she embodies one type of camp to near perfection. Indeed, Dolly Parton has done little but camp self-parody in recent years, and no one loves her less for that. At the 50th annual CMA Awards on November 2, 2016, she was presented with the Willie Nelson Lifetime Achievement Award. "I would have cried, but I didn't want to mess up my eyelashes," she said backstage.[150]

Parton wrote the song "I Will Always Love You" in 1973, a tear-jerker if ever there was one, a song that you can belt out and/or mime to while sitting in your pajamas on the carpet of your lounge, leaning against your sofa, eating chocolates or drinking wine or smoking (or all of the above), very much like Renée Zellweger as Bridget Jones in *Bridget Jones's Diary* (Sharon Maguire, 2001), finding an echo of her loneliness in "All by Myself," by Australian singer Jamie O'Neal (more of a torch song by O'Neal and by other women than by its creator Eric Carmen). It is clear that "I Will Always Love You" became even more appreciated by gay men when it was covered by Whitney Houston, but that does not mean they do not feel grateful to Dolly Parton.

At Bloomington, Indiana's famous nightclub Uncle Elizabeth's in April 2012, I watched drag queen Sasha Michaels sashay around in a gorgeous pink iridescent sheath dress and pondered a new element in her drag vocabulary, one that had most certainly not been there two months before when I had last seen her perform: in addition to her falsies, she was sporting prosthetic hips under her dress, giving her a Mae West edge. Had she thought of resting her hand on her hip at some point, the effect would have been close to perfection. Sasha has always been camp in her drag performance, but somehow those new curves, those voluptuous hips made her even camper. Before her, though, I had seen my favorite drag queen of 2012, Montana Melons, perform on the same stage. Montana not only sports prosthetic hips in her immensely camp numbers, but she systematically displays a gigantic pair of very realistic plastic breasts, clearly modeled on Dolly Parton's. Montana Melons is obviously a fan of Dolly Parton, which does not mean that Parton does not appeal to mainstream America. "Parton has a consistent fan base across a range of demographics, whether it's the heartland of America, curious feminists, or those in the gay and lesbian community and drag queens. Her persona's appeal knows no boundaries" (Havranek 2009: 326).

Diana Rigg (1938–)

Trevor Martin remembers:

I have pondered this phenomenon since I first realized I am gay. As a young child of 10, I would shut myself away during the weekends, curtains closed in the living room, and watch the triple bill of films on Saturday-afternoon BBC TV: Bette Davis. Marilyn Monroe. Judy Garland. Joan Crawford. The judo expert Emma Peel, portrayed amazingly by the inimitable Diana Rigg, in the UK-produced spy spoof *The Avengers*; I definitely wanted to be Emma Peel when I was 9 years old. Samantha from *Bewitched* was a favorite, though I secretly admired her delightfully meddling and wicked mother, Endora, the most![151]

It is true, Diana Rigg is mostly known for playing the stupendous Emma Peel in the 1960s British television series *The Avengers* (ITV 1961–1969). Some might find this unfair, considering what a talented and wide-ranging actress she is, but it was her choice: she gave up a promising Shakespearian career to embody Emma Peel, allowing Glenda Jackson to take up her roles! Emma Peel was in many ways a feminist role model and very quickly propelled Rigg to stratospheric peaks of gay iconicity, first in the UK and then all over the world.

Antonio Dominguez Leiva writes: "Like gay iconicity, camp culture [in] the sixties was to increasingly exploit the image of S&M, from leather-clad agent Mrs. Emma Peel to Bondian femmes fatales."[152] It is true many James Bond movies have their tremendously camp moments, and queer readings are easy, but they do not feature many gay icons as Bond girls, beside the arresting Grace Jones in *A View to a Kill* (John Glen, 1985), and of course, Rigg herself, who had a part in the Bond movie *On Her Majesty's Secret Service* (Peter Hunt, 1969).

In Agatha Christie's *Evil Under the Sun* (Guy Hamilton, 1982), she plays a flamboyant bitch, magnified by Anthony Shaffer's script. Clad in a heavenly evening dress, she sings Cole Porter's 1934 "You're the Top" all the way to camp heaven. In the musical *Snow White* (Michael Berz, 1987) she plays a deliciously malevolent Evil Queen. These days she is Olenna Tyrell in the cult series *Game of Thrones* (HBO 2011–2018).

Patrick Macnee, her *Avengers* partner, narrated their meeting in his memoirs. They got along well from day one, mostly because they had the same caustic humor. It was impossible not to adore her, he claims (Macnee 1988: 277). Certainly they were both extremely elegant, in extremely English ways, and it seems that they had the same flair for camp repartee both on and off the set.

Rihanna (1988–)

Not very much older than fellow gay icon Miley Cyrus, Rihanna has already had a long career, which began in 2005. A Barbadian singer, song-writer and actress,[153] by late 2017, she has released eight albums and sold more than 230 million records. She can never seem to determine what her hair should look like or what color it should be. Her gay fans have clear ideas, but she pays no heed to their Internet forum advice—although like other younger gay icons, she knows how to use social networks to her advantage. Her gay fans also like expressing their compassion for her, notably as far as her childhood is concerned, with an addict father and all that sort of thing. She started singing at age seven and apparently dropped out of school before she could graduate. Gays also enjoy her controversial style changes, especially when they involve a lot of skin and/or a lot of fetishistic fabrics—sometimes harking back to the Grace Jones of the 1980s. Some designers have greatly benefited from those changes.

Rihanna, like Whitney Houston, has been the victim of domestic abuse, at the hands of a man, Chris Brown, who shares a surname with Houston's husband Bobby Brown, attracting both a great deal of sympathy and suspicion as she went in and out of the relationship (linked with her collaboration with Eminem).[154] The Internet buzzed with more-or-less dubious notions of the willing victim and the glorification of domestic violence. In this and in other avenues,[155] Rihanna has been controversial, which is obviously a sure way not only to boost record sales but also to secure her huge gay fan base, that loves a good controversy—especially when it has to do with sex.[156] Her other relationships with baseball player Matt Kemp[157] and musician Drake[158] have been heavily publicized. The following Rihanna videos are undeniably tremendous teaching material for a queer/intersectionality studies class: "S&M" (2011), "Man Down" (2011), "Pour It Up" (2013), "Bitch Better Have My Money" (2015), and, to a lesser degree, "Love on the Brain" (2016).

Rihanna actively takes part in various charities, notably a child charity she founded in 2006, Believe. Rihanna is heavily involved in HIV activism and is a fan of fellow gay icon Elizabeth Taylor. *The Advocate* writes:

> The "Diamonds" singer is following in the footsteps of one of her role models, late actress and advocate Elizabeth Taylor, who cofounded amfAR, the Elizabeth Taylor AIDS Foundation, and other HIV organizations. In fact, at the 2014 amfAR LA Inspiration Gala, Rihanna bid $100,000 on a photograph of Taylor, which was signed by artist Willy Rizzo. "Everybody loves Elizabeth Taylor!" Rihanna said. "She's very glamorous. She's the best that's ever done it. But it was for a good cause. I didn't mind spending every penny on it, because it all went to charity."[159]

In March 2015 Rihanna gave a concert in Indianapolis, where she was determined to express her feelings about that state's "religious liberty" laws. Between two songs she declared: "Who's feeling these new bullshit laws that they're trying to pass over here? I say fuck that shit! I wanna hear you say fuck that shit! Cause we're just living our motherfucking lives, Indiana!"

She recently had a small but tremendous part in *Valerian and the City of a Thousand Planets* (Luc Besson, 2017); in an admirable piece of casting, she played Bubbles, a funny and tragic shape-shifter who works in a strip club, impersonating other people (in the strongest sense of the verb), notably rewriting *Cabaret*'s Liza Minnelli as Sally Bowles, all the better to please gays.

Joan Rivers (1933–2014)

Like many of the icons in this book (Madonna, Meryl Streep, Katharine Hepburn, etc.), Rivers was a relentlessly hard worker. This is how her daughter Melissa Rivers puts it:

Joan Rivers

My mother was a comedian, actress, writer, producer, jewelry monger, tchotchke maker, spokesperson, hand model, *Celebrity Apprentice* winner [...]. The woman was indefatigable. James Brown may have been the hardest-working man in show business, but I'm pretty sure my mother was the hardest-working woman. Even at eighty years old, she was on the go, from gig to gig, show to show, all the time. She was always working, always moving; she was like Sisyphus with jokes [Rivers 2015: 9].

Rivers put in this hard work in the service of her fans; she always had a huge gay fan base, given that what she peddled most was camp, bitchy humor. Everyone knows that she started in 1965 as a guest on *The Tonight Show*, hosted by Johnny Carson. We have watched all of her talk shows over the years. More recently, we have watched hours of *Fashion Police*, *Joan & Melissa: Joan Knows Best*, and *In Bed with Joan*, never tiring of Rivers' special brand of humor.

Arguably, Rivers would not have been half as fabulously camp if she had not owed her looks to highly prized and highly priced cosmetic surgeons. Gays who love artifice are often big fans of plastic surgery, if not for themselves, at least for their icons. She frequently commented upon those artificial looks in a distinctly camp manner. When a ciswoman reaches such a level of reconstruction, she is right up there with people like aerodynamic transwoman Amanda Lepore. One remembers fondly how Rivers used to claim that she wished she had been blessed with a twin sister who would have allowed her to form an idea of her looks unmediated by surgery in her later years.

Here are more samples of her camp humor:

"It's been so long since I made love, I can't even remember who gets tied up" [Warren 2000: 12].

Don't try to sell me that 'inner beauty' bullshit. Just call the electrolysis guy already" [Rivers 2015: 33].

"Men don't want smart. They want gorgeous. No man ever put his hand up a woman's dress looking for a library card" [Rivers 2015: 41].

"Melissa, when it comes to work, pretend you're a hooker during Fleet Week: Say 'Yes' to everything" [Rivers 2015: 50].

That humor can also be sampled in her dozen books, and to a lesser extent in her film work. I believe television was the best medium for her, though.

As she often reminisced, Rivers had two unhappy marriages, which she described very amusingly. She also had a number of lovers, whose names she sometimes disclosed. Like many practitioners of camp humor, she was very good at self-disparagement in both this and other domains. She was involved in quite a lot of philanthropy, including AIDS work.

Diana Ross (1944–)

At age 15, in 1959, Diana Ross became a member of the Primettes. They auditioned for Motown Records in 1960. They were signed in 1961 after changing their name to the Supremes. It is worth noting that in the early days of the band, Ross was everyone's stylist, hairdresser, and makeup artist, already having a sure eye for glamor. At some point in her career she became so obsessed with her appearance because of the outside pressure that she suffered from anorexia. Fragile Diana Ross writes: "Perhaps it was a form of anorexia. I was becoming skin and bones, and eating became repulsive. It was a very unhappy time for me. [...] Although the Supremes were at the top, I often felt as if I were sitting at the bottom of a deep, dark pit. It was no fun" (Ross 1993: 150–151).

The Supremes embody the Motown sound of the 1960s with a series of unforgettable hits such as "Where Did Our Love Go?" (1964), "Baby Love" (1964), "Stop! In the Name of Love" (1965), and "You Can't Hurry Love" (1966). Those songs have all been covered by various male Ross fans, notably gay ones.[160]

> The Supremes [...] helped cross racial barriers, pioneering mainstream success for black artists, and setting a new standard of glitz and glamour with their gorgeous gowns. "I think because we were so glamorous that it automatically was a great attraction for the gay community," original Supreme Mary Wilson told *GayStarNews* earlier this year. "They were the ones who were there at the door first."[161]

In 1975, as a teenager, I had an epiphany at a Cannes nightclub called The Roxy. Overnight I became fascinated by what I didn't yet call the construction of gender, by drag and alternative sexualities, etc. A tremendous creature called Angie Stardust (born Mel Michaels, 1939–2007) sang that night (as opposed to lip-synced). I was utterly convinced her pseudonym was a combination of Angie Bowie, David Bowie's wife, and Ziggy Stardust, David Bowie's persona. What a perfectly glamorous and somewhat camp name! I found out decades later that in reality, she was already using that name in New York clubs by the late 1950s (Jewel Box Review, 82 Club). When I saw her in Cannes she was living in Berlin. You can see her in the movie *Stadt der verlorenen Seelen* (*City of Lost Souls*, Rosa von Praunheim, 1983). "A short while after the movie was finished, Angie went on to have the full sex change," trans punk icon Jayne County writes (County, 1995, 148). She already sported beautiful breasts, and totally delighted her audience when she introduced herself thus (and I believe I'm quoting *verbatim*, though it was more than 40 years ago): "People often ask me, but, Angie, what are you? So I answer, here [pointing at her face] Diana Ross, here [pointing at her breasts] Jayne Mansfield, and here [pointing at her crotch] Cassius Clay!" At this point the audience collapsed with laughter, needless to say. Interestingly, Cassius Clay had changed his name to Muhammad Ali 11 years before, in 1964, and Jayne Mansfield had died in 1967, but no one seemed to hold it against Stardust. In those days I was already interested in Mansfield, and already a fan of Ross, but Stardust got me even more fascinated.

Jaap Kooijman writes: "Diana Ross's first number-one hit single 'Ain't No Mountain High Enough' (1970), a remake of the 1967 Motown duet by Marvin Gaye and Tammi Terrell, is a telling example of the flamboyant and larger-than-life Hollywood star image of Diana Ross. [...] To some, Ross's version embodied the superficiality of the Ross star image" (Kooijman in Bloch & Umansky 2005: 166).[162] Of course, more than a comment upon any feelings of love she might have had, the new version testified to Ross' professional ambition. Being superficial has rarely been an obstacle to gay iconicity. On the other hand, being a flamboyant and larger-than-life woman, as can never be stressed enough, is a requisite.

In her solo career Ross increasingly set out to please gays—who were not complaining—with songs such as "Upside Down" (1980) and the not-so-subtle "I'm Coming Out" (1980). Her cover of the gay anthem "I Will Survive" (from *Take Me Higher*, 1995) was accompanied by a very camp video featuring RuPaul and other drag queens. It is a funny lesson in artifice and glamor, literally a lesson, complete with outrageous big hair, Black-Is-Beautiful style. Ross also has a film career, notably including both *Lady Sings the Blues* (Sidney J. Furie, 1972), a biopic of fellow gay icon Billie Holiday, and *The Wiz* (Sidney Lumet, 1978), an odd movie in which she rewrites fellow gay icon Judy Garland's Dorothy.

RuPaul (1960–)

"You are born naked, the rest is drag," says RuPaul—often. And I, for one, keep quoting that line, both in and out of print. RuPaul was born Rupaul Andre Charles in San Diego and started doing drag in the 1970s. RuPaul is an African American model, actor, singer, songwriter, author, TV host, etc. Now that Divine is no longer with us, RuPaul is simply the most famous drag queen in the world. Every product associated with RuPaul is hugely entertaining, and usually successful. In the video of "Looking Good, Feeling Gorgeous" (2004), RuPaul, looking gorgeous, delivers a hilarious critique of the dictatorial beauty standards of our society while extensively quoting from the voguing classic *Paris Is Burning* (Jennie Livingston, 1990). The video features drag queen Shirley Q. Liquor as a fat woman who wants to get plastic surgery and liposuction. After all the work (bitch), she is transformed into RuPaul. The surgeon (reminiscent of the television series *Nip/Tuck*) is played by a superb male model who shows off his muscles. The video is directed by Mike Ruiz.

In addition to "Looking Good, Feeling Gorgeous," gay viewers will favor the following songs and videos: "Supermodel (You Better Work)" (1992), "Don't Go Breaking My Heart" (1994, with Elton John), "Cover Girl" (2009), "Glamazon" (2011), and "Sissy That Walk" (2014). They will also attentively watch RuPaul's cameos in *To Wong Foo, Thanks for Everything, Julie Newmar* (Beeban Kidron, 1995), *Blue in the Face* (Paul Auster, Wayne Wang & Harvey Wang, 1995), *But I'm a Cheerleader* (Jamie Babbit, 1999), and many TV series.

In *RuPaul's Drag Race* (Logo then VH1, 2009–), drag queens (usually gay men) compete in various challenges, doing everything it takes to avoid being eliminated, trying to last as long as possible in the season and if possible to win the title of "America's Next Drag Superstar." With this show, RuPaul has contributed heavily to the mainstreaming of drag in the U.S. and elsewhere. Those who don't get the proper television channel or live in the wrong country download the episodes illegally, or at least watch excerpts on YouTube. Some dislike this impressive mainstreaming, looking back with nostalgia at the years when you could only see that sort of gay drag in gay clubs. Some welcome it with open arms, and the show's competitors certainly seem to revel in the attention. *RuPaul's Drag Race* is very cleverly structured, allowing each queen to highlight her best features, whether it be acting, singing, makeup, sawing, designing clothes, etc. Some are funnier than others, some are more beautiful, some are fat, some are thin, some are white, some are non-white. RuPaul teaches a political lesson in every episode, one that comes with so many sequins and laughs that you don't necessarily realize you are being taught something. Part pageant, part improv theater, part *American Idol* for drag queens, it is also emotional reality TV at its best (or worst, depending on your point of view): there are fights, confessions, tears, everything to provide a complete spectacle. The ultimate accolade is a pronouncement such as "Congratulations, you're the baddest bitch in town," which RuPaul said to Chad Michaels in Season 4.[163]

RuPaul's Drag Race All Stars (Logo, 2012–) is basically the same as *RuPaul's Drag Race*, but with returning contestants, handpicked for the degree of cult their first appearance generated. It is very much a guilty pleasure, like drinking the second half of that bottle you were saving or starting that second pack of cigarettes or maybe coming home with an ex you know you should not see anymore. Recently RuPaul expressed interesting thoughts on the show: "I'm a marketing genius! I marketed subversive drag to 100 million muthafuckas in the world. I'm a marketing motherfuckin' genius over here."[164] Fans of the program flock to the live shows *RuPaul's Drag Race Battle of the Seasons* all over the world, even if they don't get to see RuPaul, but only other drag queens and Michelle Visage.

RuPaul's Drag Race was already queer and third-wave feminist (even though there are a few ciswomen on the set). *RuPaul's Drag U* (Logo, 2010–2012) often seemed to make a third-wave constructionist argument, and quite deliberately. RuPaul's ciswomen competed in a makeover show coached by drag queens, i.e., men, who basically taught them femininity. No need for study notes to get the point. It was less entertaining than *RuPaul's Drag Race*, but highly worth watching all the same. Some fans, needless to say, had already watched RuPaul in every single one of the 100 episodes of *The RuPaul Show* in the 1990s (VH1, 1996–1998), although that show involved less drag. Everything that RuPaul does proves that those who claim gays have no more use for camp these days are immensely mistaken.

Sheila (1945–)

When I think of French singer Sheila, I immediately think of Christian, a classmate of mine at the University of Nice in the late 1970s. He was a walking caricature, utterly queeny in every way. He spoke in a high-pitched voice, minced around campus in flashy colors, limp-wristed and swishy to the extreme. He bleached his dark hair to a golden ginger, plucked his eyebrows to near oblivion, wore great quantities of cheap foundation and favored high-heeled cowgirl boots. In the fairly safe environment of the Nice campus, he was reasonably well liked and never got into trouble. Most of us enjoyed his sense of humor. But we worried about him the minute he set foot in other neighborhoods.

He spoke English particularly rapidly, with the thickest French accent—a coked-up Maurice Chevalier after a sex change, our friends said. We felt sorry for him and wondered how he was ever going to graduate, considering the percentage of the oral exams in the final grade. We all went to the UK to spend a year as French assistants in secondary schools, and there a most extraordinary scene took place: together with a girl from our group who was also placed in Manchester, I had befriended an extremely aristocratic gentleman, with manners that would have shamed the queen and with the kind of spoken English that I had only heard in David Niven movies. Christian visited and we introduced him to the elitist gentleman, fearing the worst. To our eternal amazement, Christian spoke a ravishingly beautiful English: you would have thought he had been born and bred in the London BBC studios. At this point we realized that all this time he had simply entertained us with his fake Maurice Chevalier accent, as part of his general and incessant camping about. But the story gets better. The next year, he was conscripted, despite his varied and strenuous efforts to escape such a frightening fate. Military service was still compulsory in France in those days. We trembled for his life, certain that the illiterate beefy butch heterosexual homophobic soldiers would make mincemeat of him in the barracks, but Sheila saved him.

Some of my Anglophone readers may remember her. She was popular in France for decades, but also briefly famous in the English-speaking world under the name Sheila B. Devotion or Sheila Black Devotion (it was never clear whether Black Devotion was the name of her band or something else), produced by Chic's Nile Rodgers himself. She was especially popular in gay discos, where people whirled to "Spacer" (1980). As one might expect, Christian was a great practitioner of diva worship, and Sheila was his all-time favorite (he called her a diva, I did not); he knew all of the lyrics to her songs by heart and could reproduce her every dance move. I fancy this is what saved him from torture: he became the mascot of the regiment, entertaining the privates (pun intended) with heartfelt renditions of Sheila's oeuvre practically every evening, putting his high-heeled cowgirl boots back on for a while before bedtime. He came back unscathed after a whole year of this, and he became a "salesgirl" (as he put it) at the largest sex shop in downtown Nice—but that is another story. AIDS has taken him from us, may he rest in peace.

The question this story asks is, obviously, is this camp? Did camp save Christian? Did diva worship save Christian? Did Sheila's gay iconicity save Christian? In many respects, Christian's army days bring to mind the World War II drag shows of the British and American armies. Back in 1990 I read Allan Bérubé's *Coming Out Under Fire*, along with British actor Kenneth Williams' 1985 autobiography, which confirmed many of my intuitions. To this day I believe that had Christian been just a little bit *less* queeny, he would have been "queer-bashed" from Day One. One must boost the morale of the troops, no? What are camp followers for? In the UK, as it happens, Christian was often dubbed "camp," but as I observed early on, in the U.S. people were and are more parsimonious with the word and in that particular context would have more readily labeled him a queen, a sissy, or something of the sort. Today they might even call him "femme" or "fem."

In the 1960s, Sheila was a "yé-yé" singer. These days, she is mostly a plastic-surgery disaster, as Google Images will show you, and as she herself admits, obviously not having had access to Catherine Deneuve's surgeon. She looks like a lynx, although not as painfully so as socialite Jocelyne Wildenstein.[165] She has not really done anything interesting since 1980 by my exacting standards, but that does not mean she has not been active or that she is any less congenial. Records, tours, television shows, she has even dabbled in writing.

In July 2017, her son Ludovic Chancel apparently killed himself (although some claim it was an accident), at the age of 42, adding a layer of tragedy to her iconicity. It seemed he rarely saw his show-business mother as a child and never quite recovered.[166]

The problem is that whereas Sylvie Vartan acquired a measure of artistic credibility and Françoise Hardy is cool personified, Sheila has increasingly been seen as unsophisticated, cheesy, dim-witted, and politically dubious. If one did not fear accusations of political incorrectness one could state that in a way, she is the icon of gay French peasants. She remains in the heart of many French fans across the board, mostly over 60.

Britney Spears (1981–)

I once participated in a cultural-studies workshop in the South entitled "Going South." This title definitely inspired me. Beyond its obvious geographical meaning, "going south" also means "cunnilingus" or "fellatio." What is more, it means "taking a turn for the worse," "getting worse," "losing it," and "freaking out," among other things. That last meaning particularly interested me. I immediately thought of the late Anne Nicole Smith (1967–2007). Poor, tragic Anna Nicole Smith, born and raised in Texas, model, Playboy playmate, reality TV celebrity. Some say she is a gay icon. She had a son at age 19 and a daughter at age 39. Many people know her mostly for her marriage to billionaire J. Howard Marshall, 63 years her senior—an extreme form of sugar-babying if ever there was one. What gay fans struggling with weight issues themselves particularly remember is how she gained 60 pounds, then lost them, then gained them again ... moving from gorgeous and well-groomed to fat-slobbish-cow-lounging-in-her-slippers and back again, all in the public eye.

But more than of Texan Anna Nicole Smith, the title of the workshop made me think of Britney Spears, another woman who's often been perceived as a Southern tramp rather than a Southern Belle. I had learned with undisguised fascination in a 1999 issue of *Rolling Stone* that "Britney Spears likes to relax with candles, a bath and a Jackie Collins novel." She told the magazine: "Every night, I have to read a book so that my mind will stop thinking about the things I stress about."[167] Isn't that adorable? A gay icon reading a gay icon to find comfort. As it happens, Spears' life and career are the stuff of Jackie Collins novels and tabloids.

Many gay men love Jackie Collins novels and tabloids. In the 1920s, 1930s, 1940s and 1950s, many gay men loved movie magazines. Those were all fan magazines, quite unlike the more "serious" movie magazines that came later. Anthony Slide writes:

> An argument might certainly be made that just as the fan magazines appealed to young women, they also held a fascination for a gay readership, anxious to revel in Hollywood glamour and thrilled to find a suggestion that the film industry might very well be home to many of their orientation. As Patrick O'Connor recalled, "When I was a boy, I used to read the girl-next-door's fan magazine. I wouldn't want to be seen with one as a boy—it would have been considered sissy—but I read hers" [Slide 2010: 169].

Today's gay men are also known to buy teen fan magazines. Although such magazines still chronicle the adventures of female idols such as Spears, they also offer quite a lot of man candy that teenage girls and gay men alike love drooling over. One of the best examples in recent years is the *Twilight* craze (2008–2012), in which hundreds of magazines all over the globe published a great many pictures of a muscular and shirtless Taylor Lautner (members of Camp Jacob will know what I mean).

Spears was born in Mississippi and grew up in Louisiana. Before the age of 8 she was already a seasoned gymnast, dancer and singer. From age 11 to age 13 she worked for the Disney Channel (just like fellow pop performers Christina Aguilera and Justin Timberlake), appearing in The New Mickey Mouse Club. In 1998 she released her first single, "Baby One More Time." The album *Baby One More Time* came out in January 1999; she was 17. It was followed by *Oops!...I Did It Again* (2000), *Britney* (2001), *In the Zone* (2003), *Blackout* (2007), *Circus* (2008), *Femme Fatale* (2011), *Britney Jean* (2013), and *Glory* (2016), many of them gay favorites.

As most Americans remember, for years Spears promoted herself as a virgin. It clearly doesn't matter in the least whether she really did remain a virgin until she'd dated Justin Timberlake for a while, in her late teens, or whether she actually gave it away to Southern boyfriend Reg Jones at age 14, or to whomever. What is *really* interesting is the marketing behind it all. She was packaged as a naughty Lolita performing in a little schoolgirl uniform, looking just like a pseudo-pedophile's dream straight out of some kinky Japanese manga[168]; all the while proudly proclaiming her virginity.

She simultaneously functioned both as many an American straight male's wet dream and as a role model for Southern evangelists who preach about chastity and extol the virtues of virginity. To top it all off, she became a gay icon both because gays loved dancing to her songs and because gays approached it all with a great deal of ironic distance.

Socrates said: "an unexamined life is not worth living." Surely Spears agreed, for a certain number of years. It would seem, however, that she occasionally has severe doubts now. In "Piece of Me" (2008), she complains that the media will not let her live in peace, even when she is trying to be a decent working mother. She knows perfectly well that she has embodied the American Dream for a number of years, and she bemoans the fact that everyone insists on behaving as a cannibalistic voyeur when it comes to her career, but especially her life. In *The Truman Show* (Peter Weir, 1998), Truman Burbank famously lives in a gigantic fishbowl under the scrutiny of millions of TV viewers, unaware of the fact that his entire life (from infancy) has in fact been a vast reality show.... Like Spears, he lives in La La Land. Every object in his home and neighborhood is a prop, every person he talks to an actor. Just like Spears—at least until fairly recently. And for Spears, too, it all started at a very early age. In a very Baudrillardesque way, she continued living in Disneyland even after she quit Disney. She lived in an America that was not "real, but of the order of the hyperreal and of simulation." (Baudrillard 1981: 25). She made a lot of unreal money that her parents stashed away somewhere while they bought her plastic toys and synthetic dresses and sequined costumes. Like Truman Burbank, she literally grew up in the spotlight (so did Michael Jackson before her—and look what it did to him).

Although not exactly white-trash, originally (more middle-class, really), it is hard not to think of Spears as the epitome of Southern white trash. No disrespect intended to either Southerners or underprivileged classes. She embodies a very appealing form of Southern kitsch, similar to that of Graceland, and where would we be without Elvis Presley? Spears is a bit vulgar, her grammar is fairly bad, and her vocabulary a tad limited (after all, she did spend a lot of time reading mind-numbing lines off a teleprompter instead of learning school lessons). She is also terribly fragile and utterly endearing, in the way a lost puppy is endearing. Even when she's wearing thousands of dollars' worth of designer duds and jewelry she manages to look rather cheap (see also Dolly Parton). As revealed in the tabloids, her relatives seem to have extremely bad taste, notably in clothing.

Spears went from 1950s-style cheerleader to self-destructive walking disaster. From sweet 16 to drunk driver and "bad mom"; Success simply made her lose it at some point. She never did anything really impressive on screen (apart from some great work in her music videos, that is): in true Elvis style, she starred in a terrible movie, *Crossroads* (Tamra Davis, 2002). In January 2004 she married her childhood friend Jason Allen Alexander. The marriage lasted exactly 55 hours. In September 2004 she married Kevin Federline (an uninspired rapper, among other things). They had two children and a very messy divorce, with a highly publicized custody battle.

In September 2007 Spears staged one of her comebacks: she sang the single "Gimme More" at the MTV VMAs. It is a tremendous song, as far as her (thankfully) formatted pop vehicles go, but her performance was an absolute disaster. She couldn't lip-sync to save her life, let alone remember the dance moves. What was worse, though, was the amazing cruelty of the U.S. and UK media, which with few exceptions called her "fat," "bloated," "flabby," "pot-bellied," etc. How many of the women journalists who trashed her have a body like that after two children, one wonders. As expected, many gays were among the first to vent venomous comments, while simultaneously identifying with her and showing empathy. Everyone predicted that this was the end of her, that she would never sell a record again; yet the album sold rather well and she bounced back, just as she bounced back from every bad patch after that. She is helped by exciting videos in which she alludes to her schizophrenic tendencies and moves well compared to her performance on that infamous MTV VMA show.

In 2003, it looked like everything was going well: she was French-kissed by Madonna at the MTV VMAs in front of millions of excited viewers while participating in a very interesting hyper-referenced rewrite of "Like a Virgin" that delighted gay men all over the world. She performed with Madonna in the rather Sapphic video of "Me Against the Music"[169] and was practically hailed by all as the next Madonna, the rightful heiress to a gay-icon dynasty. Interestingly, no one made much of Christina Aguilera also being French-kissed by Madonna that day. The fact that everyone was convinced she, Christina, had lost her virginity at a very early age is one explanation.

During her worst train-wreck period it seems Spears did it all: alcohol, illegal drugs, legal drugs, dubious friendships (Lindsay Lohan, Paris Hilton), partying, clubbing, and forgetting to wear underwear when everyone knows paparazzi love taking famous girls' pictures as they climb out of cars.[170] The paparazzi never gave her a minute of respite. One infamous day she stormed into a hairdressing salon and demanded that her head be shaved. When the staff refused, she took it upon herself to shear her mane—in front of paparazzi cameras, naturally.[171] There are conflicting explanations: some say she just went berserk (shaving your head is cheaper than heroin and less permanent than wrist-slashing), others say she was trying to get rid of hair-follicle evidence of drug use in her custody lawsuit. When she was hospitalized, her confidential medical records were sold to the media.

In 2007, her hot-mess life was a 24/7 seedy peepshow. Her sartorial ventures, which had always been bad in her best periods, became simply horrendous (I can't think of any famous singer in the U.S. who is a worse dresser, even in country music). Her life was one of the Internet's top ten stories. There was even a site called whenisbritneygoingtodie.com, which has not been very active lately.

So, Spears may not be Southern white trash in the economic sense of the word, but she is kitsch, and Southern, and white, and trashy, and hyperreal. She's Vegas on legs. Sometimes fat legs, sometimes thin legs. And millions of us watch the variations in her weight with the greatest interest. She is exactly the kind of trash that makes American popular culture so great, delights gay men, and drives some of us academics to specialize in it. She has been through train-wreck periods, but then she gets up and tells herself, get back to work. Gays absolutely love diva train wrecks who pull themselves up by their garter belts.

As Joel Stein wrote in *Time* magazine in April 2011: "[All gay icons] have a much better deal than having straight-dude fans. The moment you stop playing your sport, they ignore you and your sad suburban autograph signings. But if you're a gay icon and get addicted to meth, stop working and abuse your assistant, your fans just love you more for it." Stein was astonished to find out, he remembers, that "having a penis is unappealing to gay men's iconography."[172]

It is impossible not to disagree with several passages in Daniel Harris' book *The Rise and Fall of Gay Culture*. Initially, the title itself is challenging:

it would be easy to show that gay culture has been rising for more than a century. It all depends what you mean by the expression. Over many pages, Harris describes the various mechanisms that led gay men in the pre–Stonewall years to promote the gay iconicity of some female performers. Alas, he generally takes no precautions whatsoever, oversimplifying the issue and writing very unpleasant paragraphs in which both divas and their gay admirers are reduced to boring and mindless puppets. Moreover, if Harris were right on all accounts, Britney Spears would not exist—or at any rate, she would not sell so many records. In summary, he basically claims that the whole gay iconicity phenomenon is a thing of the past, and that the only reasons gay men lionized Hollywood divas were that they were closeted, homosexuality was invisible in the media (at least in undisguised forms), and society was horribly homophobic. Gay men used divas to recognize each other, to gather at concerts, and that is all. He even goes so far as to see those diva worshippers as naïve morons[173] practicing self-deception, tricking themselves into believing that they adored their idols when they really did not, all the time implying that they were too stupid to appreciate their art, and/or that their idols were not very beautiful, talented, or anything else. More than awkward, this is seriously offensive (Harris 1997: *passim*).

Harris speaks of one single form of camp that he presents as universal. "Camp is about the death of glamor," he writes. In contrast, this book never stops associating camp and glamor. "Camp is rooted in the gay man's profound disillusionment with celebrity culture," he claims. Which gay man? Himself? This book is entirely about the unwavering gleeful engagement of gay men with celebrity culture (Harris 1997: 30). Harris is under the impression that young gays (in the 1990s) have no use for gay icons, whether of the past or of the present. We cannot have been mixing with the same young men. He sees camp as concerned with stars only if they are decaying. His presentation of the complex interaction of multifaceted drag queens with star performers is extremely reductive, as is his pronouncing gay diva worship "a religion that failed" (Harris 1997: 33). In his Introduction, he goes so far as to declare, "the love of actresses has become the ridicule of actresses," not pausing to consider whether the two might not go hand in hand (Harris 1997: 3).

With a more measured approach, Melissa Bradshaw wonders about the mechanisms that account for our tendency to chase, guzzle up and demolish our icons. She mentions a few movies that show neurotic or psychotic fans busy crawling at the feet of their idols or destroying them, sometimes both; but what of more ordinary fans such as Bradshaw or you or me? She reminds us of the crucial things queer critics such as Alexander Doty and Wayne Koestenbaum have said about the crucial role of the diva in gay culture, in the context of camp as resistance. She then undertakes a psychoanalytical reading of the diva as fetishized mother and explains that "our adoration is equivocal." She draws parallels with Roman circus games, observes how we are out for blood, and writes:

> Matt Lauer's recent *Dateline NBC* interview with Britney Spears, in which the singer—disheveled, weepy, inarticulate, smacking gum—appeared to be having a nervous breakdown on camera as she described herself as an "emotional wreck" due to the relentless pressure of constant public scrutiny, might be the contemporary equivalent of just this sort of blood-thirsty spectacle. However, for audiences trained, in part, by Madonna's *Truth or Dare* [...], to regard any claims of authenticity with postmodern skepticism and irony, this on-camera confession of emotional instability, in an interview initiated by the singer herself, reads as yet another layer of performance. Is it possible to read this "disastrous" Spears interview—at one point she cried so hard that one of her false eyelashes came loose—as a brilliant and strategic performance of the abjection central to the diva diegetic, an abjection audiences are conditioned to want and expect? [Bradshaw in Doty, *Camera Obscura* 67, 70–72].

As it happens, in 2004, Britney Spears was featured in a Pepsi commercial (Super Bowl special) together with Pink and Beyoncé. The three singers play slaves in Ancient Rome who have become gladiators and refuse to fight in the arena, instead singing Queen's "We Will Rock You" and literally overturning the Caesar played by Enrique Iglesias. Three empowering divas for the price of one and shades of sacrificial violence: how generous can you get? Whether her breakdowns are as staged as that Pepsi commercial, partially so or not at all does not matter, it is all part of one great big entertainment continuum. In the television series *Daytime Divas*, Dr. Justin Timmerman (Cuyle Carmin) tells Maxine, one of the hosts of a daytime talk show (Vanessa Williams), that he thinks "Britney Spears is hot," to which she immediately replies: "So you're gay."[174]

In the postmodern age women like Spears are hypermediatized, sacrificed on the altar of celebrity culture, and we do not even have to come out of the house to buy tabloids from the newsstand down the block anymore (though we still regularly do, of course), we simply click on the bookmark of our favorite gossip website and learn all the latest, most sensational news. The rest of the time, we can gyrate to her fabulously commercial dance tunes both in and out of clubs. It's Britney, bitch.[175]

Dusty Springfield (1939–1999)

John Forde writes in the *Routledge Encyclopedia of Queer Culture*: "Hailed as one of Britain's greatest female vocalists, Dusty Springfield [...] is also a gay icon, her status earned through memorable torch song performances and her trademark blonde bouffant hair, 'panda eye' makeup and turbulent struggles with bisexuality and alcoholism." (Forde in Gerstner 2006: 534) Part of the attraction was also the white soul[176] Springfield sold, musically emulating African American girl singers of the late 1950s and early 1960s. Some called her the "Great White Lady" of soul. During the UK's mod era she even became the Queen of Mods.

The following songs are on many a gay man's playlist: "I Only Want to Be with You" (1963),[177] "I Just Don't Know What to Do with Myself" (1964), "You Don't Have to Say You Love Me" (1966), "The Look of Love" (1967), and "Son of a Preacher Man" (1968); the latter was the reason many Europeans thought she was American (she had turned all Memphis on them) and was made popular again by *Pulp Fiction* (Quentin Tarantino, 1994).

In 1972, Springfield released an album entitled *See All Her Faces*. One of the tracks was a tremendous cover of Charles Aznavour's tremendous song "Yesterday When I Was Young" (1964). How could this song not be a gay favorite? Over the years, it has been sung by many gay favorites, including Shirley Bassey, Marc Almond and Elton John. The lyrics tell all about having once been young and egotistic, concerned only with partying a lot, without pausing to consider the meaning of existence—and then being caught up by age.

Picture an aging gay man, an aesthete forever in lust with youthful bodies, looking at his decayed body in the mirror and looking back upon his youthful years spent in bars and clubs, drinking booze, doing drugs and picking up strange men, never forming solid, lifelong attachments.

Springfield got them. Straight singer Charles Aznavour possibly got them too (he who wrote "Comme ils disent"/"What Makes a Man" in 1972, about a lonely gay man), but he didn't look half as glamorous. Gays particularly loved her hyper-sensual voice.

In 1987 she collaborated with the Pet Shop Boys, who love a good old camp icon, and who know how to stoke the fire of gay iconicity, as I already mentioned in my Liza Minnelli entry (they also produced Kylie Minogue), their single "What Have I Done to Deserve This?" was a huge success, notably with gays. Patricia Juliana Smith writes: "Dusty Springfield paradoxically expressed and disguised her own unspeakable queerness through an elaborate camp masquerade that metaphorically and artistically transformed a nice white girl into a black woman and a femme gay man, often simultaneously" (Smith in Smith 1999: 106). Pat Reid confirms "With her towering steel-blonde beehive, panda-eyed make-up and slightly grannyish gowns [Dusty Springfield was] a gift to drag queens" (Norton & Reid, 1999, 30). Indeed, she remained a model for drag queens for decades on both sides of the Atlantic, drag queens who knew that she herself had devised her look by borrowing from fellow gay icon Catherine Deneuve, along with other big-haired European blondes.

Barbara Stanwyck (1907–1990)

Every biographer agrees that Barbara Stanwyck was tough. She actually made a career out of being a strong woman both on- and off-screen. She and other tough gals were always an inspiration for gay men. "Homosexuals consumed, assimilated, and recycled Hollywood images in such vast quantities and with such intense passion," writes Daniel Harris, that it may lead one to wonder if the gay movement might have developed later if gays hadn't been stimulated by their identification with Hollywood models of strong women. "Shit-kicking amazons in sequins, ermine, and lamé became [...] integral to homosexuals' self-images [...]" (Harris 1997: 15).

Comparisons with fellow gay icon Joan Crawford are always in order. Antoine Sire writes: "Contrary to Joan Crawford who imbues all her characters with the bitter perfume of her pathological egoism, Barbara Stanwyck radiates as much generosity as strength, except in a few noir films in which plays classic monsters" (Sire 2016: 163, my translation). A Ziegfeld Follies chorus girl at 15 (still using her own name of Ruby Stevens), she fought her way to the top and was equally at ease in every movie, although we tend to favor her melodramas and noir movies. Obviously, film noir heroines often make good gay icons.

In *Stella Dallas* (King Vidor, 1937), Stanwyck plays a woman whose daughter is the only focus of her life after she separates from her husband. Stella is determined to give Laurel a more-than-decent future, and no sacrifice is too great. This movie is very much about class, and Stanwyck is excellent as the woman fighting adversity—lower-class gays identified even more. In *Ball of Fire* (Howard Hawks, 1941) she plays Sugarpuss O'Shea, a singer who teaches slang to a group of distinguished professors. At times she is both hilarious and quite delightfully vulgar. Gay men love their icons when they do vulgarity. In the noir masterpiece *Double Indemnity* (Billy Wilder, 1944), Stanwyck wears tremendous femme-fatale costumes by Edith Head, very loud lipstick and a big blonde wig. She chills the viewers to the bone. It could very well be her most iconic performance.

All I Desire (Douglas Sirk, 1953) was adapted from the eponymous novel by Carol Ryrie Brink (1953). In it Stanwyck plays Naomi, a showgirl who abandoned her husband, children and lover in small-town America to go to the big city and try to make it in the theater. She returns, and that's when the drama begins. Stanwyck is perfect as the "different" woman who escaped. In *There's Always Tomorrow* (Douglas Sirk, 1955) she plays the "other woman," as opposed to the wife played by Joan Bennett. Sirk always knew how to look at things from the feminine point of view, and that is one of the reasons he was such a good director, an icon monger and a gay favorite.

Many critics see Stanwyck's part in *Walk on the Wild Side* (Edward Dmytryck, 1962) as more annoying than anything else, a predatory lesbian procurer who fails to convince the viewers. Perhaps things are more complicated than that. It is a bad adaptation of a flawed if somewhat legendary novel (inspiring gay favorite Lou Reed's totally legendary song of the same title). Her part did little to diminish her gay iconicity, even if it is less interesting, to be honest, than Capucine's or Jane Fonda's roles.

Stanwyck added something new to westerns, notably through her part in the television series *The Big Valley* (ABC, 1965–1969), which was quite interesting. She even played Mary Carson in the four-episode series *The Thorn Birds* (ABC, 1983), adapted from Colleen McCullough. More remarkably for our purposes, she was featured in *Dynasty* (and its spinoff, *The Colbys*) in 1985 and 1986, to the delight of the millions of gay fans of the show.

When her character was shown singing in a movie, she was dubbed half the time, which was a regrettable waste. If you YouTube her and listen to her sing with that husky voice of hers, you will certainly agree. She could do accents, change social class at will—not as spectacularly as, say, Meryl Streep, but convincingly enough. She was nominated several times but never took home an Oscar for best performance (she got a lifetime achievement Oscar in 1982, which validated her gay worshippers).

She was married to actor Frank Fay (they adopted a boy whom she apparently raised with few demonstrations of affection),[178] then to actor Robert Taylor. She divorced him too. She is rumored to have had various interesting affairs, including one with Henry Fonda, who greatly admired her—and some with women (Schiavi 2011: 175).[179]

Stanwyck insisted on being dressed by Edith Head as often as possible: this is another reason gays like her. In addition, she turned cougarish in the 1950s, dating Robert Wagner when he was 22 and she 45—which many find quite lovely.

Meryl Streep (1949–)

Why is Meryl Streep a gay icon? Various websites have addressed this question over the years.[180] She herself has a few things to say about her affinity for gay people. She has been around gays for decades, beginning in childhood. She loves gays, works with gays, plays gay, etc. But if all those elements were enough to make a gay icon this book would be much thicker. She is a repressed opera diva, as it were, considering opera was her first choice as a child before she moved on to theater and film. Maybe some of it stuck.

Meryl Streep

There is every chance that the principal feature of Streep's gay iconicity is her chameleonism. She is not a chameleon in life, where on the contrary has a strong, distinct personality and never refrains from standing out and speaking her mind; but she is very possibly the best living actress. She is notorious for her accents, in particular, most of them extraordinarily convincing. She can play anything, anybody, from anywhere. Like a Protean creature, she morphs into whoever she needs to portray. She might not deal in artifice like so many other gay icons, being anti-plastic surgery, anti–L.A., and not prone to strutting around in heels and heavy makeup,[181] but she makes up for it with this magical shape-shifting talent of hers.

This is how IMDb introduces her: "Considered by many critics to be the greatest living actress, Meryl Streep has been nominated for the Academy Award an astonishing 20 times, and has won it three times."[182] She has also received 30 Golden Globe nominations, and a truckload of awards and medals. Only those shiny Streep products that have attracted a serious gay following will be reviewed below.

We should begin with *The Deer Hunter* (Michael Cimino, 1978), if only because that is when we realized Streep was hugely talented as an actress. *Kramer vs. Kramer* (Robert Benton, 1979) is the best custody battle ever filmed. *The French Lieutenant's Woman* (Karel Reisz, 1981) is a more-than-acceptable adaptation of John Fowles' eponymous novel, boasting gay favorite Jeremy Irons and featuring Streep walking around with the worst hair in her career. Then there are the great accents, regional and foreign, in *Sophie's Choice* (Alan J. Pakula, 1982), *Silkwood* (Mike Nichols, 1983), *Plenty* (Fred Schepisi, 1985), and *Out of Africa* (Sydney Pollack, 1985). In *She-Devil* (Susan Seidelman, 1989), she plays a glamorous romance writer who is obsessed with youth and beauty and plastic surgery, like many rich and famous people in our ageist, lookist and fattist society. In *Postcards from the Edge* (Mike Nichols, 1990), a Carrie Fisher story, she plays alongside Shirley MacLaine.

Mark Simpson sees a great deal of misogyny in *Death Becomes Her* (Robert Zemeckis, 1992), perhaps it is instead a movie about an extreme form of drag, and it is certainly a gay favorite (Simpson 1994: 185). In it, Streep hams it up to the max, to the utmost delight of millions of gay fans worldwide who regularly watch it. In *The Bridges of Madison County* (Clint Eastwood, 1995), Streep is terribly convincing as Francesca, a performance inspired by Italian greats such as Sophia Loren and Anna Magnani.

It's amusing to think that fellow gay icon Madonna was to play the lead in *Music of the Heart* (Wes Craven, 1999), but in the end Streep got the part and did well, although perhaps not as brilliantly as elsewhere. Curiously, three years before, Streep was considered for the part of Eva Perón in *Evita* (Alan Parker, 1996) ultimately snatched by Madonna, who energetically campaigned for it. Streep played the part of Clarissa Vaughan alongside Nicole Kidman as Virginia Woolf and Julianne Moore as Laura Brown in *The Hours* (Stephen Daldry, 2002), adapted from gay writer Michael Cunningham's novel. She played alongside Al Pacino and Emma Thompson in the adaptation of gay playwright Tony Kushner's six-hour *Angels in America* (HBO, 2003). Her role in *The Devil Wears Prada* (David Frankel, 2006) is one of her campest. The movie has become cultish, and even gay men who do not care for the novel and dislike chick lit love Streep's performance as Miranda Priestly, and not only because they admire Anna Wintour, who inspired her.

I discussed *Mamma Mia!* (Phylidda Lloyd, 2008) in the Agnetha Fält-skog entry. If Streep had not yet achieved gay iconicity, that movie might have single-handedly brought it to her. Then there was *The Iron Lady* (Phyllida Lloyd, 2011). It is said that Streep donated every penny she got from that movie to the National Women's History Museum, with which she is involved. She established in various interviews that although she was against Margaret Thatcher's politics, she admired her as a woman who reached the top and as a woman who had firm opinions, was afraid of no one, and was prepared to be disliked if that was what it took. I lived in the UK during the Thatcher years and vividly remember the hatred all of my friends felt for her. I occasionally tried to voice the opinion that she could still be a feminist role model, however anti-feminist and fascistic she was, but was vehemently rebuked.

In *Suffragette* (Sarah Gavron, 2015), she plays a small part, but because it is that of feminist heroine Emmeline Pankhurst, it seems only fitting that she should have agreed to play it—she is one herself, *mutatis mutandis*. In *Ricki and the Flash* (Jonathan Demme, 2015) she plays a rock 'n' roller who abandoned her family to pursue success as a musician. The problem with that movie is that it is a bit of a caricature, so even though she is doing her best, she cannot quite save it from mediocrity. Still, it offers her fans a rare glimpse of Streep as a funny—if aging—rock chick. In *Florence Foster Jenk-ins* (Stephen Frears, 2016) she went back to the opera-singing dreams of her youth, and must have found very amusing to play a painfully bad singer. In Streep's early days, fellow gay icon Bette Davis wrote an extremely flattering letter to her, declaring that Streep was her worthy successor as the "premier American actress." One can only hope she framed it, considering she once very famously lost an Oscar in a public bathroom.

As far as her private life is concerned, Streep engages in none of the hypermediatized *Sturm und Drang* that appeals to the gay readers of the sensationalist press. Streep had a two- or three-year relationship with actor John Cazale, who died of cancer at the young age of 42. She always refuses to discuss this with the media. Her husband is a sculptor, and she has four children, who are into modeling, singing and acting, among other things. By all accounts she leads a subdued and tranquil life, in spite of her huge stardom.

Another element of her personality gays love is her politics. She is a feminist, a very left-wing Democrat, an intellectual of sorts, etc. She has angered more than one politician, knowing that because she is so high profile, she has a forum to express her views. In February 2017, she received the HRC's Ally for Equality Award, which is basically the most prestigious LGBTQ+ award. Her devoted fans, notably gay ones, who think she is an acting genius, call themselves "Streepers." Her detractors, such as Donald Trump, think she is overrated.

Barbra Streisand (1942–)

Logically enough, this book began with Barbra Streisand, featured in the Introduction for her "role" in the movie *In & Out*. Encapsulating the use and *raison d'être* of gay icons, David Munk writes: "In my identification with Barbra Streisand, I felt two things I desperately longed for: validation and hope." Further on he adds: "The Streisand persona, a powerful tonic for all the world's exceptional outcasts, was delineated by an abiding belief that outsiders could achieve not only mainstream acceptance, but massive cultural impact."[183]

Various books insist on her Jewishness, showing how it is inseparable from her star persona—possibly like Grace Jones' blackness. Such territories are dangerous to tread, but fascinating. Many critics have commented upon Streisand's nose, which she herself calls a Jewish nose and (like Bette Midler) refused to surgically alter. Such statements are obviously problematic, politically speaking. Perhaps we could at least evoke the minority factor: Mylène Farmer explains the fact that gays love her thus: she is different, they are different, they identify with her difference. See William J. Mann's book *Hello Gorgeous: Becoming Barbra Streisand* (2012) and Neal Gabler's *Barbra Streisand: Redefining Beauty, Femininity, and Power*, in the "Jewish Lives" collection (2016).

Gay icon Dorothy Parker took part in the writing of the script of *A Star Is Born* (William A. Wellman, 1937), which starred gay favorite Janet Gaynor. Some say the story is based on the life and career of gay icon Barbara Stanwyck. It is now well documented that Gaynor was a lesbian and her husband a gay man. Seventeen years later, Judy Garland starred in the much better-known remake, *A Star Is Born* (George Cukor, 1954). It is debatable whether Streisand appropriated some of the gay iconicity of Judy Garland or whether she simply redefined gay iconicity for the 1970s (while prolonging the old Broadway/Hollywood multitalented leading lady tradition) when she was featured in the second remake, *A Star Is Born* (Frank Pierson, 1976). I recommend you YouTube "Barbra Streisand Judy Garland Ethel Merman": you're in for a nice surprise. Three gay icons bantering together can be veritably uplifting.

Amazingly, it was discovered in 2016 that Bradley Cooper had begun working on the pre-production of yet another remake, scheduled for 2018, this time with Lady Gaga. There has been Internet buzz about the project for at least six years. The mechanics of stardom and gay iconicity are so interwoven that it seems one needs a gay icon for the *A Star Is Born* story. Gay icon Beyoncé was once rumored to be the producers' choice, as was Jennifer Lopez.

Millions of gays adore Streisand's belting, love crying to her hit torch songs. "Woman in Love" (1980) remains a particular favorite. They also love her movies, delighting in her feminist gender-bending in *Yentl* (Barbra Streisand, 1983), even though she is not inordinately convincing as a boy and one has to do a sizable amount of stretching of one's willing suspension of disbelief. The same goes for Julie Andrews in *Victor Victoria*, of course, and even, perhaps a little less so, as I said earlier, for Katharine Hepburn in *Sylvia Scarlett* (George Cukor, 1935)—whereas Glenn Close, for one, is extremely credible in *Albert Nobbs* (Rodrigo Garcia, 2011).[184] Streisand's gay fans also enjoy *Funny Girl* (William Wyler, 1968) and *Hello, Dolly!* (Gene Kelly, 1969), again and again and again.

Barbra Streisand's son Jason Gould (1966-) is gay and HIV positive. Like his mother, he is an actor and a singer. Apparently he nearly published a tell-all book but finally decided against it. They performed on stage together and recorded a duet, Irving Berlin's "How Deep Is the Ocean?" (2014). It is horribly tempting to suspect that such a hugely iconic gay icon, one with such a degree of gay iconicity, could only have a gay son (as does novelist Anne Rice[185]), but we must refrain from such facile inferences. Interestingly, Christopher Andersen says that it is only when Streisand realized her son Jason was gay that she agreed to express her opinions about gay issues. "'She worked behind the scenes, sure,' said an acquaintance of Jason's. 'But she was never really *out there* until Jason told her he thought he was gay.' Jason would never take credit for his mother's support of gay rights. But, he allowed, 'she certainly got a more inside perspective from me.'" (Andersen 2006: 328) Previously she had been giving money to various charities, including AIDS-related ones, but unlike Madonna, Sharon Stone, Bette Midler and Elizabeth Taylor, she did not like to appear at galas. Now she pleases gays in every possible way, and remains on top.

Donna Summer (1948–2012)

Vicki L. Eaklor remembers that gay bars, baths and bookstores could be "arenas for politicization" and then moves on to the gay nightclubs that played disco music in the 1970s. "Popular artists and songs included Donna Summer ('Love to Love You Baby,' 'Hot Stuff,' 'On the Radio'), Sister Sledge ('We Are Family') and, of course, the Village People, whose costumes and songs 'Macho Man' and 'YMCA' were references to gay culture" (Eaklor 2011: 133). Disco was often camp, Summer was often camp. Summer was a gorgeous black diva whose music made you want either to dance or to have sex. And after you did, maybe you could go picketing.

Peter Shapiro writes about disco and Summer: "There is a ghost in disco's cyborg machine, though: camp. 'I Feel Love' was as camp as a pink poodle wandering onto the set of a Busby Berkeley musical." He explains further: "Never before, with the possible exception of Eartha Kitt, some of the French yé-yé girls, or the most over-the-top Dionne Warwick production, had a record so reveled in its own artifice" (Shapiro 2006: 50).

Donna Summer personified the gayest kind of highly artificial disco (in the best sense of the adjective). Disco music was even more artificial when it hailed from European countries such as Germany (even with American singers), as opposed to the funkier disco that stemmed from American cities. Disco was important to gays in the 1970s because clubbing was important. Because gay clubs were about the only places where you could really let your hair down. In many ways the music of Donna Summer encapsulates the gay life of the 1970s. World famous drag queen The Lady Bunny told *The Huffington Post*:

> I realized that club history is gay history. Younger gays may not need them, but clubs were where gays lived our lives prior to more mainstream acceptance. Clubs were safe spaces where we danced with or kissed a partner of the same sex, fell in love, learned gay lingo and felt safe enough to queen it up on the dance floor to the diva of the day—from Donna Summer to Madonna to Whitney. For decades, clubs were the only establishments where you could see a large group of gay men—besides AA. There was a feeling of community in the club world which I don't think you get much of on Grindr.[186]

However, strictly circumscribing Donna Summer to disco is unfair: she was equally good when she sang rock 'n' roll or show-tunes. Her version of "Don't Cry for Me Argentina" (1993) is priceless—and Goddess knows that many a gay icon recorded that ode to political gay icon Eva Perón.

I cannot avoid the polemic here, the horrible controversy that still exists: some still claim (and years later the Internet is still buzzing about it) that Summer spoke gruesomely homophobic words, at one particular place on one particular day (having become something of a fundamentalist Christian). There are different versions from various sources and I'll deliberately refrain from quoting them. Suffice it to say that some claim she declared AIDS was divine punishment, or even revenge, for gays' sins. Many gay men have been busy denying it. Possibly more gay men have boycotted her music ever since, notably some of her once most-ardent worshippers. David Munk once went to dinner with Paul Jabara and Summer, and convincingly writes:

> At some point during the meal, the conversation came around to [the] subject that seemed painful to Donna [...]. Paul practically screamed to me, "Look at this table, David," with a huge gesture pointing out six gay men, one well-adjusted husband and Donna Summer. "I ask you, is this what the dinner table of a homophobic person would actually look like?" He had a point, but then, I'd never believed the rumors in the first place. "Really, David," Donna said, her voice quiet and touched with sadness, "I love everyone," she added defensively, "I would never, ever make a comment like that." I thought it was odd that she felt compelled to set the record straight to me, a starstruck assistant. "No woman in my position could even function for a day without gay men in her life. I love my gay friends." "You see," Paul added, "She never said that about gay men. She loves us."[187]

Perhaps we'll never know exactly what transpired and whether she did indeed turn against gays when she found Jesus. I for one immediately see the disco balls rolling in the pink and blue laser rays that cut through the smoke the minute I hear the first notes of "Last Dance" (1978). She worked hard for the money.

Gloria Swanson (1899–1983)

As a silent movie star, Gloria Swanson "established herself as the paragon of DeMillean sophistication" (Rosen 1973: 102). DeMille was certainly an iconogenic filmmaker, and the movies they made together, starting with *Don't Change Your Husband* (Cecil B. DeMille, 1919), did a great deal for her career. She started appearing in shorts in 1914, and then was featured in nearly 40 movies between 1919 and 1929. During that period, she was very possibly the biggest star on the planet—and one of the richest. For various reasons, *Sadie Thompson* (Raoul Walsh, 1928) is a big gay favorite. It was based on W. Somerset Maugham's short story "Miss Thompson," aka "Rain" (1921), and the play it inspired, *Rain*, by John Colton and Clemence Randolph (1922). There are other movie versions, including *Rain* (Lewis Milestone, 1932), with gay icon Joan Crawford, and *Miss Sadie Thompson* (Curtis Bernhardt, 1953), with gay icon Rita Hayworth. Gays seem to love a good story about a prostitute seeking a change of life.

The Trespasser (Edmund Goulding, 1929) was Swanson's first talkie.

Erich Von Stroheim directed her in *Queen Kelly* (1929), a movie that cost her a lot of her own money. An excerpt from *Queen Kelly* was to be used very intertextually by Billy Wilder in *Sunset Boulevard* (1950). In that movie Swanson plays Norma Desmond, a walking disaster. A silent movie has-been, she is attempting a comeback and achieves unseen levels of gushy camp. Erich Von Stroheim plays Max Von Mayerling, Desmond's butler, who turns out to be the silent movie director who, in the distant past, discovered Norma Desmond and directed her movies.

She is immensely sad and terribly funny at the same time, and that line at the end, "Alright, Mr. DeMille, I'm ready for my close-up," so incredibly famous and so metaleptic, has contributed a great deal to her gay iconization. She is just like an old queen in tight pants and mascara, out on the town, trying to pick up one last twink before the end, overdoing it terribly and hating the competition. "[Y]ou are the diva, the victim of a conspiracy [...]. [W]hen Gloria Swanson says, at the end of *Sunset Boulevard*, 'All right, Mr. DeMille, I'm ready for my close-up,' she is speaking from the heart of diva rivalry: narcissism, a delusional godhead, makes her feel universally visible" (Koestenbaum 2001: 114). Swanson was not even 50 when she shot that movie, but 50 in 1950 is like 70 today as far as Hollywood actresses are concerned (thanks to plastic surgery, later pregnancies, increased life expectancy, and moderate improvements in women's conditions). In gay years, though, then and now, 50 is pathetically ancient.

Edward Field writes:

> After [*Sunset Boulevard*], I saw her on a TV talk show where she behaved in the same unreal manner, with that affected voice, discussing her obsession with health food to stay young, and when a handsome young actor joined the panel, she ran her forefinger around his manly jaw in admiration, and you could see her as the man eater she probably was—she'd gobble him up in a minute! A true sign of the diva! I was certain that all through the years of neglect, she'd watched her own movies over and over again and had completely identified with her performances on screen. So *Sunset Boulevard* was perfect typecasting [Field in Montlack 2009: 44].

How perfectly gay-iconic. Beside acting, Swanson was an energetic businesswoman and a pioneer of vegetarianism in the U.S. She had three children and six husbands, including two Williams, Wallace Beery, Herbert K. Somborn, Henry de La Falaise, Michael Farmer, William Davey, and William Dufty. She also had many love affairs with a wide range of men, apparently including Cecil B. DeMille and Rudolph Valentino. During her affair with Joe Kennedy, in the 1920s, Swanson actually visited the family several times, having been introduced as "a friend." It is amusing to read the relevant passages in her autobiography and in Rose Kennedy's autobiography. Surely Rose Kennedy was never as naïve as she seemed. It is also amusing to think that Joe Kennedy initiated a pattern: that of a Kennedy man dating (often cheating on his wife with) Hollywood royalty, often gay icons. Even Joe's grandson John-John prolonged the tradition when he dated Madonna.

In her song "Kill the Lights" (2008), gay icon Britney Spears alludes to the "I'm ready for my close-up" line. In that same song she also alludes to gay icon Mae West's equally famous line "Is that a gun in your pocket? Or are you just glad to see me?" Those lines are forever enshrined in the gay pantheon—however tacky the expressions or the concepts.

Elizabeth Taylor (1932–2011)

Elizabeth Taylor begins her book *Elizabeth Takes Off* (1987) thusly: "My name is Elizabeth Taylor. For almost fifty years I've been in the public eye, as child, adolescent, young woman, wife, mother and, now, grandmother" (Taylor 1987: 3). She then goes on to say that she has been under general scrutiny whether she was fat or slim. Further on, she recalls how gay icon Joan Rivers kept ridiculing her fat, claiming after Elizabeth had lost the weight that she (Joan) had performed a service for her (Taylor 1987: 56). Gays are often fans of very politically incorrect stories about weight gain and weight loss. Shamelessly, they rarely refrain from body-shaming, even if (and precisely because) they struggle with their own body image.

Elizabeth Taylor was a total fag hag: that is documented. She had a number of closeted gay actors hurled at her by the studios and learned to enjoy their company. She was a close friend of Roddy McDowall, who everybody knew was gay, although he was never officially out. She befriended James Dean, who everyone now knows was mostly gay. She was also a friend of Montgomery Clift, Rock Hudson, etc. To various degrees, she was supportive to many a gay man (and even to people like Michael Jackson, whose actual sexuality or lack thereof will probably forever remain a mystery). How could she not quickly become a gay icon? I am not claiming that her childish antics with recalcitrant dogs and horses in movies like *Lassie Come Home* (Fred M. Wilcox, 1943) or *National Velvet* (Clarence Brown, 1944) did much to endear her to gays, but soon the grown-up and smoldering Taylor played characters such as Maggie the Cat in *Cat on a Hot Tin Roof* (Richard Brooks, 1958) in her white negligée. Even the not-so-cultured gays who had not seen or read Tennessee Williams' original play could not fail to distinguish the gay (sub)text. Of course football-playing Brick and Skipper had a beautiful bromance in the beautiful pre-diegetic past. It matters little whether beautiful Brick actually ever let Skipper have any intimate access to any part of his body: clearly, Skipper was head over heels in love with him (Guilbert 2004: 87–88). In a way, Maggie could be hated by the gay viewer, because she embodies "compulsory heterosexuality" in more ways than one (Rich 1980). She signifies adulthood, responsibilities, reproduction, as opposed to the good old childish sporty fun Brick had with Skipper. But she does so in such a devastatingly gorgeous manner, with her violet eyes, her hard body (which had not yet deteriorated), and a delightful accent, that gays forgave her. Besides, the gays knew that she was often really a "Female Front" in such vehicles, hovering above the gay meaning. And Paul Newman was so exquisite, with his blue eyes that were actually shot in a close-up in cinemascope, how could gay men not understand Maggie and relate to her, what with her seduction techniques and everything?

Before Maggie, Taylor had played Angela Vickers in *A Place in the Sun* (George Stevens, 1951) alongside supremely beautiful Montgomery Clift, who was responsible for many a moviegoing boy's early discovery of gay leanings. In *Suddenly Last Summer* (Joseph L. Mankiewicz, 1959), whether she is the "Female Front" hiding/highlighting the "Homosexual Behind" or the "Female Gay Man" or the "Gay Male Woman" or whatever (Miller 1997: 34–58), she is producing the gay meaning for gay male viewers while being devastatingly gorgeous in her white swimsuit and extremely desirable to straight male viewers; "queer bait," some say. Then she played model Gloria Wandrous in *Butterfield 8* (Daniel Mann, 1960), a sugar-babying beauty who yearns for respectability.

One of the most stupendous elements in Elizabeth Taylor lore is her signification of the end of the studio system, the end of an era, in 1962.

Elizabeth Taylor

She was notoriously helped in that enterprise by fellow gay icon Marilyn
Monroe, who died in August 1962 while ruining the shooting of the aforementioned *Something's Got to Give*, as we saw earlier. After Theda Bara,
Claudette Colbert, and Vivien Leigh, it was Taylor's turn to play a Hollywood Cleopatra. What is there not to love? Artifice pushed to the extreme,
camp outfits and divine headdresses. Cleopatra is the greatest seductress
of all time: no wonder Taylor was able to appropriate her myth. And that
myth was the downfall of the tremendous myth-making factory: old Hollywood with its studio system and its star system. The shooting of *Cleopatra* (Joseph L. Mankiewicz, 1963) practically ruined 20th Century–Fox,
brought it to its knees. It marked the end of big-budget epics. Everything
that could go wrong went wrong. But what do Taylor fans remember?
That an absolute fortune was spent on her dresses and jewelry alone, and
that she looks magnificent in the movie, that she is as regal as she needs
to be, a regal queen embodying another regal queen, a historic man-eater
playing another historic man-eater. Fittingly, the Romans are shown resent-
ing Cleopatra and her ostentatious jewelry in the movie, which reflects
the way some resented Taylor and her excesses in those days.

Next, she played Martha in *Who's Afraid of Virginia Woolf?* (Mike
Nichols, 1966), adapted from Edward Albee's 1962 play. Many a critic has
read Edward Albee's play as really about two men. It is true that the story
works very well either if you change Martha's name to Martin or if you
hire a man in drag to play her. But it is reductive to suppose that it is really
only about two men: as Albee had to point out a number of times, the play
works splendidly in a heterosexual context. Naturally, in 1962, a gay couple
could not have children, but neither could many heterosexual couples.
This notion in no way accounts for gay men's enjoyment of Taylor's performance in the film, then and now, even though it cannot harm it. As
seen in the Bette Davis entry above, David Van Leer shows how *Who's
Afraid of Virginia Woolf?* is deeply immersed in gay culture, notably with
Martha's allusions to Bette Davis' career and her famous line "What a
dump." But let us not forget that, interestingly, in that movie gay icon Elizabeth Taylor appropriates the work of gay icon Bette Davis (Van Leer 1995:
22–23).

Without getting into the complicated matter of filmmaker Mike
Nichols' alleged or real sexuality, his work often feels like the work of a
gay man, notably in the way he participates in the iconization of actresses,

although perhaps with a touch of misogyny (cf. Introduction). Kathi Maio writes:

> From his first films, *Who's Afraid of Virginia Woolf?* in 1966 and *The Graduate* the following year, to his current nifty little number, *Postcards [from the Edge]*, Mike Nichols has shown an unhealthy fascination for women. I sometimes take some convincing, but after a quarter-century of gorgons, I'm beginning to think that the boy doesn't like us much [Maio 1991: 161].

Maio uses "gorgons" in a strictly negative sense, but there is a lot one could say about the Hollywood icon as gorgon. There were three gorgons in Greek mythology, one of whom, Medusa, was mortal. They had snakes in lieu of hair and they could literally petrify the men who looked at them: talk about the power of the gaze, talk about the male gaze being thrown back in men's faces. When does fascination for women start counting as "unhealthy," one wonders? Of course, all the theories of the abject and the "monstrous feminine," the writings of Julia Kristeva and Barbara Creed, do not work quite so well when it is gay men who are watching the powerful castrating/petrifying women (Creed 1986, Kristeva 2015).

In *Reflections in a Golden Eye* (John Huston, 1967), adapted from the novel by gay favorite Carson McCullers, Taylor plays the wife of a cruel, closeted homosexual. In *Boom!* (Joseph Losey, 1968), another Tennessee Williams product, she delivers her campest performance of all as Flora, in full-on broken bitch mode, complete with flamboyant outfits, competing with Noël Coward for the bitchiest queen title. It is said that Tallulah Bankhead inspired the character. Her nickname, Sissy, beyond the imperial allusion, is in itself an incursion in drag territory.

S. Elizabeth Bird has observed the "campy readings" of tabloids by gays. "Indeed, some of the most popular female celebrities in tabloids are the very stars that have enthusiastic gay followings, such as Elizabeth Taylor [and] Joan Collins [...]" (Bird 1992: 133). Understandably, tabloids have always helped stoke gay iconicity. Gay men love the twisted narratives provided by cheap celebrity magazines. They can read about their icons in chic *Vogue*, admiring their sleek appearance, with glossy hair and perfect makeup, but they can also buy the trashiest tabloids and identify with their icons who can also have bad hair days, as the vile paparazzi pictures indicate.

> Certain celebrities take on a sort of "metapersonality," as they are covered repeatedly, such as the greatest favorite of all, Elizabeth Taylor. "Liz," as she is

always called, has developed a persona in the tabloids that is part glamorous princess, part suffering heroine, as she endures constant illnesses and weight problems, and part compassionate and loving humanitarian, as she stands by her friends, even when they are pictured as degenerate and AIDS-infected gays [Bird 1992: 170–171].

Taylor was married eight times to seven men, and she was a notorious homewrecker (as the media remembered on December 27, 2016, when Carrie Fisher died, and then again on December 28, 2016, when Debbie Reynolds died). She was seen by moralists as an insatiable vixen with an unhealthy appetite for diamonds. In 2009 the Palazzo delle Esposizioni in Rome organized a Bulgari exhibition, which had an entire room—its most fascinating room—devoted to Taylor.

As fellow gay icon and competitor Joan Collins reminds us: "Realism was an unfashionable word in 1959. Actresses were supposed to be goddesses. Untouchable. Plastic." (Collins 1985: 137) Taylor evolved from untouchable plastic goddess to human being with weight and health issues, and with a complicated sexuality, right in front of our eyes; and we never stopped loving her. Over the years, she contributed vastly to the struggle against AIDS, and we are grateful.

Lana Turner (1921–1995)

In April 1958 Cheryl Crane, Lana Turner's daughter, killed Johnny Stompanato, Turner's lover. "Justifiable homicide": she was protecting her mother's life. She was 14. Like many, I bought and read her book *Detour: A Hollywood Story* in 1988. The book renewed my tenderness for Lana Turner, the "sweater girl." The whole business was the stuff thrillers are made of, the stuff of Lana Turner movies. Gays love it when gruesome stories of this sort help weld Hollywood biographies to Hollywood diegeses. Surely she was not done with the shooting of *Imitation of Life* (Douglas Sirk, 1959) when Stompanato died. One shudders to imagine a world deprived of that indispensable melodrama if he had killed her instead of being killed by her daughter. There are still those who imagine she herself killed Stompanato and let her daughter take the fall.

Fannie Hurst's novel *Imitation of Life* (1933) had already been adapted for the screen as *Imitation of Life* (John M. Stahl, 1934), with Claudette Colbert, who had not brought to the lead role the sparkle that Turner would, helped by Sirk's direction and the beautiful costumes.

Turner's gay iconicity quotient had already reached a very high level 12 years previously with the release of *The Postman Always Rings Twice* (Tay Garnett, 1946). Even 70 years later one never comes out unscathed from a viewing. The head wrap! The shoes! The shorts! That movie is a lesson in style and in it, Turner is a lesson in stylishness.

Being involved in a story as ghastly as the Stompanato murder is more than your usual run-of-the-mill train-wreck phase, it is a wet dream for tabloid journalists. Furthermore, having many husbands is always good for gay iconicity—and Lana Turner had eight.

Sontag says that there is camp in *The Prodigal* (Richard Thorpe, 1955), and if you look at the sleeve of the recent edition of the DVD, released by Warner Brothers, you see at the top "Cult Camp Classic." Does that mean the marketing people of Warner Brothers read Susan Sontag? Not necessarily. It means that they think the label will attract a certain kind of buyer, and they use "camp" *also* in the debased sense of the word, in the so-bad-it's-good sense (Sontag 1969: 286).

It is undeniable that Lana Turner reaches summits of camp in her role as the pagan Princess Samarra in *The Prodigal*. She is clearly paying the rent: this is obviously a pot-boiler for her, and she's not making much of an acting effort. But maybe that is one of the reasons it somehow works, at least in the eyes of practitioners of camp readings. Why should she strain herself too much when with the batting of an eyelash she can cause erections in straight men and tears of joy in gay men? Lana Turner is always camp, even when her daughter killed her lover she was probably perched on white heels and flailing about stylishly, as it were.

Some have pointed out her limited acting abilities, even in movies other than *The Prodigal*. They were missing the point altogether. It is like criticizing Douglas Sirk movies for the extent to which one must stretch one's willing suspension of disbelief. Mordden complains: "What's more irritating about Sirk's *Imitation of Life* is its blithe disregard for credibility. [...] This film doesn't fail to be logical—it doesn't *bother* to be." Does he not see what is problematic with his reasoning? He is providing the answer himself: it does not bother to be. Precisely. It has Lana Turner (Mordden 1988: 353).

Mae West (1893–1980)

Last but most certainly not least, Mae West concludes this analytical review of gay icons. Many people thought she was a drag queen because they could not believe a woman of her era could be so forward and so plain-spoken (always with humor), especially in matters of sexuality. Many conservatives wanted to "suppress the bawdy wit of this vampy, campy wisecracker" (Stephens 1998: 2). William Randolph Hearst even asked, "Is it not time Congress did something about Mae West?" (West 1959: 185).

West always knew on which side her bread was buttered. She was always camp, but spectacularly more so as years went by, to the delight of her largely gay audience. She is a bit of a problem for a work on gay icons, though, because of the contradictions she seemed to harbor. Surrounded by homosexuals, somehow she was a little homophobic—rather like a person suffering from ailurophobia living in a house full of cats wanting nothing but to climb on her lap. Besides, all her life she mendaciously claimed not to really understand what camp meant, and she pretended that she didn't see herself as camp anyway. In some ways she was a bit overcome by her own creation. Philip Core writes: "Mae West's camp self-creation has been obscured by its own results." I believe she really knew what she was doing, for the most part. Core believes that she was "the most consciously camp" of pre-war movie stars. "Her familiarity with homosexuals, and her delight in their humor and style, was not covert" (Core 1984: 191–192). Mark Booth calls her a "camp favorite" and discusses her "hyperbolic gestures." He speaks of "Mae West shakin' the shimmy" (Booth 1983). For someone who claimed not to really grasp camp, no one can deny she did and said an awful lot of camp things, as the following selection of quotes will demonstrate.

"In 1971, when *Playboy* asked Mae West to define camp, she responded: 'Camp is the kinda comedy where they imitate me.' By 'they' she obviously meant gay men and drag queens" [Bergman 1993: 157].
"When I'm good, I'm very good, but when I'm bad, I'm better."
"Between two evils, I always choose the one I haven't tried before." (Or "When caught between two evils, I generally like to take the one I never tried.")
"Come up and see me sometime."
"A hard man is good to find [West in Warren 2000: 105].
"To err is human but it feels divine" [West in Warren 2000: 35].

West had an ambivalent reaction to her gay cult status. On the one hand, it delighted her. It did not surprise her, considering she had written one play called *Sex* (1926) and another called *The Drag* (1927), and hired drag queens. On the other hand it sometimes seemed to irritate her. There are homophobic sentences in her autobiography, *Goodness Has Nothing to Do with It.* Jill Watts reminds us:

> Although *The Drag* was the product of a straight woman's imagination, West's attempts at genuineness made it all too real. Some have pointed out that her shrill drag queens, mentally unbalanced spurned lovers, and deceitfully closeted homosexual men conveyed homophobic messages. Yet, as Chauncey notes, in *The Drag,* for the first time, gay men played gay men [Watts 2001: 86].

It is hard to believe that she was not a straightforward fag hag considering her trade: she sold wit, sex (heterosexual and otherwise), hyperfemininity, and camp. As Claudia Roth Pierpont reminds us, the ending of West's play *The Drag* was

> a thirty-minute drag ball, largely improvised, in which giddily self-described "queens" and "queers" in gowns and floating boas performed—in a manner even then called "camping"—passable impressions of a Mae West who had not yet quite come into being. The legal reaction was prompt. West was arrested [...]. It was from The Drag and from its spin-off, entitled The Pleasure Man [...] that she added the final, transforming touches of exaggeration and irony—that is, of conscious "camping"—to her mythic self [Pierpont 2000: 85].

Comedy was the key. Most of her antics would not have led her anywhere without the humor. Thomas Doherty quotes:

> "I've developed a different way of selling my sex," she explained to a reporter in 1933. "I laugh them into it. I cover it with comedy. If you laugh with a sinner, you like her. You grow fond of her, feel sympathy for her." She continued: "There are some people who can get away with anything yet always come out on top. The worse they are the better you like them. They happen to have something different that wins you no matter what they do. No, the wages of sin in all cases is not death" [Doherty 1999: 183].

Journalists called her "buxom" or "curvy." By today's standards, Mae West was downright fat. But even by the standards of her day, if you compare her body to Garbo's or Dietrich's, it is downright plump. That did not stop her embodying irresistibility. One of the reasons she always stood with her hand on her hip was that it was supposed to make her silhouette look lither. Such artifice is the province of drag queens.[188] Booth writes that Mae West acted "like a female impersonator." As he reminds us: "She was not an attractive woman—she was heavy-featured and dumpy—but she and everyone else kept up an elaborate pretense that she was irresistible" (Booth 1983: 134). That is a prodigious achievement: West was not only a female female impersonator, she was a *plain* female beautiful female impersonator. And it worked, performatively speaking. West *declared* that she was super-sexy. In her day, she was even a fashion icon. In the 1930s fashion designers found inspiration in Hollywood movies and actresses, and Elsa Schiaparelli based a collection on the Mae West look (Gundle 2008: 189). Admittedly, West, aged 77, was certainly camp and a bit pathetic in *Myra Breckinridge* (Michael Sarne, 1970). Perhaps some of that has to do with the fact that this movie is a massacre of an adaptation of Gore Vidal's masterpiece novel (although Raquel Welsh was an interesting choice to play Myra Breckinridge). It is possible to imagine that she would have been different in a better movie.

I don't care if some, like Andrew Ross, suggest that camp and drag have been an embarrassment to politically minded gays since 1969 or maybe even since the 1950s. (Tyler 2003: 90) I don't care if they devalue camp because of what they see as "the complicity of the latter with the sexual inversion model of homosexuality." I myself see a camp tradition in male female impersonators and female female impersonators of the Mae West variety going back at least to the 1920s and that remains vibrant in the 2010s. Camp and drag are associated with gay iconicity, and vice versa. As it happens, Mae West herself believed in that "sexual inversion model of homosexuality." And the point that she made when she defended homosexuals is that it was not their fault because they had female psyches in their male bodies. And who can blame her? With the category "homosexual" invented only a few decades before, and psychoanalysis largely confirming the notion, at least she was defending them, if sometimes condescendingly and occasionally in an exploitative manner. She did not know that the concept would be later used for and by transgender people and that ideological battles would rage nearly a century later in that domain.

As a complete constructionist, I do not believe in any essential identity. To me, everything is societal. Society constructs femininity, society constructs masculinity. When you are a gay man, you do not observe strict gender roles, because to begin with you disobey the number-one commandment of the dictatorship of gender: you have sex with men. So unsurprisingly, you are going to enjoy the company or shows of strong women who disregard gender roles (to various degrees), and you are going to do and like and wear things that only women are supposed to do and like and wear in the sexist homophobic patriarchy. Back in 1982, Dennis Altman explained that the idolization of female gay icons is not over.

> Such women represent both the qualities that men are denied in this society and the defiance of traditional values, particularly through an assertion of sexuality, that have kept down both women and homosexuals. It is striking, as Michael Bronski points out, that gay men have no male cultural heroes, their idols being exclusively women. [...] Drag queens act out this veneration of the strong woman who defies social expectations to assert herself; the popular model is often a Mae West or a Bette Midler [Altman 1983: 154].

He then says, however, and this will lead us to my conclusion, that drag is waning in the U.S. Perhaps it did decline for five minutes at the beginning of the 1980s, but it is certainly doing extremely well today, happily, and a lot of it is mainstream. In March 2017 *RuPaul's Drag Race* left Logo for VH1, a move that speaks volumes.

In his book *Frightening the Horses: Gay Icons of the Cinema*, Eric Braun includes a 50-page chapter entitled "Gay Icons." He covers, in birth order Mae West, Tallulah Bankhead, Marlene Dietrich, Joan Crawford, Bette Davis, Carmen Miranda, Judy Garland, Marlon Brando, Marilyn Monroe, James Dean, Doris Day, Barbra Streisand, Bette Midler, Cher, and Madonna (Braun 2007: 51–99). He explains: "A handful of stars have qualified for the title of Gay Icon, either because of the roles they played, their outrageous mode of dressing, or by virtue of something in their personalities which appealed *instinctively* to lesbians and gays" (Braun 2007: 51, italics mine). I am not certain that dressing outrageously is enough to make a gay icon—thank you, Saint Judy—and I do hope "instinctively" is used in a wide sense here, for it would pain me to see gay worshippers of glamorous icons reduced to brainless animals who iconize because of some instinct—possibly the same instinct that made them gay in the first place.

Conclusion

This book has attempted to delineate what gay icons are and how they are constituted. I have looked at their political and artistic purposes and wondered about their participation in the formation of gender and sexual identities, showing how they are strongly linked to gay men. I have examined performers to determine what their work brought to gay culture and why it was significant. Doing so, I have also tried to establish restrictions, being miffed at the way the expression "gay icon" is used indiscriminately by the media.

I hope at this stage it has become clear that I could not include lesbian icons, queer icons and trans icons, which should have their own books. This book is more concerned with old-fashioned gay icons, as it were, however young they might be. I trust the 70 entries have also justified the decision to concentrate strictly on (mostly) female gay icons, principally American. Divas are the main focus of the demonstration. I have observed their beauty, their clothing, their glamour, their stardom, their sexuality; I have wondered about the interconnection of their biography and their work, the degree of their self-consciousness and their familiarity with gay concerns. Mostly I have scrutinized their dosage of strength and fragility and the way they made gay men's lives better.

I trust I have made a reasonably convincing argument as to why gay icons and camp practices are *not* useless, and *not* on the way out, in our changing society, as some would have us believe. "Heteroqueer ladies" and "fag hags" are here to stay, and gay iconization is not intrinsically a misogynistic phenomenon—no more than drag. To do so I have looked at academe but equally at the "real world" beyond, notably in search of that elusive commodity, the "gay sensibility." As announced in its Introduction, this book is meant to entertain and edify its readers equally. I believe gay cultural history is important, and I hope young gay men will not dismiss it.

Exacting readers might wonder about or dispute what they might perceive as glaring absences. Why were X, Y and Z not included? Some performers do not get more than a passing mention, others are entirely ignored, why is that, they may ask. True, many other women have occasionally been pronounced gay icons. The short answer is: not enough boxes checked.

I am no sociologist. I occasionally undertake informal surveys (notably of my students, who happen to have to fill in an administrative form for me, to which I often add a question such as "Who's your favorite band or singer?"), but if I use them, I do not give them too much scientific credit. However, there are some celebrities you simply know—just by talking to people, watching television, reading magazines and newspapers, and surfing the Internet—are not dear to a high enough percentage of gay men to be uncontestable gay icons. This is often attributable to subcategories in the category of gay icon. Marianne Faithfull, for instance, is enjoyed by gays who like rock 'n' roll and street cred, not so much by others. Bettie Page and her postmodern rewrite Dita Von Teese may delight thousands of gay men around the globe, but many others will not be attuned to their elaborate femininity games, seeing them merely as fodder for average straight men's average fantasies. Besides, things change and statuses evolve. "The list of gay icons is long, dynamic and in perpetual renewal," write Yann-Brice Dherbier and Charles Danna (Dherbier & Danna 2010: 3).

Some might also fault me for largely skirting class issues. What about the poor gay boy, they might ask, who cannot afford to go to concerts or movies, to buy records, DVDs, biographies and magazines? This is a less valid accusation in the cybernetic age, when all you need is a computer and an Internet connection to watch and listen to all of the women listed here for free, basically. But I guess it is true that this book is largely in keeping with a form of gay consumerism that is linked to capitalism, and I plead guilty—but the DINK gays vs. poor queers debate would be out of place here.

Others might reproach me for dealing mostly in clichés. There are thousands of gay men, they will tell me, who do not enjoy the work of a single woman in this book. Well, if that is the case, I suppose they will not attempt to read me. I do not profess, incidentally, that the average Western gay man likes all 70 of my icons, if only because there are camps, whereby some love one particular icon because they hate another, her rival. Besides, I don't suppose that Log Cabin Republicans or Mormons who claim they "suffer from same-sex attraction [SSA]" will feel particularly interested, even though they are attracted to members of their own gender. In other words, this work is about gay *culture*. I hope I have modestly contributed a little to the understanding of that culture.

"Those wonderful beings, those dream creatures, can turn out to be fragile, vulnerable. And at the same time almost superhuman. From their beauty emanates a mysterious vitality that gives the spectator the impression of being more alive. A little something more, a soul supplement that makes them become gay icons" (Dherbier & Danna 2010: 9). Perhaps when there are numerous gay singers across the mediascape who openly and clearly sing about loving men, there will be fewer female gay icon singers. Possibly when there is the same proportion of gay movies in your local movie house as the proportion of gay people in society, there will be fewer gay icon actresses. But surely they will never disappear, for reasons I hope this book has helped clarify. As long as gays are a minority, however unpersecuted, gay icons will thrive—and help gay men feel "more alive."

"Being meta is rather everyday for queers" [Dyer 2002: 201].

Chapter Notes

Introduction

1. I trust I will be forgiven for my untraditional use of the words "iconicity," "iconize," "iconization," or even "iconogenic," which should be immediately clear in the context of this book.

2. I have supervised PhD dissertations on the ways gays define themselves through what they buy, or not, at different periods in different places.

3. Evidently, even the phrase "gay community" is questionable, as is the reality or lack thereof it might cover. But this is not the place for that debate. Most of the writers who have looked at gay iconicity use the phrase. Indeed those who claim not to practice gay icon worship often claim that worshipping the same women as everybody else in that community is merely a way to conform.

4. Some prefer "constructivist," but I favor "constructionist."

5. In 2009 London's National Portrait Gallery hosted a temporary exhibition entitled *Gay Icons*. Some of the choices of its curator, Sandi Toksvig, astonished many and are still baffling (the book can still be bought from online booksellers). As *The Guardian* noted, there was "no Kylie, no Judy, no Liza and not even Barbra. But there [was] Alan Turing, Sylvia Townsend Warner, Margarethe Cammermeyer and Mstislav Rostropovich. And Will Young" (https://www.theguardian.com/artanddesign/2009/mar/27/gay-icons-national-portrait-gallery, accessed December 2, 2016).

6. The website www.storify.com proposes the following restrictive definition: "The term 'gay icon' means a public figure or celebrity, musician in [particular], who has made an impact on the gay community through entertainment and advocacy."

7. http://slavesofacademe.blogspot.fr/2006/02/how-do-i-look-gay-iconography-of-star.html, accessed October 19, 2016.

8. http://www.towleroad.com/2015/08/gay-iconography-julie-andrews/, accessed October 19, 2016.

9. I use "camp" in this book in its queerer sense, rather than the debased sense of the word, the so-bad-it's-good sense.

10. Even Hillary Clinton has been hailed as a gay icon. She is strong and resilient, she survived first-ladyship, hyper-mediatized marital infidelity and public humiliation. Even though she came to it rather late in the day, she has lately been very good indeed on LGBT issues. Her hairdos through the ages have been as wildly commented upon as those of many a more traditional icon. If she had been elected in November 2016 she might have prolonged Barack Obama's work in that domain.

11. Obviously this is modeled on the typical transgender trope of "a woman trapped in a man's body," or vice versa. This trope is immensely essentialist, and rarely uttered entirely in jest.

12. http://www.dailyrecord.co.uk/news/2005/11/10/i-m-a-gay-man-in-a-girl-s-body-86908-16352446/.

13. http://www.thefrisky.com/2011-07-10/rose-mcgowan-im-a-gay-man-in-a-womans-body/.

14. http://www.out.com/entertainment/music/2008/10/23/all-glitters-gaga http://www.music-news.com/shownews.asp?H=Lady-Gaga-a-gay-man-trapped-in-a-womans-body&nItemID=26219.

15. http://www.celebitchy.com/7961/victoria_beckham_thinks_shes_a_gay_man_trapped_in_a_womans_body/.

16. http://www.celebuzz.com/2012-06-26/mila-kunis-i-feel-like-a-gay-man-in-a-womans-body-video/.

17. http://www.people.com/people/article/0,,20177088,00.html.

18. http://www.gaystarnews.com/article/pamela-anderson-i-am-gay-man-trapped-body300712/#gs.hsCny10.

19. Here I must pause to address the vocabulary issue. I use "fag" and "fag hag" in my Introduction and elsewhere meaning absolutely no disrespect, on the contrary. I myself have no qualms "fanning the flames of my own faggotry," as Margaret Cho would put it. I do not see the hag in "fag hag," and I do not think it would be appropriate today to use yesterday's "fag moll" (like Marisa Berenson below), which was differently offensive, anyway, because it establishes a parallel between gays and gangsters. Some ill-informed people think "beard" is synonymous with "fag hag." They are very wrong: beards are something else altogether, although some fag hags may function as beards. A beard is a woman used, knowingly or not, by a (partially or entirely) closeted gay man as a (more or less) pretend girlfriend or spouse in order to pass for heterosexual. The double metonymic process at work in the expression is fascinating, although somewhat passé in this day and age when all the hipsters and all the young gays are bearded. In *The Real O'Neals*, season 2, episode 11, Kenny wrongly claims that in this day and age ("The Real Third Wheel," February 2017) "fruit fly" is less offensive than "fag hag."

20. Cf. *The Culture of Queers* (Dyer 2002: 46–48).

21. Admittedly, in some Western countries in the 21st century, gay white male privilege exists, although it is obviously far from equaling straight white male privilege. Admittedly some gay men objectify and / or exploit their icons or their fag hags (including some fashion designers), but I am utterly convinced they constitute a deplorable minority. Cf. Rohin Guha's famous *Jezebel* article "The Myth of the Fag Hag and Dirty Secrets of the Gay Male Subculture," http://jezebel.com/the-myth-of-the-fag-hag-and-dirty-secrets-of-the-gay-ma-1506868402, accessed December 1, 2016.

22. David Halperin reminds us of the fact that gay culture persists because "gay or proto-gay children still grow up, for the most part, in heterosexual families." Admittedly society has evolved, but "a culture that places less stigma on homosexuality is not the same thing as a gay culture." That is why I, like Halperin, will not restrain "gay male culture to some distant epoch" (Halperin 2012: 119).

23. https://www.queerty.com/when-luck-beats-a-lady-the-tragic-woman-as-gay-icon-20090416, accessed October 15, 2016.

24. Song "Let's Dance," by David Bowie (1983).

25. For obvious reasons when writing about divas I will use "actress" in this book to refer to a female thespian rather than the supposedly more feminist "actor."

26. http://www.independent.co.uk/life-style/diana-1961-1997-the-gay-icon-glamorous-tragic-a-drama-queen-but-never-camp-1237802.html.

27. These are the countries I am most familiar with and whose gay cultures I have observed.

28. See Erica Rand's book *Barbie's Queer Accessories* (2012). See also what gay icon Nicki Minaj makes of Barbie.

29. In his introduction to an issue of *Camera Obscura* devoted to "Fabulous! Divas," Alexander Doty writes, "I was trained by the Catholic church to be a diva worshipper" (*Camera Obscura* 65: 1). Wayne Koestenbaum speaks of the "divisions, ascensions, and arousals that shake a queer soul worshipping a diva" (Koestenbaum 2001: 116).

30. My Vietnamese grandmother could have been a local gay icon of sorts in the 1940s, if Indochina had had them. She was gorgeous and bossy, and never stopped reminding people of both. She was a local celebrity, with many men at her feet, and was involved in espionage.

31. Some would say that a huge gay fan base empowers the gay icon right back. The notion of gay men empowering woman is politically dangerous, because they are still men. In *Modern Family* Mitch says: "Wow. Another woman empowered." His husband Cam replies: "That's what we do." Mitch confirms: "Yes it is" (season 8, episode 12). The "we" may here stand for gay men in general, and it is politically dubious—if interesting.

32. Maybe in 2096 a gay president will be elected in the United States. To give but one example: On October 16, 2016, there was a demonstration in the streets of Paris to protest gay marriage, three years after it was made legal. Some of the 20,000 demonstrators held protest signs that said, "Gender studies are killing families."

33. The song "I Will Survive" was actually written by Freddie Perren and Dino Fekaris.

The Performers

1. http://www.nytimes.com/1982/03/14/movies/julie-andrews-prim-and-improper.html?pagewanted=all, accessed December 2, 2016.

2. This phrase will be used throughout this book. Obviously the Latin phrase "realitatis femina" is meant to be opposed to the more common "dramatis persona," the real woman as opposed to the character, the wearer of masks in a fiction.

3. Andrews is arguably not very convincing as a boy, but most fans are willing to forgive her.

4. https://www.theguardian.com/film/2004/oct/14/1, accessed October 27, 2016.

5. https://www.queerty.com/was-lucille-ball-a-gay-rights-advocate-plus-other-reasons-to-love-lucy-20130806, accessed November 3, 2016.

6. I apologize to all of my brown-haired readers.

7. The word "bitch" is used as a compliment in this book. It is used in the sense of Joreen's *The Bitch Manifesto* (1969), of *Bitch* magazine, etc. It is a reclaimed insult, just like "queer." A bitch lets no man step on her toes, a bitch lets no one tell her how to live her life.

8. Ball did not invent the technique, but she pioneered and popularized it.

9. Other version: "Oh goodie, I always wanted to get into Marlene's pants."

10. http://lgbt.wikia.com/wiki/Tallulah_Bankhead, accessed October 7, 2017. *New York Times* source for "Daddy warned me" story: http://www.nytimes.com/2010/02/16/theater/16tallulah.html, accessed October 7, 2017 (there are variations, depending on sources).

11. Source for priest drag story: http://lucyappert.com/TwiceBride.htm, accessed October 7, 2017. See also: http://boards.straightdope.com/sdmb/archive/index.php/t-120921.html, accessed October 7, 2017; Tallulah thread, http://www.democraticunderground.com/discuss/duboard.php?az=view_all&address=105x778416, accessed October 7, 2017; http://www.austinchronicle.com/columns/2011-01-14/after-a-fashion/print/, accessed October 7, 2017.

12. Even though Dorothy Parker is a gay icon, she does not get an individual entry in this book because I deliberately chose to limit myself to performers.

13. http://www.tcm.com/this-month/article/190997%7C0/Trivia-All-About-Eve.html, accessed October 9, 2017.

14. This proverbial expression means "even if it is not true, it is well conceived."

15. http://closetprofessor.blogspot.fr/2011/11/tallulah-bankhead-gay-icon.html, accessed December 2, 2016.

16. Rob Frydlewicz, http://thestarryeye.typepad.com/gay/2011/12/the-death-of-irrepressible-tallulah-bankhead-dec-12-1968.html, accessed October 12, 2016.

17. Cf. Sasha Torres quoting Andy Medhurst in Cleto 1999: 338.

18. All the biographies concur in this view.

19. Eccentric millionaire Howard Hughes is said to have dated many of the women featured in this book: Tallulah Bankhead, Joan Crawford, Bette Davis, Marlene Dietrich, Zsa Zsa Gabor, Jean Harlow, Rita Hayworth, Katharine Hepburn, Marilyn Monroe, Barbara Stanwyck, and Lana Turner. He is also said to have had affairs with Cary Grant and Errol Flynn (plus five dozen beautiful actresses, as if he had been checking them off of a list). Dozens of Hollywood biographies report this.

20. It is possible that Jean-Pierre is not the only drag performer who offered this version, but I never saw it anywhere else, whereas I saw the traditional Bassey version many times in several countries on three continents.

21. Some would say "sugar-daddying." The young person who gets a sugar daddy to support her/him is a sugar baby.

22. http://www.dailymail.co.uk/femail/article-3324822/Dame-Shirley-Bassey-says-women-not-pilots-police-officers.html, accessed October 18, 2016.

23. Jase Peeples, *The Advocate*, April 8, 2013.

24. There is a Valentina mural in a parking lot outside the Italian city of Volterra, in Tuscany. I once heard an American tourist exclaim "Louise Brooks!" upon discovering it.

25. Koestenbaum is an impressive authority on iconicity, as notably demonstrated by his books on Jacqueline Bouvier Kennedy Onassis and Andy Warhol.

26. http://articles.baltimoresun.com/1997-02-23/news/1997054168_1_maria-callas-gay-cult-lisbon-traviata, accessed December 1, 2016.

27. Obviously, Evita is also something of a gay icon ("I'm their savior, that's what they call me").

28. http://www.mirror.co.uk/3am/celebrity-news/naomi-campbells-roll-of-shame-read-795002, accessed November 12, 2016.

29. It is interesting to compare her very different nude work for Madonna and for *Playboy* or *Lui* or even the Pirelli calendar (1995, 1999, 2015).

30. "I love her. What we have to admit is that Madonna—our generation's Marlene Dietrich—was so fucking ballsy. Right from the get-go she did not give a fuck. She had gay motherfuckers all up in her videos. She had a black Jesus and she did not give a shit. She did not care. She pushed the envelope and she didn't do that just to be cute" (*Attitude* 274, September 2016, 124).

31. *Attitude* 274, September 2016, 134. Naomi Smalls is a drag queen who's made a specialty of looking like Naomi Campbell.

32. https://www.thegayuk.com/11-mariah-carey-songs-every-gay-boy-needs-in-his-life/, accessed June 6, 2017.

33. I apply rules that are less strict in my classifications. According to some pickier critics, the only person worthy of the high camp label in this book is Maria Callas. According to those who are more moderate, only a handful of the people in this book, women like Marlene Dietrich, qualify.

34. "The mythology of the mermaid, the virgin of the sea, is sometimes one of active villainy (as in the siren who lures the sailor to his death) and sometimes one of passive victimization (as in the fairytale heroine whose love of a mortal man is her doom). But the mermaids Cher and Winona Ryder and little Christina Ricci give us aren't interested in destroying men or themselves" (Kathi Maio 1991: 171).

35. "Before I tell you how my brush with gay iconicity both began and ended [...], lemme shout something from the rooftops: anyone attempting to be [a gay icon] should

steer clear of fag-haggery. Fag hags are called hags for a reason—much like their cousins, spinsters, fag hags are sad and desperate, and use gay men as boyfriend substitutes/ego boosters who assure them that no, those tube socks don't make their calves look chunky" (Carrie Laven, 28 March 2012, http://brokeassstuart.com/ny/2012/03/28/how-not-to-become-a-gay-icon/, accessed June 6, 2017).

36. Cher, *The Farewell Tour* DVD (2003): begins 9:26.

37. The cover of the book is by Pierre et Gilles, keepers of the flames of gay iconicity.

38. In 2017, gay showrunner Ryan Murphy produced *Feud*, an anthology television series starring Susan Sarandon as Bette Davis and Jessica Lange as Joan Crawford; it is a camp monument to the glory of camp. Murphy explained why camp heroines were popular among gays: "I think it has a lot to do with the projection of the person one wants to be in the world. You're a survivor [...]. I look at you as someone nobody could ever keep down, who has a huge reservoir of passion" (quoted in *The Gay & Lesbian Review Worldwide*, September–October 2017, 48).

39. "Don't make me go all Joan Crawford on your ass!" is the new fashionable threat.

40. http://stargayzing.com/gay-icon-quentin-crisp-on-joan-crawford/, accessed November 28, 2016.

41. http://stargayzing.com/gay-icon-quentin-crisp-on-joan-crawford/, accessed November 28, 2016. See Crisp 1984: 22.

42. Lily Allen has often good-naturedly mocked Miley Cyrus. Both have been called racists, notably for being surrounded by twerking black women in performances.

43. http://www.dailymail.co.uk/tvshowbiz/article-2409931/Miley-Cyrus-wanted-make-history-compares-VMAs-performance-Britney-Spears-Madonna.html, accessed December 12, 2016.

44. http://www.eonline.com/news/801145/miley-cyrus-talks-coming-out-as-pansexual-i-didn-t-understand-my-own-gender-and-my-own-sexuality, accessed October 9, 2017.

45. http://www.eonline.com/news/733415/miley-cyrus-and-liam-hemsworth-are-engaged-again-look-back-on-everything-that-happened-during-their-break, accessed October 9, 2017.

46. http://variety.com/2016/music/features/miley-cyrus-the-voice-donald-trump-vmas-woody-allen-coming-out-pansexual-1201884281/, accessed June 27, 2017.

47. This in spite of the fact that *Queerty*, for one, declares that she "will never be a gay icon." https://www.queerty.com/why-miley-cyrus-will-never-be-a-gay-icon-the-lady-gaga-exhibit-20091211, accessed June 26, 2017.

48. "Dalida embodies the fantasies of her gay audience, of the woman they would like to be, glamorous, strong and fragile at the same time. That audience initially got closer to her in 1967, after her first suicide attempt. She was in those days a Madonna with great tragic songs. Then a second time in the 1970s, when she became a disco vamp" (Orlando quoted in *Le Monde*, my translation). http://www.lemonde.fr/societe/article/2007/02/17/ces-chanteuses-venerees-par-les-gays_868516_3224.html#sUDlTsJ5A4Z0MGHl.99, accessed December 17, 2016.

49. http://tetu.com/2017/01/04/mais-pourquoi-les-homosexuels-aiment-ils-a-ce-point-dalida/, accessed October 9, 2017.

50. *Ibid.*

51. The cougar is often mistaken for the MILF and vice versa.

52. See Guilbert 2004, *passim*; Guilbert 2014, *passim*.

53. http://www.loverboymagazine.com/201452a-musical-education-dalida/, accessed June 27, 2017. In French the note read: "La vie m'est insupportable. Pardonnez-moi."

54. Revealingly, in French the same word, "salope," means "slut" and "bitch."

55. "Gays grow up watching heterosexual movies—*Now, Voyager*—and deciding whether they're Bette Davis or Paul Henreid" (Harvey Fierstein, *Time*, June 20, 1983).

189

56. We saw earlier that the role is apparently *not* based on Tallulah Bankhead.

57. http://www.billboard.com/video/reasons-that-prove-lana-del-rey-is-a-muse-to-gay-fans-around-the-world-billboard-news-7874016, accessed August 24, 2017.

58. http://www.heteroclite.org/2016/10/catherine-deneuve-icone-lgbt-friendly-36014, accessed July 23, 2017.

59. "Wayne Koestenbaum writes: "In Cecil Beaton's photograph of Marguerite D'Alvarez, he's trebled her face [...]. She's split into parts because Cecil Beaton, the gay photographer, loves her so intensely." This also brings to mind the Warholian repetition of Marilyn Monroe or Elizabeth Taylor.

60. http://www.parismatch.com/Culture/Cinema/Catherine-Deneuve-et-Gerard-Depardieu-couple-de-stars-a-Angouleme-1333835, accessed October 8, 2017.

61. She famously signed the *Manifesto of the 343 Sluts* in 1971, of women in favor of legal abortion who claimed they had had an illegal abortion in France.

62. Although France abolished the death penalty in 1981, Deneuve has been known to fight the death penalty elsewhere, notably in the U.S.

63. Cf. Sam Wilson's book *Let's Talk About Love: Journey to the End of Taste* (2007).

64. http://www.billboard.com/articles/news/pride/7809701/celine-dion-gay-pride-month-love-letter, accessed July 22, 2017.

65. http://archive.fabmagazine.com/features/354/CelineDion.html, accessed July 23, 2017. For Céline Dion's appeal to gay men, cf. http://www.celinedionforum.com

66. The story is more or less the same in the original musical, even if some surnames differ.

67. My nickname for Kristin Scott Thomas is "Marvelous Bone Structure," but even though she qualifies in that respect she does not fill all of the requirements to be a gay icon.

68. "Another great thing to be part of was Eurovision [...] For those of you that think it's just one night ... oh no! It's a week long camp-fest starting seven days before the final [...] If you love pop music and all its fun, try and go to it next year, it's brilliant. My highlight? Meeting Dana International. She really does think she's Madonna!" Scott Mills in *Gay Times* 395, July 2011.

69. I'll get back to this song in the Kylie Minogue entry.

70. https://www.out.com/entertainment/music/2013/05/20/comeback-abba-agnetha-faltskog, accessed July 21, 2017.

71. France 2, *Actuality*, October 2016.

72. http://www.my-gay-paris.com/gay-paris/gay-idols/my-gay-paris-mylene-farmer-frances-biggest-gay-icon.html, accessed August 8, 2017.

73. http://www.lemonde.fr/societe/article/2007/02/17/ces-chanteuses-venerees-par-les-gays_868516_3224.html, accessed October 10, 2017.

74. http://www.goodhousekeeping.com/life/entertainment/news/g3239/zsa-zsa-gabor-young-quotes/, accessed July 22, 2017.

75. http://www.forbes.com/sites/tomteicholz/2016/12/19/zsa-zsa-gabor-dead-the-last-hungarian-actress-of-her-generation/#74d213967bd9, accessed December 20, 2016.

76. http://attitude.co.uk/8-fabulous-zsa-zsa-gabor-quotes-to-help-you-navigate-your-gay-life, accessed August 24, 2017.

77. To be entirely accurate, she never actually declared, "I am a gay icon," but she did and said absolutely everything that could make anyone draw that conclusion. Moreover, she claims she is bisexual and that all of her friends are LGBT (www.news18.com).

78. http://www.attitude.co.uk/what-makes-a-gay-icon/, accessed December 12, 2016. Admittedly, some claim that Katy Perry is a gay icon.

79. I use "icon mongering" and "icon monger" in an entirely non-derogatory way. Some find that Murphy is overdoing it (notably, in the episode of *Glee* entitled "The Power of Madonna"). In *Glee* he has Kurt say, "Mercedes is black, I'm gay. We make culture." The remake of "Vogue" by Sue Sylvester/Jane Lynch is a classic of gay television. Logan Scherer

thinks there is a "problem with Ryan Murphy's wannabe divas" in his series *Scream Queens*. "The king of primetime train-wrecks and mean girls doesn't do justice to the icons he worships," he writes. "[T]he most irresistible sin at the center of the series and all of Murphy's shows isn't devil worship. It's diva worship: taking pleasure in the bad behavior of gorgeous women, like Joan Crawford abusing her children, or Naomi Campbell throwing a phone at her assistant. But Murphy's divas never quite earn icon status—their hysteria is too deliberately constructed, and their hyper-articulate speeches are so obviously written by a gay man who wants viewers to adore them. They have two things that a gay icon simply can't have: self-awareness and composure, meaning they're so in control of their own madness that they're never really at their worst" (Scherer 2015).

80. Some might even be tempted to say this piece of casting was too easy.

81. See also Todrick Hall doing Lady Gaga. In March 2017 Lady Gaga even posed as a drag queen on *RuPaul's Drag Race* Season 9. As the Unicorn Booty website says: "Lady Gaga walks in the workroom at the top of the episode like everyone else. The pop star tries to fool the contestants into thinking she is a Lady Gaga impersonator named Ronnie. How awesome is that? Lady Gaga pranking drag queens by pretending to be a drag queen pretending to be Lady Gaga. Meta as fuck!" https://unicornbooty.com/lady-gaga-drag-race/, accessed March 8, 2017.

82. As we saw in the Divine entry, Garbo was nicknamed Divine, but she was also nicknamed the Sphinx (cf. Amanda Lear entry below).

83. http://www.divamag.co.uk/category/arts-entertainment/top-10-sapphic-screen-icons-of-hollywoods-golden-era.aspx, accessed December 1, 2016.

84. http://www.refinery29.com/2013/09/53469/gay-icons-ode, accessed December 12, 2016.

85. See Rushdie 1992, *passim*.

86. The line "Toto, I've a feeling we're not in Kansas anymore," is surely one the ten most (mis)quoted cinematic (or even extracinematic) lines in the world.

87. The activist Gilbert Baker, who designed the rainbow flag in 1978, died in March 2017.

88. See Doty 2000: 49–78.

89. Surely Jane Russell's performance in *Gentlemen Prefer Blondes* (Howard Hawks, 1953) as Dorothy does no disservice to the expression, considering in particular her singing "Ain't There Anyone Here For Love?" amidst a bevy of half-naked boys more preoccupied with doing sporty things with one another than giving her love.

90. http://www.popmatters.com/column/gay-icons-judy-who/, accessed August 24, 2017.

91. https://www.carnegiehall.org/Calendar/2016/6/16/0800/PM/Rufus-Wainwright/, accessed October 29, 2016.

92. Régine also sang the extraordinarily gay 1978 song "Les femmes ça fait pédé" (Women are just like fags), written by Serge Gainsbourg.

93. https://www.youtube.com/watch?v=rtgY1q0J_TQ, accessed November 23, 2016.

94. http://www.independent.co.uk/arts-entertainment/it-was-20-years-ago-today-why-i-will-survive-did-exactly-that-1080412.html, accessed September 2, 2017.

95. http://www.vulture.com/2016/03/rupaul-drag-race-interview.html, accessed December 2, 2016. Gloria Gaynor is also hailed as the interpreter of "I Am What I Am" (1983), a song that is linked to gay culture, drag culture, etc., through the politically dubious *La Cage aux Folles*.

96. In the late 1960s and early 1970s, Mick Jagger and Françoise Hardy looked astonishingly alike in some pictures.

97. The cover by "oriental" singer Natacha Atlas is particularly noteworthy.

98. Annie Lennox, who is said by some to be a gay icon, was the lead singer of the Eurythmics.

99. http://totally-hardy.forumactif.com/t130-francoise-hardyicone-gay, accessed September 2, 2017.

100. https://blogs.mediapart.fr/yves-faucoup/blog/260315/francoise-hardy-droite-decomplexee, accessed October 9, 2017.

101. http://www.purepeople.com/article/francoise-hardy-son-pere-agresse-par-un-jeune-homme-qu-il-racolait_a172614/1; http://www.femmeactuelle.fr/culture/news-culture/francoise-hardy-se-confie-sur-l-homosexualite-de-son-pere-27609, accessed October 9, 2017.

102. http://stargayzing.com/gay-icon-quentin-crisp-on-joan-crawford/, accessed November 28, 2016. See Crisp 1984: 25.

103. http://stargayzing.com/gay-icon-quentin-crisp-on-joan-crawford/, accessed November 28, 2016. See Crisp 1984: 24.

104. https://www.theguardian.com/film/2008/jul/13/1, accessed November 2, 2016.

105. Cf. Roland Barthes's chapter on striptease in *Mythologies* (1957). Cf. also gay filmmaker and writer Pier Paolo Pasolini on Rita Hayworth in *Amado Mio* (1982)

106. http://www.newyorker.com/tech/elements/america-at-the-atomic-crossroads, accessed November 12, 2016.

107. http://www.huffingtonpost.com/trevor-martin/why-do-gay-men-historical_b_3895070.html, accessed on November 12, 2016.

108. http://www.smh.com.au/articles/2003/07/13/1058034871272.html, accessed December 2, 2016.

109. http://people.com/celebrity/bobby-brown-admits-hitting-whitney-houston-details-couples-drug-usage/, accessed October 1, 2017.

110. https://www.theatlantic.com/entertainment/archive/2012/02/the-strange-lessons-of-whitney-houstons-addiction/253087/, accessed October 1, 2017.

111. Dolph Lundgren was a walking gay fantasy in those days, particularly in the part of Drago in *Rocky IV* (Sylvester Stallone, 1985).

112. *The Shameful Life of Salvador Dalí* (1998).

113. *Coccinelle par Coccinelle* (1987).

114. *April Ashley's Odyssey* (1982).

115. She is on the cover of Roxy Music's legendary second album, *For Your Pleasure* (1973), in stiletto heels and holding a black panther on a leash. Even people who do not identify her, such as Stephen Gundle in his book *Glamour: A History* (2008), cannot help observing that she embodies glamour in that "fabulously glossy confection" (Gundle 2008: 315).

116. See *Le Dali d'Amanda* (1984), *L'Amant Dali* (1994) and *Mon Dali* (2004).

117. http://lgbt.wikia.com/wiki/Amanda_Lear, accessed October 4, 2017.

118. Before its movie adaptation as the campfest *Barbarella* (Roger Vadim, 1968), *Barbarella* was a comic book by Jean-Claude Forest.

119. Like Garbo, Lear is a mysterious sphinx.

120. https://zagria.blogspot.fr/2008/07/amanda-lear-1939-performer.html#.WdPBe UzpNE8, accessed October 3, 2017; http://lgbt.wikia.com/wiki/Amanda_Lear, accessed October 4, 2017.

121. See also *Propos secrets* (1977).

122. http://www.sylvissima.com/sylvie-vartan-arrets-sur-images/tout-le-bazar, accessed October 2, 2017.

123. http://www.canadiangay.org/GHist/Aug/17.html, accessed October 2, 2017.

124. See Deléry 2011: *passim*.

125. https://www.theguardian.com/theobserver/2000/dec/24/focus.news, accessed December 12, 2016.

126. http://attitude.co.uk/what-makes-a-gay-icon/

127. Gay Times 405, May 2012, 73.

128. http://rupaulsdragrace.wikia.com/wiki/Jaymes_Mansfield, accessed August 8, 2017.
129. http://www.culledculture.com/ethel-merman-still-the-queen-bee-of-gay-icons, accessed on December 4, 2016.
130. In the same order of ideas, gay icons David Bowie and Dalida, among others, sang "The Alabama Song," aka "Moon of Alabama," "Moon over Alabama," and "Whisky Bar," written for Bertolt Brecht and Kurt Weill by Elisabeth Hauptmann, in various contexts with varying levels of camp.
131. Both Ute Lemper and Marianne Faithfull have a strong European gay following.
132. Gay icon Sarah Jessica Parker co-starred in *Hocus Pocus* (Kenny Ortega, 1993).
133. http://www.mtv.com/news/1649140/nicki-minaj-tells-her-gay-fans-suicide-is-never-the-answer/, accessed September 2, 2017.
134. https://www.advocate.com/arts-entertainment/music/2010/10/11/liza-fesses, accessed October 10, 2017.
135. https://www.theatlantic.com/magazine/archive/2000/08/the-queen-is-dead/378302/; https://www.theatlantic.com/past/docs/issues/2000/08/gross2.htm, accessed October 10, 2017.
136. https://www.theguardian.com/music/2016/oct/06/kylie-minogue-says-she-will-not-marry-in-australia-until-there-is-marriage-equality.
137. http://www.dailymail.co.uk/tvshowbiz/article-3454016/A-look-Kylie-Minogue-s-past-loves-including-Olivier-Martinez-Andr-s-Velencoso-Michael-Hutchence.html, accessed October 1, 2017.
138. http://www.vadamagazine.com, April 26, 2013.
139. This is how *Gay Times UK* reviewed her December 2016 album *Kylie Christmas: Snow Queen Edition*: "Because Kylie is such a beloved showbiz trouper, she can be forgiven for this slightly cheeky reissue, which adds six new tracks to the very entertaining Christmas album she already released last year. [...] At 22 songs long, the *Snow Queen Edition* surely has something for every kind of guest you'll welcome this festive season. But of course, the discerning gay boy's choice remains her glitzy duet with Dannii, '100 Degrees,' a song that could only be camper if you played it while coming out to your family over Christmas dinner. Nice work as ever, Minogue sisters" (68).
140. https://www.theguardian.com/film/2016/nov/18/marilyn-monroe-happy-birthday-mr-president-dress, accessed December 1, 2016.
141. Since I am referring to Andy Warhol again, I might as well explain at this point why I deliberately left out of this book the Factory "superstars," whether born female or not, most of whom might be deemed worthy of the gay icon accolade: they are not mainstream enough, not sufficiently known. In the same way that many gay men do not particularly care about Nico and the Velvet Underground, not every gay man devours every Warhol biography and travels miles to see old Warhol movies featuring the likes of Candy Darling. In an interview he gave *High Times* in August 1977, Andy Warhol credited Jack Smith with the invention of the term "superstar."
142. *Garçon Magazine* 5, September 2016, 77.
143. The Movida was a fascinating countercultural movement that took Madrid by storm after Francisco Franco's death in 1975.
144. One can only wonder if drag queen Alaska Thunderfuck was aware of singer Alaska when she chose that pseudonym. It is said she owes it simply to a marijuana variety called Alaskan thunderfuck. Alaska the Mexican Spanish singer seemingly owes her pseudonym to Lou Reed's 1973 song "Caroline Says II" ("All of her friends call her Alaska / When she takes speed, they laugh and ask her / What is in her mind"). As we can see, all of this has a lot to do with drugs and very little with the State of Alaska. Alaska Thunderfuck has many talents, including the ability to recreate gay icons of the past, such as Mae West and Bette Davis.

145. For obvious reasons, Saint Sebastian is notoriously the gayest of saints.

146. http://www.divamag.co.uk/category/arts-entertainment/top-10-sapphic-screen-icons-of-hollywoods-golden-era.aspx, accessed December 18, 2016.

147. There have been many other covers of the song, before and after *High Heels*, but none as interesting as the ones mentioned here.

148. *Attitude* 274, September 2016, 111.

149. One only has to visit the Country Music Hall of Fame and Museum in Nashville, Tennessee, to see how camp some costumes and boots can be.

150. It is tempting to see Eva Longoria as something of a gay icon. Her parts in *Desperate Housewives* (ABC 2004–2012) and *Telenovela* (NBC 2015–2016) certainly fuel that notion. In an episode of *Desperate Housewives* she is told that she does not seem affected by the tragic events that have just transpired, to which she replies: "Oh, no, no. I'm a mess—you know, on the inside, where the mascara can't run" (season 4, episode 10).

151. Trevor Martin, *The Huffington Post*, September 12, 2013, http://www.huffington post.com/trevor-martin/why-do-gay-men-historical_b_3895070.html, accessed December 1, 2016.

152. http://etudesculturelles.blogspot.fr/search?q=camp+culture.

153. She has yet to impress us with a substantial part in a mainstream movie. Her performance in *Battleship* (Peter Berg, 2012) did not leave a imperishable mark.

154. http://www.telegraph.co.uk/women/womens-life/11916887/Rihanna-Chris-Brown-domestic-abuse-Vanity-Fair-interview-is-a-triumph.html—Accessed October 1, 2017. See singles with Eminem, "Love the Way You Lie" and "Love the Way You Lie II" (2010).

155. http://www.dailymail.co.uk/tvshowbiz/article-1150824/Pictured-Rihannas-horrific-injuries-alleged-bust-Chris-Brown.html, accessed September 30, 2017.

156. http://www.chicagotribune.com/lifestyles/chi-teen-domestic-violence-20-feb20-story.html, accessed September 30, 2017.

157. http://www.usmagazine.com/celebrity-body/news/rihanna-and-matt-kemp-call-it-quits-20102812, accessed October 11, 2017.

158. http://www.cosmopolitan.com/entertainment/celebs/a63543/drake-rihanna-relationship-timeline-love-dating-aubrih-forever/, accessed October 11, 2017.

159. http://www.advocate.com/health/here-inspire/2014/12/01/rihanna-everybody-loves-elizabeth-taylor, accessed November 26, 2016.

160. See Soft Cell's celebrated 1981 "Where Did Our Love Go?" Soft Cell's singer was Marc Almond, a male gay icon. "Where Did Our Love Go?" was preceded on the "maxi single" by a now cult cover of Gloria Jones' "Tainted Love."

161. http://www.towleroad.com/2014/08/gay-iconography-diana-ross-is-a-supreme-icon/, accessed December 2, 2016.

162. Gay icon Dusty Springfield also recorded that song.

163. *RuPaul's Drag Race* season 4, episode 11 (2012).

164. *RuPaul's Drag Race All Stars*, season 2, episode 6 (2016).

165. http://www.femmeactuelle.fr/culture/news-culture/sheila-confidences-chirurgie-esthetique-operations-nez-seins-33773, accessed October 1, 2017.

166. http://www.lefigaro.fr/culture/2017/07/17/03004-20170717ARTFIG00208-ludovic-chancel-le-fils-de-sheila-serait-mort-d-une-surdose-de-medicaments.php, accessed October 1, 2017.

167. http://randomtrivia.livejournal.com, accessed October 12, 2016.

168. This is fascinatingly pastiched by a stripper in the undeservedly little-known *Filth and Wisdom* (Madonna, 2008). In that film, writers Dan Cadan and Madonna offer a real commentary on desire in the 21st century, beyond the obvious jokes.

169. In the song Madonna intimates that Britney Spears should let herself go, and be talented and alluring right alongside her. This is one way to multiply their gay iconicity quotient, whereby 1 + 1 = more than 2, somehow.

170. Cf. Rachel Paula Abrahamson, "Commando Queens: Under Where? These Starlets Redefine Overexposed," *Us Weekly* 618, December 18, 2006.

171. Cf. *Star*, March 5, 2007, "Why Britney Snapped!" cover.

172. http://content.time.com/time/magazine/article/0,9171,2062458,00.html, accessed October 21, 2016.

173. "Poor sods," one might say in polysemic British English.

174. *Daytime Divas*, season 1, episode 2, June 12, 2017.

175. "Singer Britney Spears has been voted the greatest gay icon of all time in a new poll [1000 people in Orange County]? The hitmaker saw off competition from President Barack Obama and veteran performer Cher to take 31 percent of the vote in the Orange County Equality Project's poll to find the quintessential gay icon. Spears's idol Madonna came second with 25 percent of the vote, but a poll spokesperson insists it was a close call between the two superstars. The Equality Project's Joel Waddell says, 'When Madonna puts out a new album, she will be on top again. Madonna is the greatest icon the gay community has ever had.' Lady Gaga was voted in third with 22 percent, while 12 percent of respondents picked Katy Perry." http://www.starpulse.com/poll-britney-spears-is-the-ultimate-gay-icon-1848035126.html, accessed November 27, 2016. In the summer of 2017 she was looking very fit and in control during her Las Vegas residency.

176. White soul, sometimes called blue-eyed soul.

177. This song launched her solo career. In later decades, it was covered by many people in various languages.

178. https://backlots.net/2013/10/24/an-interview-with-victoria-wilson-author-of-a-life-of-barbara-stanwyck-steel-true-1907-1940/amp/, accessed October 12, 2017.

179. *Ibid.*

180. http://www.nydailynews.com/entertainment/meryl-streep-talks-sexting-gay-icon-article-1.2745860, accessed November 26, 2016; http://www.pridesource.com/article.html?article=77571, accessed November 26, 2016.

181. Like fellow gay icons Barbra Streisand and Bette Midler, she has kept her nose, which some may find unprepossessing.

182. http://www.imdb.com/name/nm0000658/?ref_=nmbio_bio_nm, accessed November 26, 2016.

183. http://stargayzing.com/in-honor-of-barbra-streisands-70th-birthday-how-americas-greatest-voice-helped-me-find-my-own/, accessed December 1, 2016.

184. One of the few ciswomen who are really credible in such parts in movies is Anne Carlisle in *Liquid Sky* (Slava Tsukerman, 1982).

185. For all sorts of reasons, gay novelist Christopher Rice is very popular with gay men. Anne Rice's vampire novels are gay favorites.

186. http://www.huffingtonpost.com/2014/10/05/lady-bunny-after-dark_n_5932236.html, accessed October 21, 2016.

187. http://stargayzing.com/dim-all-the-lights-for-donna-summer-one-of-our-greatest-singers-in-any-genre/, accessed November 2, 2016.

188. Cf. Alaska Thunderfuck doing Mae West in *RuPaul's Drag Race All Stars*, season 2, episode 2.

Bibliography

Books

Aldrich, Robert, ed. 2006. *Gay Life and Culture: A World History*. London: Thames & Hudson.

Altman, Dennis. 1983 (1982). *The Homosexualization of America*. Boston: Beacon Press.

Ambrose, Tom. 2010. *Heroes and Exiles: Gay Icons through the Ages*. London: New Holland.

Andersen, Christopher. 2006. *Barbra: The Way She Is*. New York: HarperCollins.

Andreoli, Richard, ed. 2004. *Mondohomo: Your Essential Guide to Queer Pop Culture*. Los Angeles: Alyson Books.

Anger, Kenneth. 1959. *Hollywood Babylon*. Paris: J.J. Pauvert.

Ashley, April, with Duncan Fallowell. 1982. *April Ashley's Odyssey*. London: Jonathan Cape.

Bacall, Lauren. 1978. *By Myself*. New York: Knopf.

_____. 1994. *Now*. New York: Knopf.

Barthes, Roland. 1993 (1957). *Mythologies*. London: Vintage.

Baudrillard, Jean. 1981. *Simulacres et Simulation*. Paris: Galilée.

Bell-Metereau, Rebecca. 1993. *Hollywood Androgyny*. New York: Columbia University Press.

Berenson, Marisa. 2009. *Moments intimes*. Paris: Calmann-Lévy.

Berger, John. 1972. *Ways of Seeing*. Harmondsworth: Penguin.

Bergman, David, ed. 1993. *Camp Grounds: Style and Homosexuality*. Amherst: University of Massachusetts Press.

Bergund, Jason, and Beverly West. 2004 (2003). *Gay Cinematherapy: The Queer Guy's Guide to Finding Your Rainbow One Movie at a Time*. New York: Universe.

Bianco, David. 1999. *Gay Essentials: Facts for Your Queer Brain*. Los Angeles: Alyson Books.

Bird, S. Elizabeth. 1992. *For Enquiring Minds: A Cultural Study of Supermarket Tabloids*. Knoxville: University of Tennessee Press.

Bloch, Avital H., and Lauri Umansky, eds. 2005. *Impossible to Hold: Women and Culture in the 1960s*. New York: New York University Press.

Booth, Mark. 1983. *Camp*. London: Quartet Books.

Bowers, Scotty. 2012. *Full Service: My Adventures in Hollywood and the Secret Lives of the Stars*. New York: Grove Press.

Boyarin, Daniel, Ann Pellegrini, and Daniel Itzkovitz, eds. 2003. *Queer Theory and the Jewish Question*. New York: Columbia University Press.

Braun, Eric. 2007 (2002). *Frightening the Horses: Gay Icons of the Cinema*. Richmond: Reynolds & Hearn.

Bronski, Michael. 1984. *Culture Clash: The Making of Gay Sensibility*. Boston: South End Press.

Browning, Frank. 1994. *The Culture of Desire: Paradox and Perversity in Gay Lives Today*. New York: Vintage.

Brownmiller, Susan. 1986 (1984). *Femininity*. London: Paladin.

Bibliography

Burston, Paul. 1995. *What Are You Looking At? Queer Sex, Style and Cinema*. London: Cassell.
_____, and Colin Richardson. 1995. *A Queer Romance: Lesbians, Gay Men and Popular Culture*. New York: Routledge.
Butler, Judith. 1990. *Gender Trouble: Feminism and the Subversion of Identity*. New York: Routledge.
_____. 2004. *Undoing Gender*. New York: Routledge.
Capote, Truman. 1986. *Answered Prayers*. London: Abacus.
Cashmore, Ellis. 2014. *Celebrity Culture*. New York: Routledge.
Cestaro, Gary P., ed. 2004. *Queer Italia: Same Sex Desire in Italian Literature and Film*. Basingstoke: Palgrave.
Clarke, Gerald. 2002 (2000). *Get Happy: The Life of Judy Garland*. London: Time Warner.
Cleto, Fabio, ed. 1999. *Camp: Queer Aesthetics and the Performing Subject: A Reader*. Edinburgh: Edinburgh University Press.
Coccinelle. 1987. *Coccinelle par Coccinelle*. Paris: Filipacchi.
Clum, John M. 2002. *He's All Man: Learning Masculinity, Gayness, and Love in American Movies*. New York: Palgrave.
Cohan, Steven. 2005. *Incongruous Entertainment: Camp, Cultural Value and the MGM Musical*. Durham: Duke University Press.
Collins, Joan. 1985. *Past Imperfect*. New York: Berkley Books.
Considine, Shaun. 1989. *Bette & Joan: The Divine Feud*. London: Sphere Books.
Corber, Robert J. 2011. *Cold War Femme: Lesbianism, National Identity, and Hollywood Cinema*. Durham: Duke University Press.
Core, Philip. 1984. *Camp: The Lie That Tells the Truth*. London: Plexus.
Creekmur, Corey K., and Alexander Doty, eds. 1995. *Out in Culture: Gay, Lesbian, and Queer Essays on Popular Culture*. Durham: Duke University Press.
Crisp, Quentin. 1984. *How to Go to the Movies*. New York: St. Martin's Press.
Deléry, Antoine. 2011. *Roger Peyrefitte, le sulfureux*. Le Triadou.
D'Emilio, John. 1983. *Sexual Politics, Sexual Communities: The Making of a Homosexual Minority in the United States, 1940–1970*. Chicago: University of Chicago Press.
Dherbier, Yann-Brice, and Charles Danna. 2010. *Icônes gays*. Paris: YB Editions.
Dickens, Homer. 1984. *What a Drag: Men as Women & Women as Men in the Movies*. New York: Quill.
Dion, Michel, ed. 1994. *Madonna: Érotisme et pouvoir*. Paris: Kimé.
Doane, Mary Ann. 1987. *The Desire to Desire: The Woman's Film of the 1940s*. Bloomington: Indiana University Press.
Doherty, Thomas. 1999. *Pre-Code Hollywood: Sex, Immorality and Insurrection in American Cinema 1930–1934*. New York: Columbia University Press.
Dollimore, Jonathan. 1991. *Sexual Dissidence: Augustine to Wilde, Freud to Foucault*. Oxford: Clarendon Press.
Doty, Alexander. 1993. *Making Things Perfectly Queer*. Minneapolis: University of Minnesota Press.
_____. 2000. *Flaming Classics: Queering the Film Canon*. New York: Routledge.
_____, ed. 2007. "Fabulous! Divas, Part 1." *Camera Oscura* 22, no. 2.
Duberman, Martin, ed. 1997. *Queer Representations: Reading Lives, Reading Cultures*. New York: New York University Press.
_____, ed. 1997. *A Queer World: The Center for Lesbian and Gay Studies Reader*. New York: New York University Press.
Dyer, Richard. 1979. *Stars*. London: BFI.
_____. 1990. *Now You See It: Studies on Lesbian and Gay Film*. New York: Routledge.
_____. 1992. *Only Entertainment*. New York: Routledge.
_____. 2002. *The Culture of Queers*. New York: Routledge.
_____. 2004 (1986). *Heavenly Bodies: Film Stars and Society*. New York: Routledge.

_____. 2009. "The Idea of a Gay Icon." In Sandi Toksvig, ed. *Gay Icons*. London: National Portrait Gallery Publications.

_____, ed. 1980 (1976). *Gays & Film*. London: BFI.

Eaklor, Vicki L. 2011. *Queer America: A GLBT History of the 20th Century*. New York: The New Press.

Epps, Brad, and Despina Kakoudaki, eds. 2009. *All About Almodóvar: A Passion for Cinema*. Minneapolis: University of Minnesota Press.

Farinelli, Gian Luca, and Jean-Loup Passek, eds. 2000. *Stars au féminin: Naissance, apogée et décadence du star system*. Paris: Éditions du Centre Pompidou.

Farmer, Brett. 2000. *Spectacular Passions: Cinema, Fantasy, Gay Male Spectatorship*. Durham: Duke University Press.

Éribon, Didier. 1999. *Réflexions sur la question gay*. Paris: Fayard.

_____, ed. 2003. *Dictionnaire des cultures gays et lesbiennes*. Paris: Larousse.

Feil, Ken. 2006. *Dying for a Laugh: Disaster Movies and the Camp Imagination*. Middletown, CT: Wesleyan University Press.

Fizgerald, Louise, and Melanie Williams, eds. 2013. *Mamma Mia! The Movie*. London: I.B. Tauris.

Fraser, John. 2004. *Close Up: An Actor Telling Tales*. London: Oberon Books.

Frederick, Kirk. 2016. *Write That Down: The Comedy of Male Actress Charles Pierce*. West Hollywood: Havenhurst Books.

Gabbard, Krin, and William Luhr, eds. 2008. *Screening Genders*. New Brunswick: Rutgers University Press.

Gabler, Neal. 2016. *Barbra Streisand: Redefining Beauty, Femininity, and Power* (Jewish Lives). New Haven: Yale University Press.

Gage, Simon, Lisa Richards, and Howard Wilmot. 2002. *Queer, the Ultimate User's Guide*. Foreword by Boy George. New York: Da Capo.

Garber, Marjorie. 1992. *Vested Interests: Cross-Dressing and Cultural Anxiety*. New York: Routledge.

Gay Left Collective, eds. 1980. *Homosexuality: Power and Politics*. London: Alison & Busby.

Gemunden, Gerd, and Mary M. Desjardins, eds. 2007. *Dietrich Icons*. Durham: Duke University Press.

Gerstner, David, ed. 2006. *Routledge Encyclopedia of Queer Culture*. New York: Routledge.

Gibson, Ian. 1998. *The Shameful Life of Salvador Dalí*. New York: W.W. Norton.

Gilbert, Sky. 2000. *Ejaculations from the Charm Factory: A Memoir*. Toronto: ECW Press.

Gill, John. 1995. *Queer Noises: Male and Female Homosexuality in Twentieth-Century Music*. Minneapolis: University of Minnesota Press.

Grandsart, Didier. 2014. *Ultra Blonde*. Éditions Nicolas Chaudin.

Greif, Martin. 1985 (1982). *The Gay Book of Days*. London: WH Allen.

Guilbert, Georges-Claude. 2002. *Madonna as Postmodern Myth: How One Star's Self-Construction Rewrites Sex, Gender, Hollywood and the American Dream*. Jefferson, NC: McFarland.

_____. 2004. *C'est pour un garçon ou pour une fille? La Dictature du genre*. Paris: Autrement.

_____. 2014. *Le Genre des objets*. Paris: L'Harmattan.

Gundle, Stephen. 2008. *Glamour: A History*. Oxford: Oxford University Press.

Haggerty, George, and Molly McGarry, eds. 2015. *A Companion to Lesbian, Gay, Bisexual, Transgender, and Queer Studies*. Chichester: Wiley Blackwell.

Halberstam, Judith. 1998. *Female Masculinity*. Durham: Duke University Press.

Halperin, David. 2012. *How to Be Gay*. Cambridge: Harvard University Press.

Hamilton, Marybeth. 1995. *The Queen of Camp: Mae West, Sex and Popular Culture*. London: HarperCollins.

Hanson, Ellis, ed. 1999. *Out Takes: Essays on Queer Theory and Film*. Durham: Duke University Press.

Bibliography

Harding, Chrishna. 2012. *The Making of Lana Del Rey*. Amazon Kindle Publishing.

Harris, Daniel. *The Rise and Fall of Gay Culture*. New York: Hyperion, 1997.

Havranek, Carrie. 2008. *Women Icons of Popular Music*. Westport, CT: Greenwood Press.

Hawley, John C. 2008. *LGBTQ America Today: An Encyclopedia*, 2 vols. Westport, CT: Greenwood Press.

Higgins, Patrick, ed. 1993. *A Queer Reader*. London: Fourth Estate.

Hoberman, J., and Jonathan Rosenbaum. 1983. *Midnight Movies*. New York: Harper & Row.

Holiday, Billie, and William Dufty. 2006 (1956). *Lady Sings the Blues*. New York: Doubleday.

Horne, Peter, and Reina Lewis, eds. 1996. *Outlooks: Lesbian and Gay Sexualities and Visual Cultures*. New York: Routledge.

Huffington, Arianna. 2002. *Maria Callas: The Woman Behind the Legend*. New York: Cooper Square Press.

Jay, Bernard. 1993. *Not Simply Divine!* London: Virgin.

Jones, Grace, as told to Paul Morley. 2015. *I'll Never Write My Memoirs*. London: Simon & Schuster,

Kaplan, E. Ann, ed. 1980 (1978). *Women in Film Noir*. London: BFI.

Keller, James R. 2002. *Queer (Un)Friendly Film and Television*. Jefferson: McFarland.

Kellner, Douglas. 1995. *Media Culture: Cultural Studies, Identity and Politics Between the Modern and the Postmodern*. London: Routledge.

Kellow, Brian. 2007. *Ethel Merman: A Life*. New York: Viking.

Koestenbaum, Wayne. 2000. *Cleavage: Essays on Sex, Stars, and Aesthetics*. New York: Ballantine.

_____. 2001 (1993). *The Queen's Throat: Opera, Homosexuality, and the Mystery of Desire*. New York: Da Capo.

Lassen, Christian. 2011. *Camp Comforts: Reparative Gay Literature in Times of AIDS*. Bielefeld: Transcript Verlag.

Lear, Amanda. 1984. *Le Dali d'Amanda*. Lausanne: Pierre Marcel Favre.

_____. 1987. *L'Immortelle*. Paris : Carrere.

_____. 1994. *L'Amant Dali*. Paris: Michel Lafon.

_____. 2004. *Mon Dali*. Paris: Michel Lafon.

_____. 2009. *Je ne suis pas du tout celle que vous croyez*. Paris : Hors Collection.

Leider, Emily Wortis. 1997. *Becoming Mae West*. New York: Farrar, Straus and Giroux.

Levy, Emanuel. 2009. *Vincente Minnelli: Hollywood's Dark Dreamer*, New York: St. Martin's Press.

_____. 2015. *Gay Directors, Gay Films? Pedro Almodóvar, Terence Davies, Todd Haynes, Gus Van Sant, John Waters*. New York: Columbia University Press.

Lewis, Lisa A. 1990. *Gender Politics and MTV: Voicing the Difference*. Philadelphia: Temple University Press.

Loren, Sophia. 2014. *Ieri, oggi, domani*. Milan: Rizzoli.

Maddison, Stephen. 2000. *Fags, Hags and Queer Sisters*. New York: St. Martin's Press.

Maio, Kathi. 1991. *Pop Corn and Sexual Politics: Movie Reviews*. Freedom, CA: The Crossing Press.

Mann, William J. 2012. *Hello Gorgeous: Becoming Barbra Streisand*. Boston & New York: Houghton Mifflin Harcourt.

McHugh, Erin. 2007. *Homo History: A Compilation of Events that Shook and Shaped the Gay World*. New York: Alyson Books.

McLean, Adrienne L., ed. 2011. *Glamour in a Golden Age: Movie Stars of the 1930s*. New Brunswick: Rutgers University Press.

Macnee, Patrick, and Marie Cameron. 1988. *Blind in One Ear*. London: Harrap.

Metz, Walter. 2007. *Bewitched* (TV Milestones). Detroit: Wayne State University Press.

Meyer, Moe. 2010. *An Archeology of posing: Essays on Camp, Drag, and Sexuality*. Madison: Macater Press.

Bibliography

_____, ed. 1994. *The Politics and Poetics of Camp.* New York: Routledge.

Mizejewski, Linda. 1992. *Divine Decadence: Fascism, Female Spectacle, and the Makings of Sally Bowles.* Princeton: Princeton University Press.

Montlack, Michael, ed. 2009. *My Diva: 65 Gay Men on the Women Who Inspire Them.* Madison: Terrace Books.

Mordden, Ethan. 1988. *The Hollywood Studios: House Style in the Golden Age of the Movies.* New York: Knopf.

Morin, Edgar. 1957. *Les Stars.* Paris: Le Seuil.

Morton, Donald, ed. 1996. *The Material Queer: A LesBiGay Cultural Studies Reader.* Boulder: Westview Press.

Paglia, Camille. 1992 (1990). *Sexual Personae: Art and Decadence from Nefertiti to Emily Dickinson.* London: Penguin.

_____. 1993 (1992). *Sex, Art, and American Culture.* London: Penguin.

_____. 1994. *Vamps & Tramps.* London: Viking.

_____. T1998. *he Birds.* London: BFI.

Parish, James Robert. 2001. *The Hollywood Book of Death: The Bizarre, Often Sordid, Passings of More than 125 American Movie and TV Idols.* New York: McGraw-Hill.

Peraino, Judith A. 2005. *Listening to the Sirens: Musical Technologies of Queer Identity from Homer to Hedwig.* Berkeley: University of California Press.

Pierpont, Claudia Roth. 2000. *Passionate Minds: Women Rewriting the World.* New York: Knopf.

Porter, Darwin. 2010. *Humphrey Bogart: The Making of a Legend.* New York: Blood Moon Productions.

Porter, Darwin, and Danforth Prince. 2007. *Blood Moon's Guide to Gay and Lesbian Film.* New York: Blood Moon.

Probyn, Elspeth. 1993. *Sexing the Self: Gendered Positions in Cultural Studies.* New York: Routledge.

Prono, Luca. 2008. *Encyclopedia of Gay and Lesbian Popular Culture.* Westport, CT: Greenwood Press.

Reid, Pat, and Graham Norton. 1999. *20th Century Icons: GAY.* Bath: Absolute Press.

Ringer, R. Jeffrey, ed. 1994. *Queer Words, Queer Images: Communication and the Construction of Homosexuality.* New York: New York University Press.

Rivers, Melissa. 2015. *The Book of Joan: Tales of Mirth, Mischief, and Manipulation.* New York: Crown.

Robertson, Pamela. 1996. *Guilty Pleasures: Feminist Camp from Mae West to Madonna.* Durham: Duke University Press.

Robertson Wojcik, Pamela, ed. 2012. *New Constellations: Movie Stars of the 1960s.* New Brunswick: Rutgers University Press.

Roen, Paul. 1994. *High Camp: A Gay Guide to Camp and Cult Films, Vol. 1.* San Francisco: Leyland Publications.

_____. 1997. *High Camp: A Gay Guide to Camp and Cult Films, Vol. 2.* San Francisco: Leyland Publications.

Rosen, Marjorie. 1973. *Popcorn Venus: Women, Movies and the American Dream.* New York: Avon.

Ross, Andrew. 1989. *No Respect: Intellectuals and Popular Culture.* New York: Routledge.

Ross, Diana. 1993. *Secrets of a Sparrow: Memoirs.* London: Headline.

RuPaul. 1995. *Lettin' It All Hang Out: An Autobiography.* New York: Hyperion.

Rushdie, Salman. 1992. *The Wizard of Oz.* London: BFI.

_____. 1994. *East, West.* New York: Vintage.

Rutledge, Leigh W. 1989. *The Gay Fireside Companion.* Boston: Alyson Publications.

_____. 1999. *Nice Girls Don't Wear Cha-Cha Heels! Camp Lines from Classic Films.* Los Angeles: Alyson Books.

Bibliography

Russo, Vito. 1987 (1981). *The Celluloid Closet*, rev. ed. New York: Harper & Row.

Schiavi, Michael. 2011. *Celluloid Activist: The Life and Times of Vito Russo*. Madison: University of Wisconsin Press.

Shapiro, Peter. 2006. *Turn the Beat Around: The Secret History of Disco*. New York: Farrar, Straus and Giroux.

Shugart, Helene A. 2008. *Making Camp: Rhetorics of Transgression in U.S. Popular Culture*. Tuscaloosa: University of Alabama Press.

Simkin, Stevie. 2014. *Cultural Constructions of the Femme Fatale: From Pandora's Box to Amanda Knox*. New York: Palgrave Macmillan.

Simpson, Mark. 1994. *Male Impersonators: Men Performing Masculinity*. London: Cassell.

_____. 1996. *It's a Queer World: Deviant Adventures in Pop Culture*. London: Vintage.

_____, ed. 1996. *Anti-Gay*. London: Freedom Editions.

_____, and Steven Zeeland. 2001. *The Queen Is Dead: A Story of Jarheads, Eggheads, Serial Killers and Bad Sex*. London: Arcadia.

Sinfield, Alan. 1994. *The Wilde Century: Effeminacy, Oscar Wilde and the Queer Moment*. London: Cassell.

_____. 1998. *Gay and After: Gender, Culture and Consumption*. London: Serpent's Tail.

_____. 1999. *Out on Stage: Lesbian and Gay Theater in the Twentieth Century*. New Haven: Yale University Press.

_____. 2004. *On Sexuality and Power*. New York: Columbia University Press.

Slide, Anthony. 2010. *Inside the Hollywood Fan Magazine: A History of Star Makers, Fabricators, and Gossip Mongers*. Jackson: University Press of Mississippi.

Smith, Jack. 2008. *Wait for Me at the Bottom of the Pool: The Writings of Jack Smith*. Ed. J. Hoberman and Edward Leffingwell. London: Serpent's Tail.

Smith, Patricia Juliana, ed. 1999. *The Queer Sixties*. New York: Routledge.

Sontag, Susan. 1969. *Against Interpretation*. New York: Laurel, 1969 ("Notes on Camp" 277–293, 1964).

_____. 1983. *A Susan Sontag Reader*. New York: Vintage Books ("Notes on Camp" 105–119, 1964).

Stein, Marc, ed. 2004. *Encyclopedia of Lesbian, Gay, Bisexual and Transgender History in America*. New York: Charles Scribner's Sons.

Steinem, Gloria, and George Barris. 1997 (1988). *Marilyn*. New York: Fine Communications.

Stephens, Autumn. 1998. *Drama Queens: Wild Women of the Silver Screen*. Berkeley: Conari Press.

Stern, Jane. 1991. *The Encyclopedia of Bad Taste*. New York: Harper.

Sullivan, Andrew. 1996. *Virtually Normal: An Argument About Homosexuality*. New York: Vintage.

Tannen, Lee. 2001. *I Loved Lucy: My Friendship with Lucille Ball*. New York: St. Martin's Press.

Tasker, Yvonne. 1998. *Working Girls: Gender and Sexuality in Popular Cinema*. New York: Routledge.

Taylor, Elizabeth. *Elizabeth Takes Off*. New York: Putnam, 1987.

Taylor, Greg. 2001 (1999). *Artists in the Audience: Cults, Camp, and American Film Criticism*. Princeton: Princeton University Press.

Tinkcom, Matthew. 2002. *Working Like a Homosexual: Camp, Capital, Cinema*. Durham: Duke University Press.

Tinkcom, Matthew, and Amy Villarejo, eds. 2001. *Keyframes: Popular Cinema and Cultural Studies*. New York & London: Routledge.

Tyler, Carole-Anne. 2003. *Female Impersonation*. New York: Routledge.

Tyler, Parker. 1985. *Myth and Magic at the Movies*. New York: Taylor & Francis.

_____. 1993 (1972). *Screening the Sexes: Homosexuality in the Movies*. New York: Da Capo Press.

Bibliography

Ursini, James, and Dominique Mainon. 2009. *Femme Fatale: Cinema's Most Unforgettable Lethal Ladies*. Milwaukee: Limelight Editions.

Van Leer, David. 1995. *The Queening of America: Gay Culture in Straight Society*. New York: Routledge.

Walker, Alexander. 1969 (1966). *Sex in the Movies: The Celluloid Sacrifice*. New York: Penguin.

_____. 1970. *Stardom: The Hollywood Phenomenon*. Los Angeles: Joseph.

Walters, Suzanna Danuta. 1995. *Material Girls: Making Sense of Feminist Cultural Theory*. Berkeley: University of California Press.

_____. 2001. *All the Rage: The Story of Gay Visibility in America*. Chicago: University of Chicago Press.

Ward, Peter. 1991. *Kitsch in Sync: A Consumer's Guide to Bad Taste*. London: Plexus.

Warren, Roz, ed. 2000 (1998). *Women's Lip: Outrageous, Irreverent and Hilarious Quotations*. London: Michael O'Mara.

Waters, John. 1987 (1983). *Crackpot: The Obsessions of John Waters*. New York: Vintage.

Watts, Jill. 2001. *Mae West: An Icon in Black and White*. Oxford: Oxford University Press.

Waugh, Thomas. 2000. *The Fruit Machine: Twenty Years of Writings on Queer Cinema*. Durham: Duke University Press.

West, Mae. 1970 (1959). *Goodness Has Nothing to Do with It*. New York: Manor Books.

Williams, John L. 2013. *America's Mistress: The Life and Times of Eartha Kitt*. London: Quercus.

Williams, Kenneth. 1987 (1985). *Just Williams: An Autobiography*. Glasgow: Fontana.

Wilson, Sam. 2007. *Let's Talk About Love: Journey to the End of Taste*. London: Bloomsbury.

Zeisler, Andi. 2008. *Feminism and Pop Culture*. Berkeley: Seal Press.

Articles

Bordo, Susan. 1999. "Gay Men's Revenge." *The Journal of Aesthetics and Art Criticism* 57, no. 1 (Winter).

Gittings, Christopher. 2001. "Zero Patience, Genre, Difference, and Ideology: Singing and Dancing Queer Nation." *Cinema Journal* 41, no. 1 (Autumn).

Bristow, Joseph. 1989. "Being Gay: Politics, Identity, Pleasure." *New Formations* 9 (Winter).

Britton, Andrew. 1979. "For Interpretation: Notes against Camp." *Gay Left* 7.

Cooper, Evan. 2003. "Decoding Will and Grace: Mass Audience Reception of a Popular Network Situation Comedy." *Sociological Perspectives* 46, no. 4.

Creed, Barbara. 1986. "Horror and the Monstrous-Feminine: An Imaginary Abjection." *Screen* 27, no. I (January).

Degen, John A. 1987. "Camp and Burlesque: A Study in Contrasts." *Journal of Dramatic Theory and Criticism* (Spring).

Dickinson, Kay. 2001. "Believe? Vocoders, Digitalized Female Identity and Camp." *Popular Music* 20, no. 3.

Geyrhalter, Thomas. 1996. "Effeminacy, Camp and Sexual Subversion in Rock: The Cure and Suede." *Popular Music* 15, no. 2.

Harcourt, Bernard E. 2004. "You are entering a gay-and-lesbian-free zone: On the radical dissents of Justice Scalia and other (post-) queers." *The Law School. The University of Chicago. Public Law and Legal Theory Working Paper* 59 (February).

Harris, Daniel. 1996. "The Death of Camp: Gay Men and Hollywood Diva Worship, from Reverence to Ridicule." *Salmagundi* 112 (Fall).

Kristeva, Julia. 2015. "Qui est Méduse." *Arts & Humanitas*.

Mallan, Kerry, and Roderick McGillis. 2005. "Between a Frock and a Hard Place: Camp Aesthetics and Children's Culture." *Canadian Review of American Studies* 35, no. I.

Bibliography

Miller, D.A. 1997. "Visual Pleasure in 1959." *October* 81 (Summer).

Mock, Roberta. 2003. "Heteroqueer ladies: Some performative transactions between gay men and heterosexual women." *Feminist Review* 75, no. 1 (December).

Ness, Patrick. 2006. "We two boys together clinging." *The Guardian* (24 June).

Scherer, Logan. 2015. "The Problem with Ryan Murphy's Wannabe Divas." *The Atlantic* (14 October).

Index

205

Index

Index

207

Index

Index

Index

Index

"Miroir" 103
Mirwais 73
The Misfits 125
misogyny 9, 10, 11
"Miss Otis Regrets" 117
Miss Sadie Thompson 89, 170
Mizejewski, Linda 121
Moby 73
Mock, Roberta 7, 8, 116
Mommie Dearest 48–49, 87
Monroe, Marilyn 7, 23, 45, 50, 57, 78, 103, 107–108, 110, 124–130, 140, 143, 174, 181
Montand, Yves 127
Montez, María 11, 130–131
Montez, Mario 131
Montgomery, Elizabeth 133
Montiel, Sara 131–132
Montlack, Michael 23, 47, 66, 89, 171
Moonstruck 40
Moore, Julianne 165
Moorehead, Agnes 133–135
Mordden, Ethan 49, 177
Morin, Edgar 6, 129
Moritz, Marguerite J. 49
Morocco 63–64, 66
Moulin Rouge 75
Mulvey, Laura 5, 29
Munk, David 50, 166, 169
Murphy, Britanny 90
Murphy, Ryan 76
Music of the Heart 165
"Music to Watch Boys to" 60
Musto, Michael 20
My Fair Lady 90
"My Heart Belongs to Daddy" 127
"My Heart Will Go On" 68
Myra Breckinridge 180
Myron 11

Nabokov, Vladimir 68
Naomi 35
Narizzano, Silvio 26
Nashville 141
Ndegeocello, Me'shell 3
Needles, Sharon 4, 135–136
Neighbours 122
Neill, Roy William 130
Ness, Patrick 18
"Never Can Say Goodbye" 83
Never Trust a Pretty Face 103
New Orleans 93
New York, New York 121
Newman, Paul 173
Newmar, Julie 99
Newton-John, Olivia 70
Nichols, Mike 164, 174–175
Nielsen, Kate 20

Nightclubbing 97
Nip/Tuck 149
Niven, David 151
"No More Tears" 67
Norton, Graham 2
Notre-Dame-des-Fleurs 69, 115
Novak, Kim 9
Now 21
Now, Voyager 57

Oakley, Tyler 68
Obama, Barack 15
Octobriana 105
Of Human Bondage 56
O'Hara, Maureen 130
On Her Majesty's Secret Service 143
Onassis, Aristotle 33
One Hundred and One Dalmatians 26
O'Neal, Jamie 142
O'Neill, Edward R. 2
Only Angels Have Wings 89
Out of Africa 164
"Over the Rainbow" 76, 80, 82–83, 114
Overland Stage Raiders 31
Ozon, François 61

Pabst, G.W. 31
Page, Bettie 104, 183
Page, Jimmy 101
Paglia, Camille 56
Pakula, Alan J. 120, 164
"La Paloma" 132
Pandora's Box 31f
Paradis, Vanessa 85, 136–137
Paredes, Marisa 138–141
Paris Is Burning 149
Parish, James Robert 110
Parker, Alan 165
Parker, Dorothy 25, 46, 81, 167
Parkinson, Michael 7
"Pars" 96
"Partition" 101
Parton, Dolly 52, 94, 141–143, 155–156
"Party" 101
Pasolini, Pier Paolo 33
Patton, Cindy 108
Paul, Billy 95
Peaches 3
Pearce, Guy 71
Peck, Gregory 90
Peeples, Jase 30
Peraino, Judith A. 83
Performance 110
Perón, Eva 34, 165, 169
Perry, Frank 48
Perry, Katy 75
Persona 140

212

Index

Index

Index

www.ingramcontent.com/pod-product-compliance
Lightning Source LLC
Chambersburg PA
CBHW020315290526
45785CB00007B/2801